Mary Jane Holmes

West Lawn

And the Rector of St. Mark's

Mary Jane Holmes

West Lawn
And the Rector of St. Mark's

ISBN/EAN: 9783744661447

Printed in Europe, USA, Canada, Australia, Japan

Cover: Foto ©ninafisch / pixelio.de

More available books at **www.hansebooks.com**

POPULAR NOVELS.
BY
Mrs. Mary J. Holmes.

I.—TEMPEST AND SUNSHINE.
II.—ENGLISH ORPHANS.
III.—HOMESTEAD ON THE HILLSIDE.
IV.—'LENA RIVERS.
V.—MEADOW BROOK.
VI.—DORA DEANE.
VII.—COUSIN MAUDE.
VIII.—MARIAN GRAY.
IX.—DARKNESS AND DAYLIGHT.
X.—HUGH WORTHINGTON.
XI.—CAMERON PRIDE.
XII.—ROSE MATHER.
XIII.—ETHELYN'S MISTAKE.
XIV.—MILLBANK.
XV.—EDNA BROWNING.
XVI.—WEST LAWN. (*New.*)

Mrs. Holmes is a peculiarly pleasant and fascinating writer. Her books are always entertaining, and she has the rare faculty of enlisting the sympathy and affections of her readers, and of holding their attention to her pages with deep and absorbing interest.

All published uniform with this volume. Price $1.50 each and sent *free* by mail, on receipt of price, by

G. W. CARLETON & CO.,
New York.

WEST LAWN

AND

THE RECTOR OF ST. MARK'S.

BY

MRS. MARY J. HOLMES,

AUTHOR OF

TEMPEST AND SUNSHINE.—'LENA RIVERS.—MARIAN GREY.—MEADOW-
BROOK.—ENGLISH ORPHANS.—COUSIN MAUDE.—HOMESTEAD.
—DORA DEANE.—DARKNESS AND DAYLIGHT.—HUGH
WORTHINGTON.—THE CAMERON PRIDE.—ROSE
MATHER.—ETHELYN'S MISTAKE.—MIL-
BANK.—EDNA BROWNING.

NEW YORK:
G. W. Carleton & Co., Publishers.
LONDON: S. LOW, SON & CO.
M.DCCC.LXXIV.

Entered according to Act of Congress, in the year 1874, by
DANIEL HOLMES,
In the Office of the Librarian of Congress, at Washington.

Maclauchlan, Stereotyper,   John F. Trow & Son, Printers,
145 & 147 Mulberry St., near Grand, N. Y.   205-213 East 12th St., New York.

CONTENTS.

CHAPTER	PAGE
I.—Dora's Diary	7
II.—Author's Journal	15
III.—Dr. West's Diary	19
IV.—Johnnie's Letter to Dora	27
V.—Dora's Diary	31
VI.—Letters	44
VII.—Dora's Diary Continued	54
VIII.—Jessie's Diary	80
IX.—Extract from Dr. West's Diary	84
X.—Dora's Diary	87
XI.—Richard's Story	102
XII.—The Shadow of Death,	119
XIII.—At Beechwood	134
XIV.—In the Spring	146
XV.—Waiting for the Answer	159
XVI.—The Engagement	169
XVII.—Extract from Dr. West's Journal	178
XVIII.—Poor Max	182
XIX.—Anna	193
XX.—Richard	209
XXI.—The Night before the Wedding	212
XXII.—Down by the Lake Shore	216
XXIII.—The Bridal Day	226
XXIV.—The Shadows of Death	235
XXV.—Breaking the Engagement	240
XXVI.—Giving in Marriage	254
XXVII.—More of Marriage	263
XXVIII.—Dora's Diary	270

THE RECTOR OF ST. MARKS.

CHAPTER	PAGE
I.—Friday Afternoon,	283
II.—Saturday Afternoon.	291
III.—Sunday	299
IV.—Blue Monday.	309
V.—Tuesday.	319
VI.—Wednesday.	328
VII.—At Newport.	341
VIII.—Showing How it Happened	354
IX.—Anna.	368
X.—Mrs. Meredith's Conscience.	379
XI.—The Letter Received	383
XII.—Valencia	393
XIII.—Christmas Day.	403

WEST LAWN.

CHAPTER I.

DORA'S DIARY.

"BEECHWOOD, June 12th,
11 o'clock P.M.

AT last, dear old book, repository of all my secret thoughts and feelings, I am free to come to you once more, and talk to you as I can talk to no one else. Daisy is asleep in her crib after a longer struggle than usual, for the little elf seemed to have a suspicion that to-morrow night some other voice than mine would sing her lullaby. Bertie, too, the darling, cried himself to sleep because I was going away, while the other children manifested in various ways their sorrow at my projected departure. Bless them all, how I do love children, and hope if I am ever married, I may have at least a dozen; though if twelve would make me twice as faded and sickly, and,—and,—yes, I will say it,— as peevish as Margaret's six have made her, I should rather be excused. But what nonsense to be written by me, Dora Freeman, spinster, aged twenty-eight,—the Beechwood gossips said when the new minister went home with me from the sewing society. But they were mistaken, for if the family Bible is to be trusted, I was only twenty-five last Christmas, and I don't believe I look as old as that."

Here there was a break in the diary, while Dora glanced in the mirror at a graceful little figure, with sloping shoulders and white neck, surmounted by a well shaped head with masses of reddish-brown hair, waving just enough to suggest an idea of the curls into which it might be easily coaxed; low forehead; piquant nose, with an undeniable curve which ill-natured people call a turn-up; bright, honest eyes of reddish-brown, like the hair; mouth which did not look as if it had ever said a disagreeable thing; rows of white, even teeth, with complexion remarkable for nothing except that it was natural, and just now a shade or two paler than usual, because its owner was weary with the months and years of care which had fallen on her youthful shoulders.

This was the picture Dora saw, and nodding to the *tout ensemble* a little approving nod, and pushing behind her ears the heavy braids of hair to see if the style were becoming, as somebody once had told her, she resumed her pen and diary, as follows :

" Where was I when vanity stopped me for an inspection of myself? Oh, I know; I had been writing things about being married, for which I ought to blush, and through which I put my pen, so— But there's what I said of Margaret; I'll let that stand, for she is peevish and cross, and it's a relief to tell it somewhere. Poor Margaret! I cannot help pitying her when I look at her now, and remember what she used to be at the dear old home,—so beautiful, so petted, and admired. Ah me! that was twelve years ago, and I was a little girl when Margaret was married, and we danced on the lawn in the soft September sunlight, with papa looking on, so happy and so proud; and then the bonfires they kindled and the bells they rang at nightfall in honor of the bride, Mrs. John Russell, Esquire. Alas! when next on a week day that bell was rung, it tolled for my dear lost father, who died with apoplexy, and left his affairs all in confusion, his property, which was reputed so great, all mortgaged, and *I* a little beggar. Shall I ever forget John Russell's kindness when, hurrying home from Europe, he came to me at once and said I should be his daughter, and should live with him and Margaret at Beechwood, where we came eleven years ago this very June,—Margaret a splendid-looking woman, who would not wear black because her bridal dresses were so much more becoming; and I a timid, awkward girl of fourteen, who cried so much for the dear father gone, and the old homestead sold, that people said I looked and acted older than my sister, the stylish Mrs. Russell. How

1*

glad I was when in the autumn Johnnie was born and Margaret left him so much with me, for in my love for him I forgot to mourn for father, and came to think of him as safe in heaven, where mother went when I was ten days old. Then those three delightful years at school, when I roomed with sweet Mattie Reed, whom I am going to-morrow to visit. No matter if there were *three* babies here instead of one when I came home; and it was very wicked in me to feel annoyed, because I was so often expected to see that nurse did her duty, or in fact turn nurse myself to the wee little things. I cannot say that I was glad when Benny came, for with the advent of each child, Margaret grew more delicate, more helpless, and more,—I wonder if it is bad to say it,—more fault-finding with her husband, who, though the very best man in the world, is not like,—like,—well, say like Dr. West."

Here the pen made three heavy strokes through that name, completely erasing it, after which it continued:

"I cannot tell why I should bring *him* up as a comparison, when I do not like him at all, even if the whole village of Beechwood is running mad about him,—I mean the old people, not the young, who sneer at him and call him stingy. If there's anything I hate, it's penuriousness, which holds so fast to a three-cent piece and hugs a battered sixpence. Don't I remember our fair last winter for the benefit of the church, and how the girls, without the slightest reason for doing so, said to me, 'Now, when Dr. West comes in, *you* take possession of him. You are just the one. He thinks more of *you* than of all of us together. You can sell him that dressing-gown and slippers. Ask *fifteen* at first, and if he demurs, fall to *ten*. They were both given, so we shall not lose. Tell him, if necessary, how shabby his present gown and slippers are looking, and how the ladies talk about it.'

"I did not believe he would come directly to my table, and, I think now, the crowd must have pushed him there, for come he did, looking so pleasant and kind, and speaking so gently when he said he hoped we should realize a large sum, and wished so much he could help us more. Of course, the gown and slippers were thrust upon his notice, so cheap, only fifteen dollars; and, of course, he declined, saying, *sotto voce:*

"'I would gladly buy them for your sake, if I could, but I cannot afford it.'

"Then I fell to twelve, then to ten, and finally to eight, but he held out firmly, notwithstanding that I told him how forlorn he looked in his old ones, patched and tattered as they were. I could see a flush on his face, but he only laughed, and said he must get a wife to mend his things. It was surely my evil genius which prompted me to retort in a pert, contemptuous tone:

"'Umph! few ladies are insane enough to marry stingy

old bachelors, who would quarrel about the pin money!'

"I shall never forget how white he grew, or how quickly his hand went into his pocket, as if in quest of his purse; but it was withdrawn without it, just as that detestable Dr. Colby came simpering along, smelling of cologne, and musk, and brandy. I knew, to a certainty, that he did not pay his board bills, and yet I felt goaded into asking him to become an example of generosity to Dr. West, and buy the gown and slippers. I'd take it as a personal favor, I said, putting into my hateful eyes as much flattery as I possibly could; and he bought them, paying fifteen dollars right before Dr. West, who said softly, sadly like:

"'I'm glad you have found a purchaser. I did not wish you to be disappointed;' and then he walked away, while that Colby paraded his dressing-gown and slippers until I hated the sight of them, and could have cried with vexation.

"Still, when later in the evening Dr. West came back and asked me to go with him for ice-cream, I answered saucily:

"'Thank you; I can't leave; and besides, I would not for the world put you to so much expense!'

"If he was white before, he was livid now, and he has never appeared natural since. I wish he knew how many times I have cried over that affair, and how I detest that pert young Colby, who never has a patient, and who called and called at Beechwood until Mrs. Markham, across the way, sent in to ask who was so very sick. After that I took good care to be engaged whenever I heard his ring. *Dr. West,*—I wonder why I will persist in writing his name when I really do not care for him in the least; that is, care as girls sometimes care for fine-looking men, with good education, good morals, good manners, and a good profession. If I could rid myself of the idea that he was stingy, I might tolerate him; but of course he's stingy, or why does he wear so shabby a coat and hat, and why does he never mingle in any of the rides and picnics where money is a necessary ingredient? Here he's been in Beechwood three, yes, most four years, getting two-thirds of the practice, even if he is a homœopathist. I've heard that he gives liberally to the church, and he attends the extreme poor for nothing. So there is some good in him. I wonder if he'll come to say good-by. I presume not, or he would have reserved that package sent by Johnnie, and brought it himself instead. It is marked 'Mrs. David West, Morrisville.' Who in the world can Mrs. David West be? I did not know he ever saw Morrisville, and I am sure he came from Boston. There's the bell for midnight. I have written the whole hour, and all of Doctor West, except the ill-natured things I said of Margaret, and for which I am sorry. Poor Madge, as Brother John calls her, she's sick and tired, and cannot help being a little fretful, while I, who never had an ache or pain, can help blaming her, and I will. I'm sorry, Sister Maggie, for what I have written about you, and humbly ask your pardon."

CHAPTER II.

AUTHOR'S JOURNAL.

IT lacked ten minutes of car-time, and the omnibus-driver was growing impatient and tired of waiting for his passenger, when a noisy group appeared upon the piazza: Mrs. Squire Russell, pale, languid, drooping as usual, with a profusion of long light curls falling in her eyes, and giving to her faded face the appearance of a poodle dog; Mr. Squire Russell, short, fat, hen-pecked, but very good-looking withal, and some half dozen little Russells, clinging to and jumping upon the young lady, whom we recognize at once as Dora, our heroine.

"You won't stay long, even if Mrs. Randall does urge you," said Mrs. Russell, in a half-complaining tone as she drew together her white wrapper, and leaned wearily against a pillar of the piazza. "You know I can't do anything with the children, and the hot weather makes me so miserable. I shall expect you in two weeks."

"Two weeks, Madge! are you crazy?" said the Squire's good-humored voice. "Dora has not been from home in ages, while you have almost made the tour of the Western Continent. She shall stay as long as she likes, and get some color in her face. She used to be rosier than she is now, and it all comes of her being shut up so close with the children."

"I think it is very unkind in you, Mr. Russell, to speak as if I was the worst sister in the world, and the most exacting. I am sure Dora don't think so. Didn't she go with us to Newport last summer, and wasn't she more than once called the belle of the Ocean House?"

John gave a queer kind of whistle, while Dora involuntarily drew a long breath as she remembered the dreary time she had passed at the Ocean House, looking after *three* nurses, six children, and her sister Margaret, whose rooms were on the third floor, and to whom she had acted the part of waiting-maid in general. But her thoughts were suddenly brought back from Newport by Margaret's next remark:

"You needn't charge the loss of her roses to me either, John. No one can expect to be young-looking forever, and you must remember Dora has passed the bloom of youth. She's in her twenty-sixth year."

"Twenty-sixth year! Thunder! that's nothing," and Squire Russell tossed up in the air the little Daisy crawling at his feet, while Johnnie, the ten-year old boy, roared out:

" Aunt Dora ain't old. She's real young and pretty, and so Dr. West told Miss Markham that time she counted on her fingers, and said, so spiteful like : ' Yes,

Miss Freeman is full thirty. Why, they've been here eleven years, and she must have been nineteen or twenty when she came, for she was quite as big as she is now, and looked as old. Yes, she's too old for the new minister, Mr. Kelley.' I was so mad I could have knocked her, and I did throw a brick at her parrot squawking in the yard. Dr. West was as red as fire, and said to her just as he spoke to me once, when he made me hold still to be vaccinated, 'Miss Freeman is not thirty. She does not look twenty, and is perfectly suitable for Mr. Kelley, if she wants him.'

"'She don't,' says I, 'for she don't see him half the time when he calls, nor Dr. Colby either.'

"I was going to spit out a lot more stuff, when Dr. West put his hand to my mouth, and told me to hush up."

There were roses now on Dora's cheeks, and they made her positively beautiful as she kissed her sister and the little ones good-by, glancing nervously across the broad, quiet street to where a small, white office was nestled among the trees. But though the blinds were down, the door was not opened, while around the house in the same yard there were no signs of life except at an upper window, where a head, which was unmistakably that of Dr. West's landlady, Mrs. Markham, was discernible behind the muslin curtain. He was not coming to say good-by, and with a feeling of disappointment Dora walked rapidly to the omnibus, which bore her away from the house where they missed her so much, Squire John looking uncomfortable and desolate, the children growing very cross, and at last crying, every one of them, for auntie; while Margaret took refuge from the turmoil behind one of her nervous headaches, and went to her room, wondering why Dora must select that time of all others to leave her.

CHAPTER III.

DR. WEST'S DIARY.

"June 13th, 10 P. M.

HOW beautiful it is this summer night, and how softly the moonlight falls upon the quiet street through the maple-trees! On such a night as this one seems to catch a faint glimpse of what Eden must have been ere the trail of the serpent was there. I have often wished it had been Adam who first transgressed instead of Eve. I would rather it had been a man than a woman who brought so much sorrow upon our race. And yet, when I remember that by woman came the Saviour, I feel that to her was given the highest honor ever bestowed on mortal. I have had so much faith in woman, enshrining her in my heart as all that was good and pure and lovely. And have I been mistaken in her? Once, yes. But that is past. Anna is dead. I forgave her freely at the last, and mourned for her as for a sister. How long it took to crush out my love,—to overcome the terrible pain which would waken me from the dream that I held her again in my arms, that her soft cheek was against my own, her long, golden curls falling on my bosom just as they once fell. I do not like curls now, and I verily believe poor Mrs. Russell, with all her whims and vanity, would be tolerably agreeable to me were it not for that forest of hair dangling about her face. Her sister wears hers in bands and braids, and I am glad, though what does it matter? She is no more to me than a friend, and possibly not that. Sometimes I fancy she avoids and even dislikes me. I've suspected it ever since that fatal fair when she urged me to buy what I could not afford ju t then. She thought me avaricious, no doubt, a reputation I fear I sustain, at least among the fast young men; but my heavenly Father knows, and some time maybe *Dora* will. I like to call her Dora here alone. The name is suited to her, brown-eyed, brown-haired Dora. If she were one whit more like Anna, I never could have liked her as I do,— brown-eyed, brown-haired Dora.

"And she has gone to Morrisville, where Anna lived. Is this Mrs. Randall very grand, I wonder, and will Dora hear of Anna? Of course she will. I knew that when I asked her to be the bearer of that package which I might have sent by express. Perhaps she will take it herself, seeing little Robin and so hearing of Anna. O Dora, you would pity me if you knew how much I have suffered. Only God could give the strength to endure, and He has done so until I carry my burden uncomplainingly.

"Will she see Lieutenant Reed, Mrs. Randall's brother? What a blow that story gave me, and yet I doubted its truth, though the possibility nearly drives me wild, and shows me the real nature of my feelings for Dora Freeman. Let me record the event as it occurred. This morning Dora went away to Morrisville, my old home, though she does not know that, because, for certain reasons, I have not chosen to talk much of my affairs in Beechwood. She went early, before many people were astir, but I saw her, and heard, as I believe, the roar of the train until it was miles away, and then I awoke to the knowledge that the world had changed with her going, that *now* there was nothing before me but the same monotonous round of professional calls, the tiresome chatter of my landlady, Mrs. Minerva Markham, and the tedious sitting here alone.

"Heretofore there has been a pleasant excitement in watching the house across the street for a glimpse of Dora, in waiting for her to come out upon the lawn where she frolicked and played with all those little Russells, in seeing her sometimes steal away as if to be alone, and in pitying her because I knew the half dozen were on her track and would soon discover her hiding-place, in wishing that I could spirit her away from the cares which should fall upon another, in seeing her after the gas was lighted going in to dinner in her white muslin dress with the scarlet geraniums in her hair, in watching her window until the shadow flitting before it disappeared with the light, and I was left to wonder if the little maiden were kneeling in adoration to Him who gave her life and being. All this, or something like it, has formed a part of my existence, but with Dora's going everything changed. Clouds came over the sun; the breeze from the lake blew cold and chilly; Mrs. Markham's talk was more insipid than ever, while the addition to my patrons of two of the wealthiest families in town failed to give me pleasure. Dora was gone, and in a listless mood I made my round of visits, riding over the Berkley hills and across the Cheshire flats, wondering if I did well to send that package by Dora, knowing as I did that it must lead to her hearing of Anna.

"It was sunset when I came home, a warm, purple sunset, such as always reminds me of Dora in her mature beauty. There was a stillness in the air, and from the trees which skirt the hillside leading to the town the katydids were biping their clamorous notes. I used to like to hear them when a boy, and many's the time I've stood with *Anna* listening to them by the west door at home; but now there was a sadness in their tones as if they were saying, 'Dora's gone; Dora's gone,' while the opposite party responded, 'And Anna too; and Anna too.'

"I had not wept for Anna since the hour when I first knew she was lost forever, but to-night in the gathering twilight, with the music of my boyhood sounding in my ears, the long ago came back to me again, bringing with it the beautiful blue-eyed girl over whose death there hangs so dark a mystery, and there was a moisture in my eyes, and a tear which dropped on Major's mane, and was shed for Anna dead as well as for Dora gone. When I reached the office, I found upon the slate a hand-writing which I knew to be Johnnie Russell's, and for a moment I felt tempted to kiss it, because *he* is Dora's nephew. This is what he had written :

"'Mother's toock ravin' with one of her headaches, cause auntie's gone, and there's nobody to tend to the young ones. Gawly, how they've cut up, and she wants you to come with some jim-cracks in a phial. Yours, with regret, JOHN RUSSELL, JR.'

" I like that boy, so outspoken and truthful, but Dora will be shocked at his language. And so my services were needed at the big house over the way. Usually I like to go there, but now Dora is gone it is quite another thing, for with all my daily discipline of myself, I dislike Mrs. Russell. I have struggled against it, prayed against it, but as often as I see her face and hear her voice, the old dislike comes back. There's nothing real about her except her selfishness and vanity. Were she raving with fever, I verily believe her hair would be just as elaborately curled, her handsome wrapper as carefully arranged, and her heavy bracelets clasped as conspicuously around the wrists as if in full dress for an evening party. To-night I found her in just this costume, with a blue scarf thrown round her, as she reclined upon the pillow. I knew she was suffering, from the dark rings beneath her eyes, and this roused my sympathy. She seems to like me as a physician, and asked me to stop after I had prescribed for her. Naturally enough she spoke of Dora, whom she missed so much, she said, and then with a little sigh continued:

"'It is not often that I talk familiarly with any but my most intimate friends, but you have been in our family so much, and know how necessary Dora is to us, that you will partially understand what a loss it would be to lose my sister entirely.'

"'Yes, a terrible loss,' I said, thinking more of myself than of her. 'But is there a prospect of losing her?' I asked, feeling through my frame a cold, sickly chill, which rapidly increased as she replied:

"'Perhaps not; but this Mrs. Randall, whom she has gone to visit, has a brother at West Point, you know, Lieutenant Reed, the young man with epaulets, who was here last summer.'

"'Yes, I remember him,' I said, and Mrs. Russell continued:

"'He has been in love with Dora ever since she was

with his sister Mattie at school. Dora has not yet given him a decided answer, but I know her preference for him, and as he is to be at his sister's while Dora is there, it is natural to fear that it may result in eventually taking Dora away from Beechwood.'

" 'It may, it may,' I responded, in a kind of absent way, for my brain was in a whirl, and I scarcely knew what I did.

"She must have observed my manner, for her eyes suddenly brightened as if an entirely new idea had been suggested to her.

" 'Now if it were some one near by,' she continued, 'perhaps she would not leave me. The house is large enough for all, and Dora will marry some time, of course. She is a kind sister, and will make a good wife.'

"At this point Squire Russell came in, and soon after I said good-by, going out again into the summer night, beneath the great, full moon, whose soft, pure light could not still the throbbing of my heart; neither could the long walk I took down by the lake, where Dora and I went one day last summer. There were quite a number of the villagers with us, for it was a picnic, but I saw only Dora, who, afraid of the water, stayed on the shore with me, while the rest went off in sail-boats. We talked together very quietly, sitting on the bank, beneath a broad grape-vine, of whose leaves she wove a sort of wreath, as she told me of her dear old home, and how the saddest moments she had ever known were those in which she fully realized that she was never again to live there, that stranger hands would henceforth tend the flowers she had tended, and stranger feet tread the walks and alleys and winding paths with which the grounds abounded. I remember how the wish flashed upon me that I might some day buy back the home, and take her there as its mistress. Of all this I thought to-night, sitting on the lone shore, just where she once sat, and listening to the low dash of the waves, which, as they came rolling almost to my feet, seemed to murmur, 'Never, never more!'

"I do not believe I am love-sick, but I am very sad to-night, and the walk down to the lake did not dispel the sadness. It may be it is wrong in me thus to despond, when in many ways I have been prospered beyond my most sanguine hopes. That heavy debt is paid at last, thanks to the kind Father who raised me up so many friends, and whose healing hand has more than once been outstretched to save when medicine was no longer of avail. As is natural, the cure was charged to me, when I knew it was God who had wrought the almost miraculous change. And shall I murmur at anything when sure of His love and protection? Be still, my heart. If it be God's will, Dora shall yet rest in these arms, which fain would shelter her from all the ills of life; and if 'tis not His will, what am *I*, that I should question His dealings?"

CHAPTER IV.

JOHNNIE'S LETTER TO DORA.

"BEECHWOOD, June 13th.
In the afternoon, up in the wood-house chaim-
ber where I've crawled to hide from the young ones.

DEAR, DEAR, DARLING AUNTIE:
"It seems to me you've been gone a hundred million billion years, and you've no idea what a forlorn old rat-trap of a plais it is Without You, nor how the Young Ones do rase Kain. They keep up the Darn-dest row—Auntie. I didn't mean to use that word, and I'll scratch it right out, but when you are away, I'll be dar—There I was going to say it agen. I'm a perfectly Dredful Boy, ain't I? But I do love you, Auntie, and last night,—now don't you tell pa, nor Tish, nor Nobody, —last night after I went to bed, I cried and cried and crammed the sheet in my mouth to keep Jim from hearing me till I most vomited.

"Ben and Burt behave awful. Clem heard their Prayers and right in the midst of Our father, Burt stopped and asked if Mr. John Smith, the Storekeeper, was related to John the baptis. Clem laughed and then

Ben struck her with his fist and Burt, who is a little red pepper any How pitched in And kicked Burt. The fuss waked up Daisy who fell out of bed and screamed like Murder, then Tish, great Tattle Tail, must go for Father who came up with a big Gadd and declared he'd have order in His own house. You know the Young Ones aint a bit afraid of Him and Ben and Burt kept on their fightin tell Clem said 'I shall tell Miss Dora how you act.' That stopped 'em and the last I heard Burt was coaxing Clem:

"'Don't tell Auntie. I'se good now, real good.'

"Maybee it's mean in me to tell you but I want you to know just how They carry on, hoping you'll pick up your traps and come home. No I don't neither for I want you to stay and have a good time which I'm sure you don't have here. I wish most you was my Mother though I guess girls of 25 don't often have great strappin Boys like me, do they? I asked Dr. West and he looked so queer when he said, 'It is possible but not common.' Why not, I wonder? Now, Auntie, I don't want mother to die, because she's Mother, but if she should, *you'll* have father, won't you? That's a nice Auntie, and that makes me think. Last night mother had the headache and Dr. West was here. It was after the Rumpus in the nursery and I was sitting at the head of the stairs wishing you was come home when I heard 'em talking about you and what do you think mother told Doctor? A lot of stuff about you and that nasty Reed who was here last summer. She talked as if you liked him,—said he would be at Mrs. Randall's and she rather expected it would be settled then. *I was so mad,* I bumped right up and down on the stairs and said Darn, Darn, as fast as I could. Now, Auntie, I didn't mean to lie, but I have. I've told a whopper and you can bite my head off if you like. Dr's voice sounded just as if he didn't want you to like that Reed and I diddent think it right to let it go. So this morning I went over to the office and found Dr. West looking pale as if he diddent sleep good.

"'Doctor,' says I, 'do I look like a chap that will lie?'

"'Why, no,' says he, 'I never thought you did.'

"'But I will,' ses I, 'and I am come to do that very thing, come to tell you something Aunt Dora made me promise never to tell.'

"'John, you mussent, I can't hear you,' he began, but I yelled up, 'you shall; I will tell; it's about Dora and that Reed. She don't like him.' Somehow he stopped hushin' me then and pretended to fix his books while I said how last summer I overheard this Reed ask you to be his wife, and you told him no; you did not love him well enough, and never could, and how you meant it too. There diddent neither of you know I was out in the balcony, I said, until he was gone, and I *sneazed* when you talked to me and made me promise never to tell what I'd heard to father, nor mother, nor nobody. I never did tell them, but I've told the doctor, and I ain't sorry, it made him look so glad. He took me, and Tish, and Ben, and Burt, all out riding this afternoon and talked to them real nice, telling them they must be good while you was gone. Tish and Jim are pretty good, but Ben has broken the spy-glass and the umberill, and Burt has set down on the kittens, and oh I must tell you; he took a big iron spoon which he called a *sovel* and dug up every single gladiola in the garden! Ain't they terrible Boys?

"There, they've found where I be, and I hear Burt coming up the stairs one step at a time, so I must stop, for they'll tip over the ink, or something. Dear Auntie, I do love you ever and ever so much, and if you want my Auntie and a grown up woman I'd marry you. Do boys ever marry their aunts?

"Your, with Due Respect,
"JOHN RUSSELL.

"p.s. Excuse my awful spellin. I never could spel, you know, or make the right Capitols.

"p.s. No. 2. Burt has just tumbled the whole length of the wood-house stares, and landed plump in the pounding barrel, half full of water. You orto hear him *Yell*."

CHAPTER V.

DORA'S DIARY.

"MORRISVILLE, June 13th.

WAS too tired last night to open my trunk, and so have a double duty to perform, that of recording the events of the last two days. Can it be that it is not yet forty-eight hours since I left Beechwood and all its cares, which, now that I am away from them, do seem burdensome? What a delicious feeling there is in being referred to and waited upon as if you were of consequence, and how I enjoy knowing that for a time at least I can rest; and I begin to think I need it, for how else can I account for the languid, weary sensation which prompts me to sit so still in the great, soft, motherly chair which Mattie has assigned me, and which stands right in the cosey bay-window, where I can look out upon the beautiful scenery of Morrisville?

"It is very pleasant here, and so quiet that it almost seems as if the town had gone to sleep and knew nothing of the great, roaring, whirling world without. Not even a car-whistle to break the silence, for the nearest station where I stopped, after my uneventful ride, is eight miles from here. There was Mattie herself waiting for me on the platform, her face as sunny as ever, and her greeting as cordial. Her husband, Mr. Randall, is a tall, well-formed man, with broad shoulders, which look a little like West Point discipline. It was very silly in one to contrast him at once with Dr. West, but I did, and Dr. West gained by the comparison, for there is an expression in his face which I seldom see in others, certainly not in Mr. Randall. *He* looks, as I suspect he is, proud, —and yet he is very kind to me, treating me with as much deference as if I were the Queen of England. They had come in their carriage, and the drive over the green hills and through the pleasant valleys was delightful. I could do nothing but admire, and still I wondered that one as fond of society as Mattie should have settled so far from the stirring world as Morrisville, and at last I asked why she had done so.

"'It's all Will's doings,' she answered, laughingly. 'He is terribly exclusive, and fancied that in Morrisville he should find ample scope for indulging his taste,—that people would let him alone,—but they don't. Why, we have only lived there three months, and I am sure half the town know just how many pieces of silver I have,— whether my dishes are stone or French china,—what hour we breakfast,—when we go to bed,—when we get up, and how many dresses I have. But I don't care, I rather like it; and then, too, Morrisville is not a very small town. It has nearly three thousand inhabitants, and a few as refined and cultivated people as any with whom I ever met.'

"'Who are they?' I asked, and Mattie began:

"'There's the Verners, and Waldos, and Strikers, and Rathbones in town, while in the country there's the Kingslakes, and Croftons, and Bishops, and Warings, making a very pleasant circle.'

"I don't know why I felt disappointed that she did not mention *Mrs. David West* as among the upper ten, but I did, and should have ventured to speak of that lady, if I had not been a little afraid of Mr. Randall, who might think my associates too plebeian to suit him.

"We were entering the town now, and as we drove through what Mattie said was Grove Street, I forgot all about Mrs. David West in my admiration of the prettiest little white cottage I ever saw. I cannot describe it except that it seemed all porticoes, bay-windows, and funny little places shooting out just where you did not expect them. One bay-window opened into the garden, which was full of flowers, while right through the centre ran a gurgling brook, which just at the entrance had been coaxed into a tiny waterfall. I was in ecstasies, particularly as on a grass-plat, under a great elm-tree, an oldish-looking lady sat knitting and talking to a beautiful child reclining in a curious-looking vehicle, half wagon, half chair. I never in my life saw anything so lovely as the face of that child, seen only for a moment, with the setting sunlight falling on its golden curls and giving it the look of an angel. The lady interested me greatly in her dress of black, with the widow's cap resting on her gray hair, while her face was familiar as if I had seen it before.

"'Who are they?' I asked Mattie, but she did not know.

"Neither did her husband, and both laughed at my evident admiration.

"'We will walk by here some day, and maybe you can make their acquaintance,' Mattie said, as she saw how I leaned back for a last glance at the two figures beneath the trees.

"'There is West Lawn!' Mattie cried at last, in her enthusiastic way, pointing out a large stone building which stood a little apart from the town.

"I knew before that 'West Lawn' was the name of Mr. Randall's home, and when I saw it I comprehended at once why it was so called. It was partly because of the long grassy lawn in front, and partly because it stood to the westward of the village, upon a slight eminence which overlooked the adjacent country. It is a delightful place, and Mattie says they have made many improvements since they bought it. But it must have been pleasant before, for it shows marks of care and cultivation given to it years ago. Like that cottage by the brook, it has bay-windows and additions, while I think I never saw so many roses around one spot in my life. There is a perfect wilderness of them, in every shade and variety. These reminded me of Dr. West, who is so fond of roses, and who said once that he would have *his* home literally covered with them. 'West Lawn' would suit him at this season, I am sure. Here in Morrisville I find myself thinking a great deal about Dr. West, and thinking only good of him. I forget all I ever fancied about his littleness, and remember instead how kind he is to the Beechwood poor, who have named at least a dozen children after him. *Mrs. David West!* I do not see as I shall be able to meet her ladyship, as she evidently does not belong to the Vernor and Randall clique.

"But let me narrate events a little more in the order in which they occurred, going back to last night, when we had tea in what Mattie calls the 'Rose Room,' because the portico in front is enveloped with roses. Then came a long talk, when Mr. Randall was gone for his evening paper, and when Mattie, nestling up to me, with her head in my lap, just as she used to do in school, told me what a dear fellow her husband was, and how much she loved him. Then some music, I playing my poor accompaniments while Mattie sang her favorite Scotch ballads. Then, at an early hour for me, I went to bed, for Mattie does not like sitting up till midnight. I have a large, airy chamber, which must have been fitted up for a young lady, there are so many closets, and shelves, and presses, with a darling little bath and dressing-room opening out of it. Mattie, who came in to see that I was comfortable, told me this was the only room in which the paper had not been changed.

"'It's old-fashioned, as you see,' she said, 'and must have been on before the time of Mr. Wakely, of whom we bought the house, but it is so pretty and clean that I would not have it touched.'

"It is indeed pretty, its ground a pure white, sprinkled here and there with small bouquets of violets. Just back of the dressing-table and near the window are pencil-marks, 'Robert, Robert, Robert,' in a girlish hand, and then a name which might have been 'Annie,' though neither of us could make it out distinctly. Evidently this room belonged to a maiden of that name, and while thinking about her and wondering who she was, I fell asleep. I do not believe in haunted houses, nor witches, nor ghosts, nor goblins, but last night I had the queerest dreams, in which that woman and child beneath the trees were strangely mingled with Dr. West and a young lady who came to me with such a pale, sad face, that I woke in a kind of nightmare, my first impression being that I was occupying some other room than mine.

"This morning Mattie was present while I unpacked my trunk, and coming upon that package, I said, as unconcernedly as possible, 'Oh, by the way, do you know such a person as Mrs. David West ? I have a package for her, entrusted to me by a—a friend in Beechwood.'

"'Mrs. David West?' and Mattie seemed to be thinking as she examined the package, which felt like a small square box. 'Mrs. David West? No, I know no such person; but then I've only lived here three months. There's Bell Verner now coming in the gate. Maybe she will know, though they have only been here since last autumn. I'll ask her, and you be in readiness to come down if she inquires for you, as she certainly will. You look sweet in your white wrapper, with the blue ribbon round your waist. I wish blue was becoming to me— Yes, yes, Dinah, I'm coming,' and she fluttered down to the hall, where I heard a sound of *kissing*, accompanied with little cooing tones of endearment, such as Mattie has always been famous for; then a whisper, and then I shut the door, for I was sure they were talking of me. As a general thing I dread to meet grand people, I had enough of them at Newport: and so I hated to meet Miss Bell Verner; and after I was sent for I waited a little, half wishing myself away from Morrisville.

" I found her a stylish, cold-looking girl, who, after taking me in, at a glance, from my head to my slippers, said rather abruptly :

"'Excuse me, Miss Freeman, but weren't you at Newport last summer ?'

"'Yes,' I answered, now scanning her, to discover, if possible, some trace of a person seen before.

"'I thought so,' she continued. 'We were at the Atlantic. We could not get in at the Ocean House, it was so full. Pardon me, but I am afraid I felt slightly ill-natured at your party—the Russells, I believe—because they took so many rooms as to shut us out entirely. If I remember rightly, there were nine of you, together with three servants, and you stayed two months. I used to see you on the beach, and thought your bathing-dress so pretty. We were a little jealous, too, at our house of Miss Freeman, who was styled the belle.'

"'Oh, no,' I exclaimed, feeling very much embarrassed, 'I couldn't be a belle. I did not go much in society. I stayed with Margaret who was sick, or helped take care of the children.'

"'Oh, yes,' she rejoined, 'I heard of the invalid Mrs. Russell, who exacted so much of her sweet-tempered sister. The gentlemen were very indignant. By the way, how is Mrs. Russell?'

"I did not like the way she spoke of Margaret, and with as much dignity as possible I replied that Mrs. Russell was still out of health, and I feared would always remain so. Somehow I fancied that the fact of there having been nine of us, with three servants, and that we stayed at the Ocean House two months did more towards giving Miss Vernor a high opinion of me than all Mattie must have said in my praise, for she became very gracious, so that I really liked her, and wished I had as fine and polished an air as she carried with her. When we had talked of the Strykers, and Waldos, and Rathbones, Mattie suddenly asked if Bell knew a Mrs. David West in town.

"'Mrs. David West? Mrs. David West?' It did seem as if Miss Verner had heard the name, and that it belonged to a widow living on the Ferrytown road. 'But why do you ask?' she said. 'It can't be any one desirable to know.'

"Mattie explained why, and Miss Verner good-naturedly offered to inquire, but Mattie said no, their man Peter would ascertain and take the package. So after Miss Verner was gone, and Peter came round to prune a rose-bush, Mattie put him the same question:

"'Did he know Mrs. David West?'

"'Yes, he knew where she lived; she had that handsome grandchild.'

"Of course Mattie deputed him at once to do my errand, and I consented, though I wished so much to go myself. Running up-stairs I wrote on a card:

"'Dr. West, of Beechwood, commissioned me to be the bearer of this little package, which I should have brought to you myself had Mrs. Randall known where to find you.

"'DORA FREEMAN, West Lawn.'

"I did not see Peter again until long after dinner, and then I asked if he had done my errand.

"'Yes, miss,' he replied. 'She was much obliged. She's a nice woman.'

"'Peter, don't those verbenas need sheltering from the hot sun?' Mr. Randall called out, his manner indicating that by volunteering information respecting Mrs. David West, Peter was getting too familiar.

"Mr. Randall is very proud, and so is Mattie, but in a different way. If she knew how much I wish to see Mrs. West, or at least learn something of her, she would never rest until the wish was gratified. We took a walk after tea to the village cemetery, of which the people are justly proud, for it is a most beautiful spot, divesting the dark, still grave of half its terrors. There are some splendid monuments there, one costing I dare not tell how much. It was reared to the memory of General Morris, for whom the town was named, but this did not impress me one half so much as a solitary grave standing apart from all the others and enclosed by a slender iron fence. The grass in the little yard was fresh and green, and there were many roses growing there. The stone was a plain slab of Italian marble, with only these words upon it:

"' Anna, aged 20.'

"Even Mattie was interested, and we leaned a long time on the gate, speculating upon the Anna sleeping at our feet. Who was she, and whose the hand of love which had been so often busy there? She was young, only twenty when she died. Had many years been joined to the past since she was laid to rest? Was she beautiful, and good, and pure? Yes, she was all that, I fancied, and I even dared to pluck a rose-bud whose parent stalk had taken root near the foot of the grave. I can see it now in the glass of water where I put it after returning home. That rose and that grave have interested me strangely, painfully I may say, as if the Anna whom they represented were destined to cross my path, if ever the dead can rise up a barrier between the living.

"June 15th.

"A steady summer rain has kept us in-doors all day, but I have enjoyed the quiet so much. It seems as if I never should get rested, and I am surprised to find how tired I am, and how selfish I am growing. I was wicked enough to be sorry when in the afternoon Bell Verner came, bringing her crocheting and settling herself for a visit. She is very sociable, and asks numberless questions about Beechwood and its inhabitants. I wonder why I told her of everybody but Dr. West, for I did, but of him I could not talk, and did not.

"SATURDAY, June 16th.

"A long letter from Johnnie, and so like him, that I cannot find it in my heart to scold him on paper for his dreadful language. I will talk to him on my return, and tell him he must be more choice of words and must make an effort to learn to spell, though I believe it is natural to the Russells to spell badly. I can see just how they miss me at home, and I cried over the letter till I was almost sick. I am sure they want me there, and I wonder what they would say if they knew how the Randalls, and Verners, and Strykers are plotting to keep me here until September, Mattie and Bell saying they will then go with me to Beechwood. Just think of those two fine ladies at our house. To be sure, it is quite as expensively furnished as either Mattie's or Bell Verner's, and we keep as many servants; but the children, the confusion! What would they do? No, I must not stay, though I should enjoy it vastly. I like Bell Verner, as I know her better. There is a depth of character about her for which I did not at first give her credit. One trait, however, annoys me excessively. She wants to get married, and makes no secret of it either. She's old enough, too,—twenty-eight, as she told me of her own accord, just as she is given to telling everything about herself. Secretly, I think she would suit Dr. West, only she might feel above him, she is so exclusive. I wonder Margaret should tell him that story about Lieutenant Reed, and I am glad Johnnie set him right. I would not have Lieutenant Reed for the diamonds of India, and yet he is a great, good-natured, vain fellow, who is coming here by and by. I think I'll turn him over to Bell, though I can fancy how her black eyes would flash upon him.

"I have had a note from Mrs. David West, inviting me to come and see her, and this is the way it reads:

"'My Dear Miss Freeman:

"'I am much obliged for the trouble you took in bringing me that package, and did I go out at all, except to church, I would thank you in person. If you can, will you come and see me before you return to Beechwood? I should like to talk with you about the Doctor. Any one interested in him has a sure claim upon my friendship.

"'Yours respectfully,

"'Helen West.

"'Grove Street, No. 30.'

"Nothing can be more ladylike than the handwriting, and, indeed, the whole thing. Mrs. David West may be poor and unknown, but she is every whit as refined and cultivated as either Mattie or Bell. I shall see her, too, before I leave Morrisville; but why does she take it for granted that I am interested in Dr. West? I am not, except as a good physician; and what is she to him? Here I am puzzling my brain and wasting the gas, when I ought to be in bed; so with one look at that rose, which I have been foolish enough to press,—the rose from Anna's grave,—I'll bid the world good-night."

CHAPTER VI.

LETTERS.

No. 1.

Mrs. David West's Letter.

MY DEAR RICHARD:
"Your package of money and little note, sent by Miss Dora Freeman, was brought to me with a line from the young lady by Mr. Randall's colored servant Peter. I know you could not afford to send me so much, and I wish you had kept a part for yourself. Surely, if the commandment with promise means anything,—and we know it does,—you, my son, will be blessed for your kindness to your widowed mother, as well as your unselfish devotion to those who have been, one the innocent, the other the guilty, cause of so much suffering. God reward my boy—my only boy as I sometimes fear. Surely if Robert were living he would have sent us word ere this. I have given him up, asking God to pardon his sin, which was great.

"And so the debt is paid at last! Dear Richard, when I read that I shed tears of gratitude and thanksgiving that you were free from a load you never should have borne. It was a large sum for you to earn and pay in less than seven years, besides supporting me and Robin. He grows dearer to me every day, and yet I seldom look at him without a great choking sob rising to my throat. He is like his mother, and I loved her as if she had been my daughter. O Anna, lost darling, was she as pure and sinless when she died as when she crept into my arms and whispered of her newly found hope in Him who can keep us all from sin? God only knows. Alas! that her end should be wrapt in so dark a mystery; and ten times alas! that any one should be malignant enough to blame you, who had well-nigh died when the trouble fell upon us.

"And so you fear you are more interested in this Dora than you ought to be, or rather that she is far too good for you.

"She must be very, very good, if my boy be not worthy of her.

"Yes, the Randalls are very grand, fashionable people, as you may know from the fact that the Verners and Strykers took them up at once. I don't know what influence they may have over Dora; not a bad one, I hope. I think I saw her the other night riding by on horseback, in company with Bell Verner. It was too dark to see her distinctly, but I heard Miss Verner say, in reply evidently to some remark, 'I never trouble myself to know or inquire after any one out of our set,' and then they galloped on rapidly. As I am not in Miss Verner's 'set' she will not probably bring Dora to see me, but I have obviated that difficulty by writing her a note and inviting her to call on me. Did I do right? I am anxious to see her, for a mother can judge better than her son of what is in woman.

"Yours affectionately,

"HELEN WEST."

"By the way, did you know that Mr. Randall was the purchaser of West Lawn, our old home?

"H. W."

No. 2.

Extract from Dr. West's reply.

"DEAR MOTHER:—Your letters do me so much good, and make me strong to bear, though really I have perhaps as little to trouble me as do most men of my years. If the mystery concerning poor Anna were made clear,— if we were sure that she was safe with the good Shepherd, and if we knew that Robert, whether dead or alive, had repented of his sin, I should be very happy.

"There's *Dora*, I know,—a continuous trouble, but one with which I would not willingly dispense. You ask if you did right to invite her to call. You seldom do wrong; but in this case, O mother, I have become a perfect coward since Dora left me. I thought I wanted her to know all that we know of Anna and Robin; but now the very possibility of her hearing the little you can tell, and then giving it the natural construction which she might, makes the cold sweat ooze out in drops upon my face. If she comes, tell her as little as possible. It gives me a thrill of satisfaction to know that she is at West Lawn, enjoying the roses I planted. Dear West Lawn! but for that terrible misfortune which prompted us to sell it, you might have belonged to Miss Bell Verner's set. But don't tell Dora. I'd rather she should like me for myself, and not for what I used to be." * * * *

No. 3.
Extract from Margaret's letter to Dora.

* * * * "I do think you might come home, instead of asking to stay longer. It's right shabby in you to leave me so long, when you know how much I suffer. The children behave dreadfully, and even John has acted real cross, as if he thought all ailed me was nervousness. You cannot love me, Dora, as much as I do you, and I think it's downright ungrateful after all I've done for you since father died. If you care for me at all, you'll come in just one week from to-day. I have about decided to go to Saratoga, and want you to go with me. Be sure and come."

No. 4.
Extract from Mattie's letter to Margaret.

"DEAR MRS. RUSSELL:—Excuse the liberty I am taking, but really if you and your husband knew how much Dora has improved since leaving home, and how much she really needs rest, you would not insist on her coming home so soon. Husband and I and Bell Verner all think it too bad, and I for one veto her leaving us."

No. 5.
Extract from Mr. Randall's letter.

"MRS. RUSSELL.—MADAM:—Both myself and Mrs. Randall are exceedingly loth to part with our young guest, whom rest is benefiting so much. You will do us and her a great favor to let her remain, and I may add I think it your duty so to do."

Scene in Mrs. Russell's parlor one morning about the first of July.

Squire John nervously fumbling his watch-chain, looking very hot and distressed; Johnnie all swollen up, looking like a little volcano ready to explode; Mrs. Russell crying over Mr. and Mrs. Randall's letters, wondering what business it was of theirs to *meddle* and talk, just as if she did not do her duty by Dora. Who, she'd like to know, had supported Dora these dozen years, sending her to school, taking her to Newport, and buying her such nice dresses? It was right mean in Dora, and she would not stand it. Dora should come home, and John should write that very day to tell her so, unless he liked Dora better than he did her, as she presumed he did—yes, she knew he did.

"Thunderation, mother, why shouldn't he like Auntie best?" and with this outburst, Johnnie plunged heart and soul into the contest. "Who, I'd like to know, makes the house decent as a fellow likes to have it,—a married old chap, I mean, like father. 'Tain't you. It's *Auntie*, and so the whole co-boozle of servants say. You ask 'em. Talk about what you've done for Dora these dozen years, taking her to Newport, and all that! I think *I'd dry up* on that strain and tell what she'd done for me. Hasn't there been a baby about every other week since she lived here, and hasn't Auntie had the whole care of the brats? And at Newport how was it? I never told before, but I will now. I heard two nice gentlemen talking over what a pretty girl Miss Freeman was, and how mean and selfish it was in her sister to make such a little *nigger* of her. They didn't say *nigger*, but that's what they meant. Dora ain't coming home, no how. You can go to Saratogo without her. Take Clem, and Daisy, and Tish, and Jim. You know they act the best of the lot. Leave me and Burt and Ben at home. I'll see to them, and we shall get on well enough."

By this time Margaret was in hysterics, to think a son of hers should abuse her so, with his father standing by and never once trying to stop him. Possibly some such idea crept through Squire John's brain, for, putting into his voice as much sternness as he was capable of doing, he said, "My boy, I'm astonished that you should use such shocking words as *thunderation, co-boozle, dry up,* and the like. Your Aunt Dora would be greatly distressed; but, Madge," turning to his sobbing wife and trying to wind his arm around her waist, "Johnnie is right, on the whole ; his plan is a good one. We'll take Clem, and Rosa, too, if you like, leaving Johnnie, Ben, and Burt at home, and Dora shall stay where she is. She was tired when she went away, and very pale. You are not selfish, Madge ; you'll let her stay. I'll write so now,—shall I ?" and there was a sound very much like a very large, hearty kiss, while a moment after Johnnie, in the kitchen, was turning a round of somersaults, striking his heels in the fat sides of the cook, and tripping up little Burt in his delight at the victory achieved for Dora.

No. 6.

Extract from Johnnie's letter to Dora.

"July 7th.

"DEAR AUNTIE:—The house is still a as mouse, and seems so funny. The old folks, with Tish, Jim, Daisy, Clem, and Rosa, have cut stick for Saratoga, leaving me with Ben and Burt. You orto have seen me pitch into mother about your staying. I give it to her good, and twitted about your being a drudge. I meant it all then, but now that she is gone, I'll be—I guess I'll skip the hard words, and say that every time I rem'ber what I said to her, there's a thumpin' great lump comes in my throat, and I wish I hadn't said it. I've begun six letters to tell her I am sorry, and she only been gone two days, but I've tore 'em all up, and now when you see her you tell her I'm sorry,—'cause I am, and I keep thinkin of when I was a little shaver in pettycoats, how she sometimes took me in her lap and said I was a preshus little hunny, the joy of her life. She says I'm the *pest* of it now, and she never kisses me no more, nor lets me kiss her 'cause she says I slawber and wet her face, and muss her hair and dress. But she's mother, and I wish I hadn't sed them nasty things to her and maid her cry.

"Dr. West was here just now, and wanted to borrow a book, but when he found it was yourn he wouldn't take it; he said he'd write and ask permission.

"We get on nice, only cook has spanked Ben once and Burt twice. I told her if she did it agen I'd spank her, and so I will. I think I've got her under, so she knows I'm man of the house. The old cat has weened her kittens. Burt shut one of 'em up in the meal chest, and the white-fased cow has come in, which means she's got a calph." "Yours,
"JOHNNIE."

No. 7.

Dr. West's letter, on which he spent three hours, wasting half a dozen sheets of note-paper, and which when finished did not please him at all.

"MISS FREEMAN:—You probably do not expect me to write to you, and will be surprised at receiving this letter. The fact is I want permission to go to that little library, which, until this morning, I did not know was yours. There are some books I would like to read, but will not do so without leave from the owner.

"I hear you are enjoying your visit, and I am glad, although *I* miss you very much. Of course you know your brother and sister are at Saratoga, and that Johnnie is keeping house, as he says. If you have not time to answer this to me, please say to Johnnie whether I can read the books or not.

"Yours truly,
"RICHARD WEST."

No. 8.

Dora's reply, over which she spent two hours and wasted five sheets of note-paper.

"DR. WEST.—DEAR SIR:—You really were over-nice about the books, and I should feel like scolding were it not that your fastidiousness procured me a letter which I did not expect from you. Certainly, you may take any book you like.

"And so you miss me? I wonder if that is true. I should not think you would. I'm not worth missing. I hope you will see Johnnie as often as possible.

"Yours respectfully,

"DORA.

"P. S.—I am going to-morrow to see Mrs. David West."

CHAPTER VII.

DORA'S DIARY CONTINUED.

IT is a long time since I wrote a word in this book; I have been so happy and so busy withal; visits, rides, picnics, and everything. I did not know that life was so bright and pleasant as I have found it here in Morrisville, where everybody seems trying to entertain me. Mattie's brother Charlie is here, but he behaves like a man; does not annoy me one bit, but flirts shockingly with *Bell Verner,* who flirts as hard in return. He teasingly asked me one day about *Dr. West,* and when Bell inquired who he was, he said he was 'a country doctor of little pills; a sort of lackadaisical chap, who read service very loud, and almost touched the pew railing when he bowed in the Apostles' Creed.'

"I grew so very angry defending Dr. West that Bell honestly believes I care for him, and kindly stops Lieutenant Reed when he begins his fun. I like Bell Verner more and more, only she is too proud. How I cried over that letter from Margaret telling me to come home, and how I tried not to have Mr. and Mrs. Randall answer it; but they did, and there came back such a nice response from

John. What a dear, unselfish man he is, and how smooth he made it look,—so smooth that I really felt as if doing him a favor by staying until Johnnie's letter was received, and I guessed at once the storm through which they had passed.

"Will I ever forget the day I received a letter from *Dr. West?* I could scarcely credit my own eyes, yet there was his name, Richard West, looking so natural. I felt the blood tingling in my veins, even though he merely wrote to ask me if he might read my books, the foolish man! Of course he might. He says he misses me, and this I think is why the letter is worth so much, and why I answered it. Perhaps it was foolish to do so, but I can't help it now. It is not at all likely he'll write again, though I find myself fancying how I shall feel, and what he would say in a second letter. Bell Verner knows he wrote, for I told her, but pretended I did not care. To-morrow I am going at last to see Mrs. David West.

"July 15th.—I have seen Mrs. David West; have looked into her eyes, so like the doctor's; have heard her voice; have seen the child; and oh! why *am* I so wretched, and why, when I came back, did I tear up that rose from Anna's grave and throw it to the winds? I hate this room. I cannot bear it, for Anna used to occupy it; she haunts me continually. She died in this room. *Richard kissed her here,* and here that child was born. Oh, what am I to think except what I do? And yet it is all suspicion, based on what a gossiping woman told me. I wish she had never come here. I would rather have cooked the dinner myself than have heard what I have.

"It was arranged that Mattie should go with me to see this Mrs. David West, and I thought of little else all the morning; but when dinner came Mattie had been seized with one of her violent headaches, and it was impossible for her even to sit up. Knowing how much I had anticipated the call, and not wishing to have me disappointed, she insisted that I should go without her, Peter acting as my escort there, while the new cook, a Mrs. Felton, who, it seems, had business on that street, would call for me on her way home. This was the arrangement, and at about four o'clock I started. I had in some way received the impression that Mrs. David West lived on Elm Street, and when we passed that point I asked Peter if we were right.

"'Yes, miss, Grove Street,—just there a ways in the neatest little cottage you ever set eyes on, I reckon.'

"Involuntarily I thought of the woman and child seen that first evening of my arrival at Morrisville, and something told me I was going straight to that cottage with its roses, its vines, and bay-windows. The surmise was correct. I knew the house in an instant, and had there been a doubt it would have been dispelled by the widow's cap and the little child out on the grass-plat, just where they were that other summer day so like this and yet so unlike it, for then I never guessed how sharp a pang I should be suffering now.

"'There she is. That's Mrs. West with Robin,' Peter said, and the next moment I was speaking to Mrs. David West, and before she said to me, 'You know my son,' I felt sure she was the doctor's mother.

"The same fine cast of feature, the same kind, honest expression beaming in the dark eye, and the same curve of the upper lip,—said by some to be always indicative of high breeding. The mother and son were very much alike, except that she as a female was noticeable for a softer style of beauty. I never saw one to whom the widow's cap was so becoming. It seemed peculiarly adapted to her sad, sweet face and the silken bands of grayish hair, which it did not conceal. There was also in her manner and speech a refinement which even Bell Verner might have imitated with advantage. My heart went out to her at once, and by the time I was seated in the rustic chair, for I preferred remaining in the yard, I felt as much at ease as if I had known her all my life.

"'This is Robin,' she said, turning to the child, who I now discovered was a cripple in its feet, and unable to walk. 'Did Richard ever tell you of Robin?'

"There was a hesitancy now in her voice, as if she knew Richard had never told me of him, and doubted her own integrity in asking the question.

"'No,' I replied, 'the doctor never told me of Robin, nor yet of himself.'

"'Richard is very reticent,' she answered; and then as she saw my glance constantly directed to Robin, she evidently tried to keep me from talking of him by asking numberless questions about Richard, and by telling me what a good, kind child he was to her.

"It is true I did not suspect her then of such a motive, but I can see now how she headed me off from the dangerous ground on which I leaped at last, for I could not resist the expression of that child's face, and breaking away from what she was telling me of Richard, I knelt by his chair, and kissing his round cheek, asked:

"'Whose boy are you?'

"'Papa Richard's and grandma's,' he replied, and then there flashed upon me the thought that in spite of his deep blue eyes and soft golden curls he was like Dr. West. For an instant I was conscious of a sharp, stinging pain, as I said to myself, 'Was Dr. West ever married?' Surely he would have told of that,—would at some time have mentioned his wife, and with the pain there came the knowledge that I did care more for Dr. West than I had supposed; that I was jealous of the dead woman, the mother of this child. Mrs. West must have divined a part of my thoughts, for she said half laughingly, like one under restraint:

"'He has always called my son "Papa Richard," as he

is the only father the child ever knew,' and a shadow flitted across her face as she directed my attention to a tall heliotrope near by. But I was not to be evaded; curiosity was aroused, and replying to her remark concerning the heliotrope, I turned again to Robin, whose little hand I now held in mine, and said, 'He is your grandchild?'

"Suddenly the dark eyes looked afar off as if appealing to something or somebody for help; then they softened and tears were visible in them.

"'Poor little Robin, he has been a source of great sorrow as well as of comfort to me, Miss Freeman,' and Mrs. West's delicate hand smoothed and unwound the golden curls clustering around Robin's head. 'So I used to unwind her curls,' she continued abstractedly. 'Robin's mother. I must show you her picture when we go in. She was very beautiful, more so than any one I ever knew, and Richard thinks the same.'

"Again that keen pain, as of a sharp knife gliding through my flesh, passed over me, but I listened breathlessly, while still caressing the child she continued:

"'His mother was my adopted daughter: I never had one of my own. Two sons have been born to me; one I have lost,—and her breath came gaspingly like speaking of the dead,—'the other you know is Richard. To all intents and purposes Anna was my daughter, and I am sure no mother ever loved her own offspring more than I did Anna. O Anna darling, Anna darling! I never dreamed, when I took her to my bosom, that she could —O Anna!' and Mrs. West's voice broke down in a storm of sobs.

"After this I could not ask her any more questions, and in a kind of maze I followed her into the house, which was a perfect little gem, and showed marks of most exquisite taste. Some of the furniture struck me as rather too heavy and expensive for that cottage, but I gave it but little thought, so interested was I in what I had heard and seen.

"'That is *Anna*,' Mrs. West said, pointing to a small portrait hanging upon the wall just where the western sunbeams were falling upon it and lighting it up with a wonderful halo of beauty.

"Instantly I forgot all else in my surprise that anything so perfectly beautiful could ever have belonged to a human being, and with a scream of delight I stood before the picture, exclaiming, ' It is not possible that this is natural!'

"'It is said to be,' Mrs. West rejoined, ' though there is a look in her eye which I did not notice until a few months before she died. She was crazy at the last.'

"'Crazy!' I repeated, now gazing with a feeling of pity upon the lovely face, which seemed imbued with life.

"I cannot describe that face, and I will not attempt it, for after I had told of the dark blue eyes and curls of golden hair, of the pure white skin and full ripe lips, you, my journal, would not have the least idea of the face, for the sweet, heavenly expression which made it what it was can never be described on paper. The artist had put it on canvas, so at least said Mrs. David West, and I believed her, drinking in its rare loveliness and repeating again, 'Crazy—poor Anna! Was it for long?'

"'No, not long; she died when Robin was born.'

"'And her husband; he must have been heart-broken,' I ventured to say next, but if Mrs. West heard me, she made no reply, and with my thoughts in a tumult, I continued looking at the portrait until, suddenly remembering the grave which had so interested me, I asked, 'How old was Anna when she died?'

"'Just twenty,' was the reply; while I rejoined, 'I am sure then I have seen her grave. It says upon the stone, "Anna, aged 20."'

"'Yes, that's all Richard would have on the marble. It almost killed Richard, but God has healed the wound just as He will heal all hearts which go to Him.'

"I don't know why I said what I did next, unless it were that I should have died if I had not. The words were wrung from me almost against my will:

"'Was Richard Anna's husband?'

"'No, no, oh no, Richard was not her husband!' Mrs. West replied, quickly.

"Heretofore she had answered my queries concerning Anna with hesitancy, but the 'No, no, oh no, Richard was not her husband,' was spoken eagerly, decidedly, as if it were a fact she would particularly impress upon my mind. Then, as I stood looking at her expectantly, she went on, but this time in the old, cautious manner:

"'I never knew who Anna's husband was. It is a sad story, which I would gladly forget, but Robin's presence keeps it in my mind,' and bowing her head over the child, the poor woman wept passionately.

"'Poor grandma, don't cry. I love you! What makes grandma cry over me so much, and look so sorry at me? Is it because I am a little lame boy?'

"This Robin said to me, while he tried to brush away the tears of her he called grandmother. He had not talked much before, but what he said now went through my heart, and kissing his forehead, I whispered:

"'People sometimes cry for joy.'

"'But she don't,' he said, nodding toward Mrs. West, who left us alone while she bathed her face and eyes. 'She looks so sorry, and says, "Poor Robin," so often. I guess it's because my feet will never walk, that she says that. I should cry too, but Papa Richard talked to me so good, and said God made me lame; that up in heaven there were no little cripples; that if I loved the Saviour, and didn't fret about my feet, I'd go up there some day; and since then I've tried hard not to mind, and ever so many times a day I say softly to myself, "Will Jesus help Robin not to fret because he's a poor lame boy, of no use to anybody." I say it way in my mouth, but God hears just the same.'

"I could not answer for my weeping, but kneeling beside the lame boy, I wound my arms around his neck, and laid his curly head upon my bosom, just as I would have done had it been Johnnie, Ben, or Bertie thus afflicted.

"'Seems like you was most my mother,' he said, caressing my cheek with his soft little hand. 'You don't look like her much, only I dreamed once she came to me and loved me, as you do, and kissed my twisted feet, oh! so many times. It was a beautiful dream, and next day I told it to grandma, and asked her if she wasn't sure my mother was in heaven! She did not answer until I said again, "Is she in heaven?" Then she said, "I hope so, Robin;" but I wanted to know sure, and kept on asking, until she burst out with the loudest cry I ever heard her or anybody cry, and said, "God knows, my little Robin. He will take care of her. I hope she's there!" but she wouldn't say for sure, just as she did when the minister and Mrs. Terry's baby died. Why not? Why didn't she? Lady, you look good. You look as if you prayed. Do you pray?'

"'Yes,' I answered, wondering if he would call my careless words a prayer.

"'Then lady,' and the deep eyes of blue looked eagerly, wistfully at me, 'then tell me true, is my mother in heaven, sure?'

"What could I do,—I who knew nothing to warrant a different conclusion,—what could I do but answer, 'Yes.' He believed me, the trustful, innocent child, clapping his hands for joy, while the picture on the wall, wholly wrapped in the summer sunshine, seemed one gleam of heavenly glory, as if the mother herself confirmed the answer given to her boy. He did not doubt me in the least, neither did I doubt myself; Anna was safe, whatever her sin might have been; whether the wife of one husband or six, like the woman of Samaria, she surely was forgiven.

"Mrs. West had now returned, her face as calm and placid as ever, and her voice as low and sweet.

"'You have had a sad call, I fear,' she said. 'Richard would not like it if he knew how I had entertained you, but I'll promise to do better next time, though I cannot talk of Anna. Some day perhaps, you may know all, but I would rather it should be Richard who tells you.'

"She kept associating me with Richard, and though the association was not distasteful, it puzzled me somewhat, making me wonder if he had ever told her much of me.

"At that moment Mattie's new cook, Mrs. Felton, appeared, curtseying with a great deal of humility to Mrs. West, who did not seem especially pleased to meet her. Still she greeted her kindly, and suffered her to caress Robin, whom she called a 'precious lamb,' a 'poor, little, stunted rosy,' and numerous other extravagant names.

"'I'm back to the old place,' she said to Mrs. West, when through with Robin, 'but my, such a change! 'Tain't much such times as when you were there, I tell you. Then we had a head; now we've none.'

"Mrs. West stopped her at this point by asking me to come again, and saying she did not know Mrs. Randall or she would call on me.

"'You might make the first advance,' I said. 'You have surely lived here longer than Mrs. Randall.'

"'Yes, I know,' and her pale face flushed up to her soft grey hair. 'But times have changed with me. I do not go out at all.'

"'Come again,' Robin said, as I turned towards him; 'come again, lady; I likes you,' cause you seem some like Papa Richard.'

"It grated harshly to hear the child say Papa Richard, and involuntarily I asked, 'Why he did not say Uncle Richard? He is not your father,' I added, while the child's eyes grew big with wonder, as he replied:

"'Then where is my father, I'd like to know?'

"Mrs. Felton laughed a hateful, meaning laugh, and said:

"'Come, Miss Freeman, it's time we were going.'

"With another good-by for Robin I shook Mrs. West's proffered hand, and was soon out in the street with Mrs. Felton, who, when we were at a safe distance from the house, remarked in a very disagreeable tone:

"'The cutest thing you ever did was to tell that child not to call the doctor papa. I'd have broke him of it long before this. It don't sound well, 'specially after all's been said about Mr. Richard and Miss Anna.'

"I wouldn't question her, neither was there a necessity for it, as she was bent on talking, and of the Wests, too.

"'I s'pose you know the doctor and his mother used to own West Lawn?' was the next remark, which brought to my mind the conversation between her and Mrs. West.

"'Used to own West Lawn!' I repeated, surprised out of my cool reserve.

"'To be sure they did; but, for some unaccountable reason which nobody ever knew, they sold it about the time Anna died, and bought the place where they live now. Of course when a person jumps right out of a good nest with their eyes wide open, nobody but themselves is to blame for where they land. Mrs. West held her head as high as the next one, drove her carriage, and used solid silver every day, and now its all gone. I lived with her as chamber-maid for a whole year. I was Sarah Pellet then.'

"I was too much interested to stop her, and suffered her to go on.

"'I loved Miss Anna, even if she did turn out bad. She was the sweetest-tempered, prettiest-wayed girl you ever seen, and when they took her to the hospital I felt as bad as if she'd died.'

"'To the hospital? The lunatic asylum? Did she go there?' I asked; and Sarah Felton replied:

"'Oh yes; they hoped 'twould cure her. Seems's if the trouble all come to once. First, there was Robert, Richard's twin, who went off, or was murdered, and has never been heard of since.'

"'Richard's twin brother ran off? When? How long ago? How long before Anna died, I mean?' I asked, stopping suddenly as a new light dawned upon me, only, alas! to fade into darkness at the answer.

"'Oh, better than a year. Yes, a full year; for he'd been gone a good spell before it was known to many. He didn't live here; 'twas in New York, and he hardly ever come home. He was a wild one, not much like Richard, who was engaged to Anna, and that's what I can't make out,—why he didn't marry her.'

"We were crossing a common now, where there were rustic benches beneath the trees; and feeling that unless I stopped I should fall, I was so faint and sick with what I had heard, I said that I was tired; and seating myself upon a bench, loosened my hat-strings and leaned against a tree, listening, while my loquacious companion continued:

"'He was engaged for years, so I've heard, and I know he thought a sight of her. It was fairly sickish to see 'em together, he with his arm round her and she a lettin' her head, with them long curls, loll on his shoulder. They was to be married the very day she died. 'Twas an awful sight. I went away from them about the time they sent her to the hospital; but I was back a spell, as the chamber-maid was took sick, and so I was in it all. Dr. Richard kissed her when she was dyin', and she whispered something in his ear.'

"'But Robin,' I gasped; 'Anna was surely married to somebody.'

"Again the smile I had seen before and hated curled her lip as she answered:

"'Yes, of course she was married, for she was a very pious girl, runnin' Sunday-schools, belongin' to the church, tendin' to the poor, and all that.'

"I knew that woman did not believe in Anna's piety, but I did, and the belief gave me comfort as I gazed up into the clear blue sky and said to myself, 'She is there.'

"Dimly I began to perceive why Mrs. West could not tell Robin that his mother was in heaven sure; but I was glad I had done so, without reasoning in the least upon the matter. I exonerated Anna, and only wrote bitter things against poor Richard, saying to the woman, 'An Richard kissed her when she was dying?'

"'Yes, up there where you sleep. That was Anna's room, where she died, and where Robin was born. I didn't see it, but them that told me did. Richard fell as flat as if struck with lightning when he came up from the office and heard what had happened, and six hours after, when they said she was dyin' and had asked for him, he had to be carried, he was so limpsy and weak. She never noticed the child an atom, or acted as if there was one, but would whisper, 'Forgive,—I can't tell,—I promised not. It's all right,—all right.' What she meant nobody knows, for she died just that way, with Richard's arm around her, and the doctor a-holdin' him, for he was whiter than a rag, and after she was dead he went into a ravin' fever, which lasted for weeks and weeks, till the allopaths give him up. Then the homopaths come in and cured him, and that's why he turned into a sugar-pill doctor. He was one of the blisterin' and jollup kind before his sickness, but after that he changed, and they do say he's mighty skilful. As soon as he got well they ld West Lawn, and Mrs. West has never seemed like the same woman since. Folks thinks they's poor, though what's become of the property nobody knows. Anyways the doctor supports his mother, sendin' her money every now and agen.'

"'But why,' I asked, 'did Mrs. Randall and Bell Verner never hear of all this?'

"'Easy enough,' was the reply. 'Judge Verner only

moved here last fall, and Mr. Randall last spring. West Lawn has changed hands three times since the doctor owned it; so it's natural that his name shouldn't appear in the sale. Then, it's seven years since it all happened, and a gossiping place like Morrisville, where there are upwards of three thousand folks, don't harp on one string forever; only them that was interested, like me, remembers.'

"This was true in detail, and was a good reason why neither Bell nor Mattie had ever heard of Anna West, I thought, as I dragged my steps homeward, hardly knowing when I reached there, and feeling glad that Mattie was still confined to her bed, as this left me free to repair at once to my own room,—Anna's room,—where she died, with her head on Richard's arm, and he so weak that he had to be supported. Poor Richard! I do pity him, knowing now why he so often seems sad. But what was it? How is it, and what makes my brain whirl so fast? Anna said with her dying breath that it was all right, and I believe her. I will not cast at her a stone. She is in heaven sure; yes, Robin, sure. And Richard fell as if smitten with lightning when he heard of it! That betokened innocence on his part. Then why this horrid feeling? Is it sorrow that he cared for and loved her? I don't know; everything seems so far off that I cannot find it. What is the record? Let me see.

"Richard once lived here in this grand house; he has

met with reverses, nobody knows what; he has a brother somewhere, nobody knows where; he supports his mother, and this accounts for what I termed his stinginess. How I hate myself, and how noble Dr. West would appear were it not for,—for,—I cannot say it,—the horrible possibility, and I,—I guess,—I think,—I am very sure I did care for him more than I supposed.

"July 23d.

"I have been sick for many days, swallowing the biggest doses of medicine, until it is a wonder I did not die. It was a heavy cold, taken when sitting upon the common, I heard Mattie tell Bell Verner when she came in to ask after me, and so I suppose it was, though I am sure my head would never have ached so hard if I had not heard that dreadful story. I have thought a great deal while Mattie believed me sleeping, and the result of it is this: *I hate Dr. West*, and never desire to see him again! There is something wrong, and I've no faith in anybody.

"There's a letter from Margaret lying on the table. They are at the Clarendon, which is a new hotel, smaller than either the United States or Union Hall, but makes up for its size in its freshness, its quiet, and air of homelike comfort. At least so Margaret says; and although she complains that she does not see so many people as she would at the larger houses, she seems contented, and speaks in raptures of her nice large rooms and their gentlemanly host. I am glad she is satisfied, and that Johnnie, at home, is, as he expresses it in a letter just received, 'as happy as a clam.'

" Accidentally I have heard that Robin is sick and has sent for me. I must have slept for many hours, I think : not a heavy, stolid sleep, as I was vaguely conscious that Mattie stole in to look at me, and that Bell Verner, too, was here. But I did not realize it all until at last I woke and felt that I was better. The pain from the head was gone, and the soreness from the throat, leaving only a pleasant, tired feeling which I rather enjoy.

" In the other room Mattie and Bell were talking, as it seemed, of me, for I heard Mattie say :

" 'I wonder if she really does care about him ? '

" ' I think she does,' was Bell's reply, ' for I remember how annoyed she was when your brother teased her by ridiculing his peculiarities. Poor girl ! I half suspect this has something to do with her illness. Mrs. Felton has confessed having told her what she knew.'

" ' She has ? When ? ' and Mattie seemed surprised.

" ' Why,' returned Bell, ' that night I sat with Dora, Mrs. Felton, you know, was with me a part of the time, and once when Dora, in her disturbed sleep, was talking, she moaned about Dr. West and Anna. " Poor lamb, she's dwellin' on the young lady who died in this very room," Felton said ; and when I inquired what young

lady, she told me all she knew, and more too, I think.
Afterwards I asked Mrs. Stryker if she ever heard of
Anna West, and she said, " Oh yes; she died just before
we came here. Everybody was talking about it;" and
then she told her story, which, of course, differed from
Mrs. Felton's about as much as is the difference in the
social position of the two women,—Felton seeing things
from her stand-point, and Mrs. Stryker repeating them
from hers. She said Mrs. West used to give elegant parties, and Anna was always the star of the company. She
was so beautiful and attractive that young men could not
help admiring her, while Richard loved her very much,
and nobody now believes—'

"I covered up my head at this point, for I would not
listen to any more. After a little I heard some one coming up the stairs, not quietly, soberly, as Mattie and Bell
had come, but noisily, rapidly, two steps at a time, trilling a few notes from some opera, and when the music
ran high, absolutely breaking into a clear, decided whistle!
I was amazed, particularly as the next moment Bell
Verner said:

"'Hush-sh! Miss Freeman's asleep. You'll wake her
with your boy-ways!'

"'I don't care!" and the whistler evidently cut a pirouette. 'I'll try to wake her, unless you tell me quick
who is the handsomest man in town, the most *distingué*,
for I met him just now in the street, and fell in love at

once! Tall, broad-shouldered, with brown, dreamy eyes, and the whitest teeth! Tell me quick, Bell! You ought to know every marriageable man between the two poles, for here you've been out just as many years as you are older than I am, to wit, *ten.* Say, who was it?'

"'Jessie, do be quiet. How do I know?' Bell began, and then I knew the noisy girl was Bell's young sister, Jessie, who had just been graduated in Boston, and had of course come home.

"She was a wild, rattle-brained creature, I was sure, but her flow of spirits suited my mood, and for the sole purpose of seeing her I called to Bell, who, the next moment, was asking anxiously what I wanted.

"'I am better,' I said. 'Am well; and I want you to open the blinds so I can see; then all come in where I can hear you talk. Who is that with the cheery whistle?'

"'*Eureka!* she thinks my whistle beautiful!' I heard from the next room, while Bell replied:

"'It's sister Jessie. She came last night, and has nearly driven us wild already with her fun and spirits. She stopped for a few days at Saratoga, and saw your sister. Shall I call her?'

"'Yes,' I said; and Jessie came at once,—a little fairy, hoydendish creature, with the sauciest, merriest face, the roundest black eyes, and a head covered with short, black curls, which shook as she talked, and kept time with the twinkle of her eyes.

"She kissed me heartily, and then, perching herself upon the foot of the bed, told me about Saratoga,—what a little paradise it was at the Clarendon,—so clean and nice; what a splendid man the proprietor was, treating his boarders as if they were invited guests; humoring everybody's whim, even to muzzling the poor dog who barked at night, thereby disturbing some nervous invalid,—told me too what a love of a man she thought Squire Russell.

"'Mrs. Russell is your sister,' she went on, 'and so I say nothing of her, *pro* nor *con*, except that it must be good pious work to live with her,' and the curls and the eyes danced together.

"I could not be angry, and the gypsy rattled on:

"'But that Mr. Russell is my *beau-ideal* of husbands. I made him promise if he ever was a widower, he'd take me for his second wife. There's nothing I'd like better, I told him, than to mother his six children. You ought to have seen my lady then!' and the queer, little face put on a look so like Margaret's that I could not forebear laughing, knowing, as I did, how shocked my sister must have been.

"'"Husband," she said, "I think it's wrong to trifle with matters so sacred!" Whereupon the husband meekly subsided, and fanned her connubially with the Saratoga paper. Oh, he's a splendid fellow, but I used to pity him evenings when I saw him standing over his wife's chair, looking so wistfully at the dancers. She wouldn't let him waltz,—thought it was very improper, and I was told made several remarks not very complimentary to my style of tripping the light fantastic toe. She is rather pretty, and one night when she wore a pale blue silk, with all her diamonds and point-lace, she was the finest-looking woman in the room.'

"'She used to be very beautiful,' 1 said, feeling that I must defend her, 'but she is sadly broken, and no wonder,—six children in twelve years!'

"'Yes, I know. It's perfectly dreadful, but if I had forty children, I'd let my husband waltz and smoke. Oh, I forgot, she don't let him smoke if she knows it, and if by chance the poor fellow drew a whiff or two down in the office, he had to walk round the south-east corner of the building sixteen times to air himself. There's the gate,—who's come?' and with this she bounded from the bed and ran to the window to reconnoitre.

"'As I live,' she exclaimed, drawing back from the window, 'it's the very man I told you about, and he's coming here.'

"'Don't be angry with her: she's a crazy child,' Bell whispered, and I had just time to reply that I was not angry, when the peal of the door-bell was distinctly heard, and Jessie, by leaning over the bannisters, tried to hear what was said.

"'It's about you,' and she darted back to my side. 'He certainly said Miss Freeman.'

"I don't know that I expected what followed, but my breath came heavily, and I was not surprised when Sarah, the maid, came up and handed me a card bearing the name of *Dr. West*. He was in the parlor, and if I could not go down he wished to see Mrs. Randall. Instantly Mattie and Bell exchanged glances, while the former said in an aside:

"'Can it be the child is so sick they have sent for him?'

"'What child?' I exclaimed. 'Who is sick. Is it Robin?'

"'Yes,' Mattie answered, hurriedly. 'We did not think best to tell you when the message came, four days ago. Robin West is very sick, and keeps asking for the lady who said his mother was in heaven sure. As you could not go, I went myself, learning by that means many things concerning the family which I never knew before. I liked Mrs. West very much. But what shall I tell the doctor for you?'

"I felt irritated and annoyed that Mattie and Bell, and so many, should know and talk about that story, and more than all I was vexed that Bell should believe I cared for the doctor, whose heart was buried in Anna's grave, and I answered pettishly:

"'You needn't tell him anything.'

"Bell looked surprised, Jessie whistled, and Mattie laughed, as she walked downstairs to receive her visitor.

"'I have only known you for half an hour, Miss Dora Freeman,' Jessie said, saucily, 'but if I am any judge of the genus female-homo, you are desperately in love with that man, and are jealous of somebody.'

"Bell shot at her a warning glance, which silenced her for a moment, and in the pause I distinctly caught the tones of Dr. West's familiar voice, though I could distinguish nothing he said. He did not stay long, and the moment his step was heard in the hall Jessie was at her post at the window, ready to watch him as he went down the walk. I think Bell wanted to look out, but she was far too proud, and in spite of Jessie's entreaties that she would come just for a minute and say if she ever saw a more perfectly splendid man, she sat where she was and waited for Mattie, who soon appeared, joining with Jessie in praises of Dr. West. The most agreeable person she had ever met, she said, and she wondered I had not told them about him.

"I was so unamiable that I would not even ask when he came to Morrisville, nor why he had called; but Jessie asked for me, and so I learned that he arrived at his mother's the night previously, and in compliance with Robin's repeated request that some one should go for *the lady*, he had come himself. Robin was better, Mattie said, and if no new symptoms appeared the doctor would return to Beechwood the next day.

"All this while I asked no questions and volunteered

no remark, though in my own mind I resolved that so soon as I was able, I would go to see Robin West. I suppose I was beginning to look tired, as Bell said they were worrying me too long, and, after some coaxing and scolding, she persuaded her sister to leave with her.

"'Mind, now,' Jessie said to me, as she stood with her hat poised on her short, thick curls, 'if you are sure you do not like this doctor, and wish to be rid of him; I'll take him off your hands, and thank you, too. I've a great mind to try the effect of my charms upon him: shall I? You see, I am not going to wait, like Bell, till I verge upon the *serious* yellow leaf. I am going to be married. *Au revoir!*' and whistling 'Hail to the Chief,' she bounded down the stairs, three at a time, I verily believe, for I trembled lest she should break her neck, and felt relieved when her gay laugh sounded upon the walk.

"The next thing which I heard was that Dr. West was at Mr. Verner's, prescribing for Jessie's father, who had been taken violently ill."

CHAPTER VIII.

JESSIE'S DIARY.

JULY 24th.—The richest thing has happened; the best joke I ever heard of; and I give myself great credit for having been the direct cause of its happening! If there is any one thing which father hates more than another, it is a homœopathic physician.

"'Quacks, humbugs, impositions, loggerheads, ignoramuses!'

"These are very mild names compared with what I've heard him call them, declaring he would show the door to the first one who should ever come round him with their two goblets, two spoons, two little plates for covers, and one pill dissolved in a hogshead of water, half a drop to be taken once in six hours! That's the way he talked, submitting to any amount of blistering, bleeding, drugging, and torturing, and thinking it felt nice. But I've played him a trick which will do him good for the remainder of his natural life.

"When I came home last night from Mr. Randall's, I found him groaning, sweating, and almost swearing with the colic, brought on by too much fruit at dinner, followed by two saucers of cream. He never was in such pain in his life; he should die, he knew he should; and somebody must go for the doctor. Of course every servant was out of sight and hearing, and so I went myself for Dr. Lincoln, who was off in the country miles away, and would not be home for hours. Here was a dilemma; and as I was wondering what to do next, I saw that paragon of M.D.'s, Dr. West, coming down the street. Instantly my decision was made; and looking as anxious as I could, I accosted him at once, begging him to go and prescribe for my father, Judge Verner. He looked at me a little curiously, but acceded to my request, and in less than five minutes I had ushered him into the room, where father was enacting a round of *colicky* gymnastics, and where Bell looked up in wonder, actually starting to her feet when I introduced *Dr. West.*

"'Dr. Lincoln was gone, and I brought this one,' I whispered to father, who was in too much pain to notice particularly, and who thought it Dr. Lincoln's student.

"'I shall need some water, a spoon, and two goblets,' the doctor said, and I hastened to execute the orders, watching father as the stirring process went on, and almost screaming when he swallowed the first spoonful.

"'I'm afraid it ain't strong enough, doctor. It hasn't much taste,' he said, smacking his lips, as he missed the flavor of Dr. Lincoln's bottles.

"'We'll see what effect it has,' was the doctor's reply; and in a few moments down went another drop of the sweetened water; then another, and another, until the groaning and flouncing ceased, and father lay upon his pillow as well-behaved a patient as one would wish to see.

"He was very quiet, and after waiting half an hour the doctor said he did not think he was needed any longer, and would leave.

"'Should the paroxysms return,' he said to Bell, 'give him six of these pills,' and he placed upon the table a tiny phial, which at once caught father's eye and set him to raving like a madman.

"'Bell! Jessie!' he gasped, as the gate closed after the doctor, 'who was that chap?—what persuasion, I mean? Was he a rascally—'

"He was in too great a rage to say the words, and so I said it for him.

"'He was a homœopathist, father. Didn't he help you quick? You never groaned a groan after the third swallow.'

"'Third swallow be—no, I won't swear, but I will say Thunder and Mars!' he roared; 'have I been insulted in my own house? I won't stand it! I'll gag, I'll heave, I'll puke, but what I'll get rid of the stuff! Give *me* water for the colic,—*me!*'

"'But if the water answered the purpose, why do you care?' Bell asked, and father gave her a look very like, '*Et tu Brute.*'

" He could not deny that he was better,—that something had helped him; but it wasn't sweetened water; no indeed; and I might heave it out of the window.

"I took up the goblet to do so, when he yelled :

" 'Don't be a fool because you made one of me! Set that glass down and bring me that phial.'

"I obeyed, and he read on the little yellowish paper : 'For Colic. For an adult, take six every hour. For children from two to three, according to age. Prepared by R. West, M.D., Beechwood.'

"He read it aloud twice, then asked, 'Who the —— was *R. West, M.D.*, and how the plague came he there ?'

"The hurricane was over, and I ventured to explain, asking if he were not very gentlemanly and pleasant.

" 'He's well enough for a *fool!*' he replied, declaring he should have been better without the truck; that had nothing to do with it.

"This morning I missed the little phial, and when I asked where it was, father told me to mind my business, and then I knew he had it safe in his vest pocket, a charm against future attacks of colic. How Bell scolded when we were alone, and how I rolled on the floor and laughed. Bell is smitten; I can see it in her face and manner. She does nothing but think of Dr. West, who has returned to Beechwood. Will I ever see him again? and does Dora Freeman hate or like him, which?"

CHAPTER IX.

EXTRACT FROM DR. WEST'S DIARY.

"BEECHWOOD, July.

DID not see Dora after all, and I had thought so much about it, feeling, I am afraid, more than willing that Robin should be sick, and so give me an excuse for going to Morrisville. Since receiving that little note from Dora, I have frequently dared to build castles of what might some day be, for something in that message led me to hope that I am not indifferent to her. The very fact that she answered my informal letter asking the loan of a book would prove it so, so I sit and think and wonder what the future has in store for me, until my patients are in danger of being neglected.

" Poor Robin, I fear he is not long for this world, and when I remember how perfectly helpless he is, and must always remain, I say to myself:

" 'It is well that the child should follow the mother, if indeed, as Dora told him, she is in *heaven sure.*'

" Darling Dora, I am glad you told him so. You have no reason to think otherwise. Does Dora know how much I once loved Anna? I fancy not, and yet there are those in Morrisville who remember the sad story, but she is not thrown much in their society. The Randalls and Verners and Strykers form a circle into which outsiders are not often admitted. I liked that Mrs. Randall, and so did mother. How familiar the old place looked to me, and how natural it seemed that I should be there, and Dora too. Will she ever be the mistress of my home? If so, that home I know will not be West Lawn, but there is still a cherished hope of one day redeeming that old homestead of which she talks so much. Then, *Dora*, brown-eyed, brown-haired Dora, your little feet shall dance again upon the greensward and your merry laugh awaken the echoes of the olden time. Dear Dora, I trust she is not very sick, and I wish I could have seen her.

"Judge Verner,—by what chance came I in his presence, and that of his regal daughter Bell? I suspected then I was the victim of a joke, perpetrated by that saucy-looking, black-eyed elf, whom they called Jessie, and now I am sure of it, for here this morning comes a letter from the judge, worthy, I think, to be preserved as a curiosity.

"'Mr. West,' he writes, with the *Mr.* heavily underscored, as if to make it doubly evident that he ignored the title of Dr. in my case: 'Enclosed find five dollars for professional services rendered to self July 22d. If

I hadn't had such a confounded stomach-ache I suppose I should have marched you out-doors in double-quick time, as that is what I've threatened to do with all kinds of quacks; but I'm glad I didn't, as my remembrance of you *is* that you are a gentleman, even if you have a soft spot in the brain. Jessie,—that's my youngest,—insists that your spoon victuals did me good, and prides herself on having cajoled you into the house,—but she needn't tell me; I know better. Bell, too,—that's my eldest,—has partially gone over to the enemy, but I'll stick to my principles. It's all a piece of tomfoolery, though if you'll never breathe a word of it to Bell, nor Jessie, there *is* something about those paltry little pills in that phial that will stop the tallest kind of a gripe! I'd like to know you better, young man, and so would my daughters. Come here in the autumn, when the shooting is fine. We have splendid woods for hunting, if you enjoy it.

"'Yours truly,
"'THOMAS VERNER.'

"This is a judge's letter, and I rather like him for it. He is not to be convinced in a hurry, but those little pills will do the work. I'd like to know him better, and his daughters too. There was something fascinating in that haughty Bell's manner, while the mischievous Jessie attracted me at once. I may some time improve the acquaintance commenced under so very singular circumstances."

CHAPTER X.

DORA'S DIARY.

IT seems to me a year since I last wrote, and yet 'tis only three short weeks. But in that time so much has happened that I scarcely can realize it at all. Morrisville was very lonely after the doctor left, and but for that wild Jessie, who keeps one so constantly stirred up, I could hardly have borne the loneliness. She is so full of life, and she has made me laugh so much as she described her father's conversion to homœopathy, and then went off into ecstasies over Dr. West.

" But there came a day when even the gleeful Jessie's laugh was hushed, and her merry eyes were dim with tears, as she helped me array a little crippled form for the grave. Robin is dead! I can write about it now, can speak of the darling composedly, but at first the thought of him brought a great choking sob, and I could only weep, so fast he grew in my love during the few days I watched over him. He was worse I heard, and in spite of Mattie's assertion that I was not able to endure it, I went to see him. Nor was I sorry when I met the look of love which beamed in his soft blue eyes, as folding his arms around my neck, he said:

"'I knew you'd come, for I asked God would He send you to little Robin, and He did. You'll stay, too, won't you, till Robin's dead? and you'll tell me again of my mother in heaven?'

"I might not have stayed with him to the last, but for a dream I had that night, in which Anna came to me, her robes all white and pure as are the robes of the redeemed, a halo of glory round her head, and a look of love in her eyes as she bent over me and said:

"'There's a little harp in heaven waiting for my boy, and ere many days his baby hands will sweep its golden strings; but till that time arrives, he wants you, Dora Freeman,—wants you to lead him down into the river, across whose waters I shall wait to meet him. For Richard's sake, you'll go.'

"The beautiful vision faded from my view, and I awoke from what seemed more reality than a dream.

"'Not for Richard's sake,' I said, 'but for Anna's;' and so next day I went again to where the little sick boy lay, watching and waiting for me.

"'I don't call him Papa Richard now,' he said, when my wrappings were removed, and I sat down beside him. 'I told him what you said, that he was not my father, and he told me, "No, Robin, I am not," but he wouldn't say where papa was. Do you know, lady, is he in heaven, too?'

"I could not tell, and I tried to divert his mind into some other channel, getting him to speak of Richard, and, vain girl that I was, laying ingenious snares for ascertaining if Richard had mentioned me when he was home.

"'He talked of "Dora." Is that you, and may I call you so?' Robin said, in reply to my direct interrogation as to what Richard had talked about; and so after that I was Dora to the child, who would scarcely let another wait upon him. 'You seem like mother. You'll stay,' he kept repeating, when Mattie came at nightfall after me.

"I thought of Anna in my dream; thought of the little golden harp, and stayed, while people talked, as people will, wondering what kept me at that child's sick-bed, and associating me at last with Richard, for whose sake they said I had turned nurse to Robin. This piece of gossip proved the resurrection of the old story, which was told and retold in a thousand different forms, until madcap Jessie Verner threatened to box the first one's ears who should say Anna West to her again. This she told me herself, watching with me by Robin, and that was all that passed between us on the subject. It seemed to be tacitly understood that neither Mattie, Bell, nor herself were to speak of the story to me, and they did not. Somehow it would have been a great relief to know just what they thought, but I would not ask, and on this point surrounded myself with so strong a barrier of reserve, that they never tried to break it down.

"Jessie had come to Mrs. West's unsolicited, and it was strange how the quiet, sad woman opened her heart at once to receive the wild young creature, while Robin turned to her trustingly, and whispered when she was gone:

"'I don't mind—her seeing my feet. She laughs at most everything, but she wouldn't at my poor, twisted toes.'

"Precious Robin ! I would he could have seen the gush of tears with which Jessie baptized those twisted toes when first the shrivelled things met her view; but he was then where the halt and maimed are made whole, and the feet which here had never stepped a step were treading the golden streets. It was strange that one so young should be so sensitive about his deformity, but he had been so from the time he first learned that he was lame, and when, sitting in his chair upon the lawn, he would often ask his grandmother if she supposed the passers-by guessed that he was not like them.

"It is frequently the case that a deformity of the body manifests itself in the expression of the face, but it was not so with him. A more beautiful face I never saw, and I loved to watch it as he lay sleeping upon his pillow, wondering if the mother could have been as beautiful as the child, and then speculating bitterly upon the father, wherever he might be. I had said in my heart that I exonerated Richard, but at times I experienced a feeling which I called hatred for the man whom Mrs. West was almost hourly expecting, and who, when he came, found me with Robin on my lap, his head nestled upon my bosom, while I sang to him of the Heavenly City, where his mother waited for him.

"It was just at the setting of the sun that I heard the coach stop before the gate, and a rapid step upon the walk. My voice must have trembled, for Robin unclosed his eyes as if to ask the cause, but I hushed him gently, while in the adjoining apartment a low conversation was carried on for twenty minutes or more. At last the doctor started for the room where I was sitting, but I gave no sign of consciousness until he was close beside me and I met the glance of his eyes,—a glance in which for an instant I fancied I read more than a friendly interest; the blood surged hotly through my veins; but thoughts of Anna, whom dying he had kissed, holding her as I had held Robin, froze it back from my face, which must have turned very white, for after his first words of greeting, he said to me, 'I cannot thank you enough for what you have been to mother. She has told me of your kindness; but Dora,' and his hand touched my hair lightly, 'I fear you are overtaxing your strength. You are very pale to-night. Let me relieve you of Robin.'

"I was not tired, I said, and my manner was so chilling

that his hand slid from my hair, while he began speaking to Robin, who only complained of weariness.

"'I am glad you have come, Uncle Richard,' Robin said, putting out his thin fingers and playing with the heavy beard of the doctor, who had knelt beside me the better to see the child. 'I call you uncle all the time because Dora wanted me to.'

"Instantly our eyes met, and I saw his face crimson with emotions whose nature I could not guess. I only knew they hardened me into stone, and I was glad when at last Jessie came in, for she relieved me from all necessity of talking. Richard liked Jessie; her sprightly manner amused and rested him, I could see, and it made me half angry to hear how merrily he laughed at her remarks, even when he knew that Robin's days were numbered. How I clung to that child, refusing to give him to the care of Mrs. West. He could not lie upon the bed, and I felt a kind of fierce pleasure in holding him, and in knowing that Richard knew what I was doing for Anna's child.

"Slowly the summer night darkened around us, and the August moon cast its beams across the floor, even to where I sat singing the low lullaby. And out upon the piazza Dr. West and Jessie talked and laughed together, until the sick boy whispered moaningly, 'It's very cold and dark in here. Cover me closer, Dora, and light the candles now.'

"I covered him up, and saw upon his face a shadow, whose import I could not mistake, and half bitterly, half reproachfully, I exclaimed:

"'Dr. West, if you can spend the time, I think Robin needs you.'

"He was at my side in an instant, and so was Jessie; her eyes filling with tears when she, too, saw and recognized the shadow which had alarmed me. Robin was dying! We all knew it now, and Robin knew it, too, and still refused to leave me for the arms which Richard stretched out to him.

"'It's nicer here,' he said, and there was a world of love in the soft blue eyes as he nestled closer to me. 'I guess I'm dying. It's all so dark and queer. Is it very far to heaven, and will I lose the way?'

"'No, darling, for Jesus will go with you,' Richard answered, now pressing so close to Robin that his shoulder touched mine, and I felt his breath upon my hair.

"'And I won't be a cripple any more? I'll walk in heaven, and mother's there sure?' was the next remark, to which there came no response, except a moan from Mrs. West, until I answered:

"'Yes, *sure, Robin, sure.*'

"'I'll tell her how good you was, and how much I loved you, too. What shall I say for you, Grandma West? What word shall I carry mother?'

"Mrs. West was weeping bitterly, with her head upon the pillow, where Robin's had lain so long, and when he thus addressed her, she answered:

"'Tell her, if you meet her, how I mourned for her till my hair all turned white, and tell her how if in thought I ever wronged her, I am so sorry now.'

"'I'll tell her,' Robin whispered; 'and you, Uncle Richard, what for you?'

"The doctor's frame shook, and his face was white as ashes as he was thus appealed to for a message to the dead, but he did not speak until Robin twice repeated, 'And what for you?'

"Then with a sob, he said:

"'Nothing, Robin; nothing from me.'

"'Why! didn't you love my mother?' the dying boy asked, the look of surprise for a moment mastering the look of death upon his face.

"'Yes, he did,' I said. 'He loved her better than his life. He loves her still. Tell her so.'

"Again my eyes met those of Dr. West, but in the expression of his there was something which subdued all my pride, and brought a rain of tears upon my face. I did not longer refuse to let him take the child, nor did Robin refuse to go; and I leaned back in my chair sick and faint, while that great struggle went on between death and the little life whose lamp had burned so feebly.

"It was not long, but while it lasted I knew that Richard was praying softly, and that his words were soothing to the sufferer, who suddenly exclaimed:

"'I see my mother! She's like the picture in the frame! She's waiting for me over there where the banks are so green! She is in heaven sure; but I don't see my father anywhere! He is not there! Oh, where is my father?'

"That was the last; and two hours later, Robin lay quietly upon his couch, his golden curls all smooth and shining, just as Jessie had made them, his blue eyes closed, his tiny hands folded upon his bosom, his poor, crippled feet hidden from curious sight.

"That night I began to love Jessie Verner, and so I fancied did Dr. West. All her levity was gone for the time, and in its place there came a tender, motherly manner, which brooded over and encircled all in its careful forethought. Even Mrs. West became a very child in the hands of this girl of eighteen, while Richard, too, was brought within her influence. He was weary with his long ride of a hundred and thirty miles, but no one save Jessie seemed to think of this. She remembered everything, and when I would have worried Mrs. West with questions as to where Robin's clothes were kept, she hushed me gently, going about the house in quest of what was needed, with as much assurance as if she had been the daughter instead of a perfect stranger.

It was Jessie who made Richard lie upon the lounge in the quiet sitting-room; Jessie who arranged his pillows for him, covering him up with his travelling-shawl, and then brought him tea and toast she herself had made, and which he so much needed after his wearisome ride. I did not marvel that he followed her movements with eyes in which I read, as I believed, more than an ordinary interest; while at me, still keeping a useless watch by the dead boy, he seldom glanced. There was a pang at my heart which I suppose was jealousy, though I did not so define it, and I rather enjoyed thinking that Anna, and Robin, and myself, were in some way wronged by this new interest of Richard's. I had cared for Robin to the last, but with his life my usefulness had ceased. I was not needed longer, I thought, and so next morning I went home, saying to Mrs. West and Richard, when they asked if I would soon be back:

"'I shall attend the funeral, of course. There in no necessity for coming before. Jessie will do everything.'

"Mrs. West did not urge me to return, neither did Richard, but he went with me to the gate, opening it for me, and then, standing a moment as if there was something he would say, 'You do look tired, *Dora*,—more so than I thought. You are not strong enough for all you have gone through. I think I must prescribe,' and he took my hand to feel the quickened pulse. 'You are feverish,' he continued. 'You ought to rest, but we shall miss you so much. It's a comfort to know you are here.'

"I was very foolish, very nervous, and the tears started, but I dashed them away, and taking the offered medicine, answered back, 'I leave to Jessie the task of comforter. She will do better than I.'

"The next moment I was walking rapidly down the street, never looking back until the corner was reached, when, glancing over my shoulder, I saw the doctor still standing where I had left him, leaning upon the gate. I never remember a time when I was so childish, or more unhappy, than I was that day and the following, which last was the day of Robin's funeral. There was no parade, no display,—only a few friends and neighbors, with Jessie, presiding genius, telling everybody what to do, while, stranger than all, Judge Verner himself was there as director, his carriage bearing Mrs. West and Richard to the grave where they buried Robin.

"There was something in the young man which he liked, he said, even if he was a fool, and so he had offered no objections to Jessie's proceedings, and was himself doing what he could for the family. There was room in the carriage for four, and greatly to my surprise the Judge whispered to me:

"'That chap they call *Doctor* wants you to go with them. He says, next to his mother, the child loved you the best.'

5

"I was very faint for an instant, and then shrinking back into the corner I answered no, so decidedly that the judge hastened away, repeating his ill success to Richard, who had risen, and with his mother on his arm was advancing to the door. As he passed me he stopped, and reaching his hand said gently, '*Dora*, come with us; for Robin's sake.'

"I could not resist that voice, and I went forward taking his other arm, and so out into the yard, past the groups of people who speculated curiously as to why Miss Freeman should go with the chief mourners. Behind us came Mr. Randall's carriage, with Mattie, and Bell, and Jessie, and that in a measure relieved me of my rather awkward position.

"'Mother,' Richard said, as we drew near the cemetery, 'it is seven years to-day since Anna died. Do you remember?'

"'Yes,' she answered sadly, while I remembered that seven years ago was also to have been his bridal.

"Did he think of it as we wound round the gravelled road, past the willow and the cedar, past the box, the pine, and fir, to where Anna lay sleeping? Did he look back with anguish and regret to that other day, when, with the August sunshine falling upon him as it was falling now, he listened to the solemn words, 'Ashes to ashes, dust to dust,' and heard the cold earth rattle down upon the coffin-lid? Yes, he did, I was sure, and this was what blanched his cheeks so white and made his lips quiver so, as we returned to the carriage and were driven from the yard, leaving Anna and Robin there alone.

"That afternoon I was restless and wretched. I could not remain quietly in any place, but wandered uneasily about until near nightfall, when I stole out unobserved and took my way to the burying-ground, where Anna and Robin were. Just outside the iron railing which enclosed their graves there was a rude, time-worn seat, placed upon the grass-plat years ago, it would seem, from the names and dates carved upon it. Here I sat down, and leaning my face upon my hand, tried to think of all that had transpired since I had come to Morrisville. Had I known all I was to see and hear, would I have wished to come? I asked myself; but could find no satisfactory answer. I was glad I had known Robin, for his memory would be a sacred thing to me, and I said I was glad I had heard of Anna ere I learned to think too much of Richard. Then thoughts of Jessie arose, and I said aloud, 'Can he ever forget Anna, who died in his arms?'

" 'No, Dora, I shall never forget her, neither can I mourn for her always, as I mourned when we first laid her here, and I sat nearly all the night just where you are sitting, watching the stars as they held their first vigil over Anna's grave, and almost impiously questioning the Providence which had dealt so strangely with me.'

"I knew it was Richard's voice speaking to me, and I gave a little start of surprise, but did not lose a word which he had spoken.

"'I half believed I should find you here,' he said, sitting down beside me, and drawing a little more about my neck the shawl which had fallen off. 'Something told me I should find you, and so I came quite as much to join the living as the dead. Dora, you will forgive the familiarity,—I never called you so at home, but here, where you have done me and mine so much good, you will surely let me use a name which mother and Robin adopted.'

"I bowed, and he went on.

"'You do not know how glad I am that you were with us when Robin died, or how it lessens the smart to have you sitting with me in sight of Robin's grave.'

"'And Anna's?' I said, looking at him for the first time.

"'Yes, Anna's,' he continued in the same kind tone; 'and it is of her I would tell you, Dora,' and he spoke hurriedly now. 'How much do you know of Anna, and who told you?'

"'Sarah Felton; and I know more than I wish I did,' I answered, my voice full of tears, which I could not repress.

"'Felton!' he repeated in dismay. 'Unless her reputation for veracity has improved, I would not vouch for the truth of what she might say, though she liked Anna. Shall I tell you her history, Dora?'

"I knew it would cost him a mighty effort to do so, but I must hear the story. I should never be happy till I had, and I answered eagerly:

"'Yes, tell me of Anna.'

CHAPTER XI.

RICHARD'S STORY.

E was very white, and his voice trembled, while his eyes had in them the far-off look I had once or twice observed before.

" 'There are some things in our family history,' he began, ' which I shall omit, as they have nothing in particular to do with Anna and myself. For instance, you know, perhaps, that we once lived at West Lawn in different circumstances from what mother is living in now, and that we suddenly sold the place, purchasing a smaller one, and living in a cheaper, plainer way. Why we did this I need not say, except that Anna was in no way connected with it.

" ' She was my adopted sister; and she came to us when only six years old. I was twelve, as was my twin-brother Robert. He went from us years ago, and has never been heard from since. We fear he is dead, and the uncertainty is killing my mother. I shall soon be all alone. But I was telling you of Anna, who grew so fast into our hearts, my brother and I quarrelling for the honor of drawing her to school. This was in her childhood, but as she grew older Robert professed to care less for her than

I. "She was a doll-baby," he said; "a compound of red and white, and yellow curls." He would not even acknowledge that she was beautiful, but said she could not compare with the maidens of New York, where he went to live when Anna was fourteen and we were twenty. His coldness troubled me at first, but when I came to think of her as something dearer than a sister, I was glad that he so seldom came to Morrisville, for he was far finer-looking than I am. Put us side by side, and nineteen out of twenty would have given him the preference. But he did not care for Anna, and when she was sixteen I asked her to be my wife. It was here, too, Dora, on this very bench, where you are sitting with me, and it was eleven years ago this very day.

"'Something most always happens to me on this day—something which leaves its impress on my mind. One year ago we went to that picnic by the lake. Do you remember it, Dora?'

"'Yes,' I gasped, while my cheeks burned painfully. 'Yes, but go on with Anna.'

"He was silent a moment, and then continued:

"'We were in the habit of coming here to sit, she little dreaming how near we were to the spot of earth where she would ere long be lying. I have told you that I asked her to be my wife, but I have not told you how much I loved her, for I did—oh, so much, so much! And she was worthy of my love. Whatever happened afterward she was worthy then. You have seen her picture. It hardly does her justice, for no artist can ever give a correct idea of what that face was when lighted up with life, and health, and love. I have never seen a face one-half as beautiful as Anna's. She knew that she was beautiful, but it did not make her vain, for she knew that God had given her the dangerous gift of beauty, and she tried to keep His gift unsullied, just as she tried to keep her heart pure in His sight. I cannot think of a single fault she had unless it were that she sometimes lacked decision, and was too easily swayed by those in whom she had confidence. But in all essential points she was right, serving God with her whole soul, and dedicating herself early to His service.'

" 'Then why,' I exclaimed, 'when Robin asked if she was in heaven sure, why did you hesitate to tell him yes?'

"A look of pain contracted his features as he replied:

"'I am speaking of Anna as she was when I asked her to be my wife. We read of angels falling,—then why not a mortal man? though Heaven knows that I cannot fully believe that Anna fell. I could not live if I believed it. Mother's religious creed and mine differ in one point, although we profess the same holy faith. To me a child of God is a child forever, just as no act of mine can make me cease to be my mother's son. But to go on. I loved her with my whole soul, and I told her so, while for a moment she made no reply, except to lay her head upon my arm and weep. Then lifting up her eyes she said she was too young to know her own mind yet; that she loved me, and always had,—like a brother at first, but latterly in a different way, and if I would not require her to be my wife at once, and would promise to release her should she ever come to think that she could not be mine, she would answer yes. And so we were engaged.

"'After that I seemed to tread on air, so happy and so full of anticipation was my whole being. I had been graduated the previous year, and I was then a student in Dr. Lincoln's office, but I boarded at home, and saw Anna every day, counting the hours from the time I left her in the morning until I returned late in the afternoon to our fashionable dinner, for we observed such matters then. I shut my eyes at times, and those days come back again, bringing with them Anna as she used to look when she came out to meet me, her curls falling about her childish face, and her white robes giving her the look of an angel. I loved her too much. I almost placed her before Him who has declared He will have no idols there, and so I was terribly punished. We were to be married on her twentieth birthday, and until about a year previous to that time I had not the shadow of a suspicion that Anna's love was not wholly my own. I well remember the time, a dreary, rainy autumn day, when she came

5*

nto my room, and leaning one hand on my shoulder, parted my hair with the other, as she was wont to do.

"'"Richard," she began, "isn't it just as wicked to act a lie as it is to tell one?"

"'"I supposed it was," I said, and she continued:

"'"Then you won't be angry when I tell you what I must. I was very young when I promised to be your wife, and I am afraid I did not quite know what I was doing. I love you dearly, Richard, but you seem more like my brother; and, Richard, don't turn so white and tremble so,—I shall marry you if you wish it; but please don't, oh! don't—"

"'She was weeping bitterly now,—was on her knees before me, my Anna, my promised wife. I had thought her low-spirited for some days, but had no thought of this, and the shock was a terrible one. I could not, however, see her so disturbed, when I had the power to relieve her, and after talking with her calmly, dispassionately, I released her from the engagement and she was free. I did not even hint at the possibility of her learning to love me in time, because I fancied she would be more apt to do so if wholly untrammelled; but that hope alone kept my heart from breaking during the wretched weeks which followed, and in which Anna's health seemed failing, and her low spirits to increase. A change of air was proposed, and she was sent to Boston, where my mother has relatives. It was on the eve of the new year when she came back to us, with a white, scared look upon her face, which became at last habitual, making it painful to look at her, she appeared so nervous and frightened. It was as if some great terror were continually haunting her, or some mighty secret, which it was death to divulge and worse than death to cover up. I supposed it to be a fear of what I might require of her, and so I said to her one day that if the thing preying upon her mind was a dread lest I should seek to make her my wife, she might put that aside, as I should not annoy her in that way.

"'Never to my last hour shall I forget the look in her eyes,—a look so full of anguish and remorse, that I turned away, for I could not meet it.

"'"O, Richard," she moaned, drawing back so I could not touch her, "you don't know how wretched I am. It almost seems as if God had forgotten that I did try to serve Him, Richard. What is the unpardonable sin? Is it to *deceive?*"

"'I thought she referred to her relations with me, and I tried to soothe her agitation, telling her she had not deceived me; that she had told me frankly how she felt; that she was wholly truthful and blameless.

"'With a cry which smote cruelly on my ear, she exclaimed:

"'"No, no, you kill me! Don't talk so! I am not blameless; but, oh! I don't know what to do! Tell me,

Richard, tell me, which is worse, to deceive, or break a solemn vow?"

"'I had no idea what she meant, and without directly answering her questions I tried to quiet her, but it was a useless task. She only wrung her hands and sobbed more passionately, saying God had cast her off, and she was lost forever. This seemed to be the burden of her grief for many days, and then she settled down into a stony calm, more terrible than her stormy mood had been, because it was more hopeless. She did not talk to us now except to answer questions in monosyllables, and would sit all day by the window of her chamber, looking afar off as if in quest of some one who never came.

"We thought when she came home that we had as much as we could bear, for a domestic calamity had overtaken us, involving both ruin and disgrace, unless it were promptly met; but in our concern for Anna, we forgot the other trouble, else we had fainted beneath the rod. At last the asylum was recommended, and the first of March we carried her there, taking every precaution that her treatment should be the kindest and most considerate.'

"'How long ago was that?' I asked, starting suddenly, as a memory of the past swept over me.

"'Seven years,' he replied, and I continued:

"'Was it in Utica? If so, I must have seen her, for seven years this summer Mrs. Randall and I visited a schoolmate in Utica, and one day we went from curiosity to the lunatic asylum, but I did not see a face like Anna's in the portrait. Oh yes,' and I started again, 'I remember now a young girl with the most beautiful golden hair, but her face was resting on the window-sill, and she would neither look up nor answer my questions,— that was Anna,' and in my excitement I could scarcely control myself to listen, while Richard continued :

"'It is possible, and seems like her, as she would not answer any one.

"'Every two weeks mother and I visited her, but after the first time she never spoke to us, but tried to hide away where we could not see her. She gave them no trouble whatever, as she seldom left her chair by the window, where she sat the live-long day, looking westward, just as she did at home. She had written one letter, they said, and when we asked to whom, the matron could only remember that she believed it was to California, adding that the attendant who then took the letters to the office had sickened since and died. It was to some imaginary person, no doubt, she said, and so that subject was dismissed by my mother, but I could not so soon forget it, and when next I visited her, I said abruptly:

"'"Anna, what correspondent have you in California?"

"'Instantly her face was pallid with fear, and she fell

at my feet senseless. This was a mystery upon which I dwelt day and night, finding no solution whatever to it, and forgetting it at last as the terrible tragedy drew to a close.

"'Late in July mother went again to visit Anna, and when she returned her hair was almost as white as you now see it, while her whole appearance was indicative of some great, crushing sorrow which had fallen suddenly upon her. Anna had asked to be taken home, she said, —had fallen on her knees, and clasping her dress had kissed it abjectly, crying piteously, "Home, mother; take poor Anna home; let her die there."

"'It was the first time she had spoken to us in months, and we could not refuse. So she came,—the seventh day of August,—travelling by railroad to the station, and coming the remainder of the way in our carriage. Her last fancy was that she could not walk, and I met her at our gate, carrying her into the house—and upstairs to her old room, which had been made ready for her. As I laid her upon the bed, she clasped her arms tightly round my neck, and whispered, "God has forgiven me, Richard, will you?"

"'I kissed her, and then went down to mother, who needed my services more than Anna, and who lay all that evening on the lounge as white and rigid as stone. The next day I saw a good deal of Anna, and hope whispered that she was getting better. The scared, wild look was gone, and a bright, beautiful color burned upon her cheeks. Her hair, which had been cut, was growing out again more luxuriant than ever, and curled in short ringlets about her head. She talked a little, too, asking if we had ever heard from Robert, and bidding me tell him, when he came back, that she spoke kindly of him before she died. This was the eighth. The next day was her birth-day, the one fixed upon for our bridal. I do not know if she remembered it, but I thought of nothing else as the warm, still hours glided by, and to myself I said it may be some other day. Anna is better. Anna will get well. Alas! I little dreamed of the scathing blow in store for me; the frightful storm which was to rage so fiercely round me, and whose approach was heralded by the arrival of Dr. Lincoln, who had been there before, holding private consultations with my mother, and looking, when he came from them, stern, perplexed, mysterious, and sorry.

"'Dora, you know what all this portended, but you do not know, neither can you begin to guess, how heavy, —how full of agony was the blow which awaited me, when just at nightfall I came up from the office where I had been for several hours. "Anna was dying." This was the message which greeted me in the hall, and like lightning I fled up the stairs, meeting on the upper landing with my mother, who had grown old twenty years since morning.

"'" Richard, my boy, my poor boy, can you bear it? have they told you? do you know?"

"'"Yes," I said, "Anna is dying. I must see her; let me go," and I tore away from the hands which would have held me back until I was to some extent prepared.

"'I did not heed her voice, for through the half-closed door I caught a glimpse of Anna. She saw me, too, and her hand was beckoning. I was half-way across the room, when a sound met my ear which took all consciousness away, and for the next three hours I was insensible to pain. Then came the horrid waking, but the blow had stunned me so, I neither felt nor realized as I did afterwards. I went straight to Anna, for she was asking for me, she from whom the rest stood aloof as from a polluted thing. Through all the horror she had never spoken a word, or made the slightest sound, and this suppression of feeling was hastening her end. Nothing but the words, "Tell Richard to come," had passed her lips since, and when I went to her she could only whisper faintly, "Forgive me, Richard. It's all right, but I promised not to tell. It's right, it's right." Then she continued, entreatingly, " Let me lay my head on your arm as it used to lie, and kiss me once in token of forgiveness."

"'Dora, you are a woman, and women judge their sex more harshly than we do, but you would not have had me refuse that dying request?'

"'I should hate you if you had,' I sobbed, while he continued:

"'Mother made a motion of dissent. She was casting a stone, but I did not heed her. I lifted Anna up; I held her on my bosom; I pushed away the clustering curls; I kissed the quivering lips sueing for forgiveness and assuring me all was right. I forgave her then and there as I hoped to be forgiven; I said I would care for her baby; I received her last injunction; I kept her in my arms until the last fleeting breath went out, and when I laid her back upon the pillow she was dead!

"'Death wipes out many a stain, and Anna, by her dying, threw over the past a veil of charity, which only a few of the coarser, unfeeling ones ever tried to rend. There was gossip and talk, and wonder, and pity, and surmise, and something suspicious thrown upon me, the more readily as people generally did not know that our engagement had been broken; but I outlived it all, and when, three months after Anna died, I rose from a sickbed, and went forth among people again, they gave me only sympathy and friendly words, never mentioning either Anna or Robin in my presence.

"'During that sickness, my opinion with regard to the practice of medicine underwent a change, and greatly to the horror of good old Dr. Lincoln, with whom I studied, I became a homœopathist. This furnished me with an excuse for leaving Morrisville, as I wished to investigate that mode of treatment, and gain every possible information from physicians whom I knew to be intelligent and thorough. I went first to New York, and after a few months commenced my new practice in Boston; thence, as you know, I went to Beechwood. Once I hoped mother might be persuaded to go with me, but she said:

"'"I would rather stay here, where people know all about it. I could not bear to be questioned concerning Robin."

"'Women are different from men; it takes them longer to rise above anything like disgrace, and mother has never been what she was before Anna's death. She came in time to love Robin dearly, but his misfortune added to her grief, until her cup seemed more than full. Her health is failing rapidly, and a change of place is necessary. For a long time past I have had it in my mind to sell the cottage and take mother to Beechwood. A friend of mine stands ready to purchase at any time. I saw him two hours since, and to-morrow the papers will be drawn which will deprive us of our home.'

"'And your mother!' I exclaimed, 'will she go to Beechwood?'

"'Not at present. Not until she is better, Dora. I am going with mother to California as soon as I can arrange my affairs at home. I may not return for a long time, certainly not for a year.'

"There was a tremulousness in the tone of his voice as he told me this, while to me the world seemed changed, and I felt how desolate his going would leave me. Still I made no comment, and after a moment he continued:

"'And now, Dora, comes the part which to me is most important of all. Men do not often lay bare their secrets except to one they love! It has cost me a great effort to go over the past, and talk to you of Anna, but I felt that I must do it. I must tell you that the heart I would offer you has on its surface a scar, but, Dora, only a scar; believe me, only a scar. It does not quicken now one pulse the faster when I remember Anna, who was to have been my wife. I loved her. I lost her; and were she back just as she used to be, and I knew you as I know you now, I should give you the preference. You are not as beautiful as Anna, but you are better suited to my taste,—you better meet the requirements of my maturer manhood. I cannot tell when my love for you began. I was interested in you from the first. I have watched and pitied you these four years, wishing often that I could lighten the load you bore so uncomplainingly, and when you came away this time, life was so dreary and monotonous that I said to myself, "Whether Dora hears of Anna or not, I'll tell her when she returns, and ask her to be my wife." At first I was a very coward in the matter, and cautioned mother against revealing anything, but afterward thought differently. If you are to be mine, there should be no concealments of that nature, and so I have told you all, giving you leave to repeat it if you please. There is one person whom I would particularly like to know it, and that is Jessie Verner.'

"The mention of that name was unfortunate, for it roused the demon of jealousy, and when he continued:

"'Dora, will you be my wife? Will you give me a right to think of and love you during the time I am absent?'

"I answered pettishly:

"'If I say no, would you not be easily consoled with Jessie? You seem to admire her very much.'

"While he was talking to me he had risen, and now he was leaning against the iron fence, where he could look me directly in the face, and where I, too, could see him. As I spoke of Jessie, an amused expression flitted over his features, succeeded by one more serious as he replied:

"'I never supposed Jessie could be won even if I wished to win her, flut now that I am at the confessional, I will say that next to yourself Jessie Verner attracts and pleases me more than any one with whom I have met since Anna died. There is about her a life and sparkle which would put to rout a whole regiment of blues, while her great kindness to mother and Robin show her to be a true, genuine woman at heart. I have seen but little of her. I admire her greatly, and had I never met you, Dora, I might have turned to Jessie. Surely this should not make you jealous.'

"I knew it should not, but I think I must have been crazy; certainly I was in a most perverse, unreasonable mood, and I answered:

"'I am not jealous, but I have seen your great admiration for Jessie, and if on so short an acquaintance you like her *almost* as well as you do me, whom you have known for years, it would not take long for you to like her better, so I think it wise for you to wait until you know your mind.'

"I wonder he did not leave me at once; he did move away quickly, saying:

"'It is not like you, Dora, to trifle thus. You either love me or you do not. I cannot give you up willingly. You are tired, weak, excited, and you need not answer me now, though I hoped for something different. I shall think of you, love you, pray for you, while I am gone, and possibly write to you; then, when I return, I shall repeat the question of to-day, and ask you again to be my wife.'

"He was perfectly collected now, and something in his manner awed me into silence. The sun had already set, and the night dews beginning to fall. He was the first to notice it, and with tender care he drew my shawl a second time about my neck, and then taking my arm in his, led me away from Anna's grave out into the streets, where more than one turned to look inquiringly after us, whispering their surmise that we were really engaged.

"He stayed in Morrisville three days after that, and Mattie invited him to tea, with Judge Verner's family and Dr. Lincoln. He came, as I knew he would, but the judge and the doctor kept him so constantly talking of homœopathy that I hardly saw him at all till just as he was going, when he held my hand in his own and looked into my eyes so kindly that I could scarcely keep back the tears which would have told him that I loved him now, and he need not wait a year. A bad headache had prevented Bell from coming, and as the judge was called away on business, the doctor walked home with Jessie, while I watched them as far as I could see, feeling myself grow hot and angry when I saw how Jessie leaned upon his arm, and looked up in his face as confidingly as a child.

"Remembering that he wished her to know of Anna, I tried one day to tell her, but she knew it already from Mrs. West, and exonerated Richard from all blame. She is at the cottage a great deal, and Mattie thinks her greatly interested in Dr. West. I wish he had not said that next to me he preferred Jessie, for it haunts me continually, and makes me very unamiable."

CHAPTER XII.

THE SHADOW OF DEATH.

Telegram to Dora Freeman, Morrisville.

" 'SARATOGA, August 25th.
" ' Come immediately. Madge is very sick, and cannot possibly live. " ' JOHN RUSSELL.'

HIS is the telegram which I received this morning, and to-morrow I am going to poor Margaret. God grant she may not be dead! Dear sister, what would I not give if I had never written those dreadful things of her in my journal. Poor Margaret! her married life has not been very happy with all those children born so fast, and if she lives how much I will love her to make amends for the past. My trunks are packed and standing in the hall, and I am looking, for the last time it may be, on the woods and hills of Morrisville, where the moonlight is falling so softly. I can see a little of the cemetery in the distance, and I know where Anna's grave is so well. I have been there but once since that day, and then I found Jessie with Mrs. West planting flowers over Robin. Mrs. West loves that young girl, and so do I, in spite of what the doctor said; but she does shock me with her boyish, thoughtless manners, actually whistling *John Brown* as she dug in the yellow dirt. Jessie is a queer compound. She and her father and Bell are going on with me to Saratoga. Oh, if Dr. West could be there too, he would cure Margaret. I have been half tempted to telegraph, but finally concluded that brother John would do so if desirable. Poor John! what will he do if he is left alone? and does Jessie remember the foolish thing she said about his second wife? I trust not, for that would be terrible, and Margaret not yet dead.

"CLARENDON HOTEL, SARATOGA.
August 30th.

"My heart will surely break unless I unburden it to some one, and so I come to you, my journal, to pour out my grief. Margaret is dead; and all around, the gay world is unchanged; the song and the dance go on the same as if in No.— there were no rigid form, no pale Margaret gone forever,—no wretched husband weeping over her,—no motherless little children left alone so early.

"It was seven when we reached Saratoga, and I stepped from the car into the noisy, jostling crowd which Judge Verner pushed hither and thither in his frantic efforts to find his baggage, and secure an omnibus. How sick of fashionable life it made me, to see the throng upon the sidewalks and in front of the hotels, as we drove along the streets, and how anxiously I looked up at all the upper windows as we stopped before the Clarendon, saying to myself, 'Is this Margaret's room, or that?'

"I knew there was a group of men on the piazza, and remembering how curiously new-comers are inspected, I drew my veil before my face and was following Judge Vernor, when Jessie suddenly exclaimed, 'Perfectly splendid!' and the next moment my hand was grasped by Dr. West. He was waiting for us, he said; he expected us on that train, and was staying downstairs to meet us.

"'And Margaret?' I asked, clinging to his arm, and throwing off my veil so I could see his face.

"'Your sister is very sick,' he replied, 'but your coming will do her good. She keeps asking for you. I arrived yesterday, starting as soon as I received your brother's telegram. Johnnie is nearly distracted, and nothing but my telling him I was sure you would prefer to have him remain at home, was of the least avail to keep him from coming with me.

"All this he told me while we waited in the reception-room for the keys to our apartments.

"'It is very crowded here,' he said, 'but by a little engineering I believe you are all comfortably provided for. Your room especially,' and he nodded to me, 'is the most desirable in the building.'

"I did not then know he had given it up to me, going himself into a little hot attic chamber. Kind, generous

Richard, you are a great comfort to me these dreadful days. As he had said, my own room was every way desirable, but I only gave it at first a hasty glance, so anxious was I to get to Margaret. She knew I had come, and was asking continually for me. How sadly she was changed from the Margaret who stood upon the piazza and said good-by one morning last June. The long curls were all brushed back, and the blue eyes looked so large, so unnaturally bright, as they turned eagerly to me, and yet I liked her face better than ever before. There was less of self stamped upon it, and more of kindly interest in others.

"'Dora, darling sister,' was all she said, as she wound her arms about my neck, but never since my childhood had she called me by so endearing a title, and I felt springing up in my heart a love mightier than any I had ever felt for her, while with it came a keen remorse for the harsh things written against my dying sister.

"I knew she was dying; not that instant, perhaps, but that soon, very soon, she would be gone, for there was upon her face the same pinched look I had seen on father and Robin just before the great destroyer came.

"'Dora,' she whispered at last, 'I am so glad you are here. I was afraid I might never see you again, and I wanted so much to tell you how sorry I am for the past. I did not make your home with me as happy as I might. Forgive me, Dora. I worried you and John so much.

He says I never did, but I know better. I've thought it all over, lying here, and I know you cannot be so sorry to have me die as I should if it were you.'

"I tried to stop her,—tried to say that I had been happy with her,—but she would not listen, and talked on, telling me next of the little life which had looked for half an hour upon this world, and then floated away to the next.

"'I called it Dora for you,' she said, 'for something told me that I should die, and I thought you might love baby better if she bore your name. But I am glad she died; it makes your burden less: for Dora, you will be my children's mother,—you will care for them.'

"I thought of Dr. West, and the year which divided us, but I answered, 'Yes, I will care for the children;' and then, to stop her talking, I was thinking of leaving her, when Jessie's voice was heard in the hall, speaking to the chamber-maid.

"'Who is that?' Margaret asked, her old expression coming back and settling down into a hard, unpleasant expression, when I replied:

"'That's Jessie Verner. The family came with me, or rather I came with them. You know her; she was here a few weeks since.'

"'The dreadful girl! Why, Dora, she *whistles*, and romps with the dog, and talks to the gentlemen, and goes down the sidewalk *hip-pi-ti-hop*, and up the stairs two at a time; and *joked* with John about being his second wife right before me! Actually, Dora, right before *me!*' and Margaret's voice was highly indicative of her horror at this last-named sin of Jessie's.

"'It was better to joke before you than when you were absent. Jessie is at least frank and open-hearted,' I said, but Margaret would not hear a word in her favor, so deeply prejudiced had she become against the young girl, who half an hour later inquired for her with much concern, and asked if she might see her.

"'I did not know,' I said, 'I'd ask.'

"'Never, Dora, never!' and Margaret's lips shut firmly. 'That terrible girl see me! No, indeed!' and in this she persisted to the last, Dr. West telling Jessie that he did not think it best for her to call on Mrs. Russell, as it might disturb her.

"That night, tired as Jessie was, she danced like a top in the drawing-room, meeting many acquaintances, and winning a host of male admirers by her frankness and originality. Next morning I counted upon her table as many as six bouquets, the finest of which she begged me carry Margaret, with her compliments.

"Margaret was weaker this morning than she had been the previous night, but her eyes lighted up with a gleam of pleasure when I appeared with the flowers, and she involuntarily raised her hand to take them.

"'Miss Jessie sent them,' I said, and instantly they dropped from Margaret's grasp, while she exclaimed:

"'That dreadful girl? Put them out of my sight. They make me sick. I can't endure it!'

"So I put the poor discarded flowers away in the children's room, and then went back to Margaret, who kept me by her the live-long day, talking of the years gone by, of our dead parents, and finally of the rapidly coming time when she would be dead like them. Then she spoke of Johnnie and the little boys at home, and gave to me messages of love, with sundry injunctions to mind whatever I might tell them. Remembering Johnnie's letter, in which he had expressed so much contrition for the saucy words said to her when he did battle for me, I told her of his grief and his desire that I should do so. Margaret was beautiful then, with the great mother-love shining out upon her face, as with quivering lip she bade me tell the repentant boy how she forgave him all the past, and only thought of him as her eldest-born and pride.

"'And, Dora, when I'm dead, cut off some of my curls, and give the longest, the brightest to Johnnie.'

"I assented with tears, and received numerous other directions until my brain was in a whirl, so much seemed depending upon me.

"Hovering constantly over and around her was brother John, doing everything so clumsily and yet so kindly, that Margaret did not send him from her until the day was closing. Then as I came back to her after a short absence, during which I had gone with Bell and Jessie to the Congress Spring, she said to him softly:

"'Now leave me with Dora.'

"He obeyed silently, and I fancied there was a flush upon his cheek as he closed the door upon us. All thought of that, however, was forgotten in Margaret's question:

"'Dora, are you engaged?'

"How I started, standing upon my feet, so that from the window I saw Dr. West leaning against a tree, and talking to Jessie, who sat with Bell upon the piazza. I thought she referred to him, and I answered her no, wondering the while if it was a falsehood I told her.

"'I am glad,' she said, reaching for my hand. 'When I heard he was at his sister's in Morrisville, I thought it might end in an engagement, particularly as he admired you so much when he visited us last summer.'

"I knew now that she was talking of Lieutenant Reed, and that no suspicion of my love for Dr. West had ever crossed her mind, and so I listened, while she continued:

"'I told you last night that you must be my children's mother, and you promised that you would. Tell me so again, Dora. Say that no one else shall come between you, and if, in after years, children of your own shall

THE SHADOW OF DEATH. 127

climb your lap, and cling about your neck, love mine still for your dead sister's sake. Promise, Dora.'

" For an instant there flashed upon my mind a thought, the reality of which would prove a living death, and in that interval I felt all the sickening anguish which would surely come upon me were I to take her place in everything. But she did *not* mean that. She could not doom me to such a fate, and so when she said to me again faintly, oh! so faintly, while the perspiration stood on her white lips, and her cold hand clasped mine pleadingly, ' Promise, Dora, to be my children's mother.'

" I answered, ' Yes, I will care for and be to them a mother.'

" ' You make me so happy,' she replied ; ' for, Dora,' and her dim eyes flashed indignantly, ' you may say it was all in a jest, but I know that dreadful *whistling* girl meant more than half she said. She fancied John, and sometimes I thought he fancied her. Dora, I should rise out of my grave to have her there, in my room, riding in my carriage, sporting my diamonds, and using my dresses, the whistling hoyden ! '

" I shed tears of repentance over Margaret's dead body for the merry laugh I could not repress at the mere idea of her being jealous of Jessie Verner, who was only eighteen years of age, while brother John was almost forty. My laugh disturbed her, and so I forced it back, going at her request for John, who, when next we met alone, stroked my hair kindly, saying to me :

"'You are a good girl, Dora, to make Madge so easy about the children.'

"Again that torturing fear ran like a sharp knife through every nerve, and hurrying on to the farther end of the long hall, I sat down upon the floor and wept bitterly as I thought, 'What if Margaret did mean that I should some time be his wife. Am I bound by a promise to do so?'

"From the busy street below came up a hum of voices, among which I recognized the clear, musical tones of Dr. West, while there stole over me a mad desire to fly to him at once, to throw myself into his arms and ask him to save me from I knew not what, unless it were the white-faced sister going so fast from our midst. And while I sat there crouching upon the floor, Jessie came tripping down the hall, her bright face all aglow with excitement, but changing its expression when she saw and recognized me.

"'Poor Dora!' she whispered, kneeling beside me and pressing her warm cheek against my own; 'I am so sorry for you. It must be dreadful to lose one's sister. Why, only this afternoon, when I was talking and laughing with those young men downstairs, whom I can't endure, only I like to have them after me, I was thinking of you, and the tears came into my eyes as I tried to fancy how

I should feel if Bell were dying here. Death seems more terrible, don't it, when it comes to such a place as this, where there is so much vanity, and emptiness, and fashion? I have been saying so to Dr. West, who talked to me so Christian-like. Oh! I wish I was as good as Dr. West! I should not then be afraid to lie where your sister does, and go out from this world alone in the night, leaving you all behind. Is she afraid, do you think?'

"I did not know, and I answered only with a choking sob, as I gazed up into the clear evening sky, where the myriads of stars were shining, and thought of the father and mother already gone, wondering if we should one day all meet again, an unbroken family. For a long time we sat there, I listening while Jessie talked as I had not thought it possible for her to talk. There was more to her even than to Bell I began to realize, wishing Margaret might live to have her prejudice removed. But that could not be. Even then the dark-winged messenger was on his way, stealing noiselessly into the crowded house and gliding past the gay throng, each one of which would some day be sent for thus. Up the winding stair he went and through the upper halls until Margaret's room was reached, and there he entered. Dr. West was the first to detect his presence, knowing he was there by the peculiar shadow cast by his dark wing upon the ghastly face and by the fluttering of the feeble pulse; and

Margaret knew it next, and asked for me and the children.

"I was sitting with Jessie at the window, watching the glittering stars, when a step came hurriedly towards us, and Dr. West's voice said to me, pityingly:

"'Dora, your sister has sent for you. I believe she is dying.'

"I had expected she would die,—had said I was prepared to meet it; but now when it came it was a sudden blow, and as I rose to my feet I uttered a moaning cry, which made the doctor lay his hand on my head, while, unmindful of Jessie's presence, he passed one arm round my waist, and so led me on to where the husband and the children wept around the dying wife and mother. The waltzing had commenced in the parlor below, and strain after strain of the stirring music came in through the open windows, making us shudder and grow faint, for standing there, with death in our midst, the song and the dance were sadly out of place. For a moment I missed the doctor from my side, and afterwards I heard how a few well-chosen words from him had sufficed to stop the revellers, who silently dispersed, some to the other hotels, where there was no dying-bed, some to the cool piazzas, where in hushed tones they talked together of Margaret, and others to their rooms, thinking, as Jessie had done, how much more terrible was death at such a place as this, than when it came into the quiet bed-chamber of home. And the great hotel was silent at last, every guest respecting the sorrow falling so heavily on a few, and even the servants in the kitchen catching the pervading spirit, and speaking only in whispers as they kept on with their labor. And up in Margaret's room it was quiet, too, as we watched the life going out slowly, very slowly, so that the twinkling lights were gone from the many windows, and the *nuns* in the convent across the street had ceased to tell their beads ere the chamber-maid in our hall leaned over the bannisters, and whispered to a chamber-maid below, 'The lady is dead.'

"There had been a last word, and it was spoken to *me*, ringing in my ears for hours after the stiffening limbs were straightened, and the covering laid over the still, white face of her who said them.

"'Remember your promise, Dora,—your promise to your dead sister.'

"Yes. I would remember it, as I understood it, I said to myself, hugging little Daisy in my arms, and soothing her back to the sleep which had been broken that her mother might kiss her once more. And while I cared for Daisy, Jessie cared for Margaret, just as she had for Robin. Jessie was a blessing to us then, and we could not well have done without her. Bell, though ten years older, was helpless as a child, while her young sister ordered all, thought of all, even to the bereaved husband sobbing so long by the side of his lost wife. In the gray dawn of the morning, as I passed the room, I saw her standing by him, and knew she was comforting him, for her small hand was smoothing his hair as if he had been her father. Involuntarily I looked to see if from the dead there came no sign of disapprobation; but no, the wife was lying there so still, while Jessie comforted the husband.

"They have put Margaret in her coffin; it is fifteen hours since she died, and to-morrow we shall go with her back to the home she left a few weeks since, and whither a telegram has preceded us telling them of our loss. Jessie would gladly accompany me, but I do not think it best, neither does Bell, and so she will remain behind, and visit me in the winter with her sister. I shall need her then so much, for the world will be doubly lonely,—Margaret gone, and the California sun shining down on Richard. Do I love him now? Yes, oh yes, and I am not ashamed to confess it here on paper, while more than once I have wished so much to tell it to him,—wished he would ask me again what he did by Anna's grave, and I would not answer angrily, jealously as then. I would say to him:

"'Wait, Richard, a little time till Margaret's children are a few years older, and then I will be yours, caring still for the little ones as I promised I would.'

"But he gives me no chance, and talks with Jessie and Bell far more than he does with me. He is going with us to Beechwood, and then in a few weeks' time he too, will be gone, and I left all alone. Oh, if he would but give me a right to think of, and talk of him as of one who was to be my husband, that terrible something would not haunt me as it does, neither should I ask myself so constantly:

"' Did Margaret mean anything more than that as a mother I should care for her children?'"

CHAPTER XIII.

AT BEECHWOOD.

The Author's Story.

THE great house at Beechwood was closed, and the first September sunshine which lay so warmly on the grassy lawn and blooming flower-garden, found no entrance through the doors and curtained windows of what had been Margaret Russell's home, and whither they were bringing her lifeless form. During the past week there had been hot, passionate tears wept in that desolate home, and touching childish prayers made that God would spare the sick mother till her broken-hearted boy could tell how sorry he was for the angry words spoken to her, and for the many acts of disobedience which came thronging around him like so many accusing spirits. Poor Johnnie's heart was almost crushed when he heard that his mother must die, and calling Ben and Burt to him, he bade them kneel with him, and ask that God would give her back to them alive. And so with concern for Johnnie on their baby faces, rather than concern for their mother, the two little boys prayed that "God would make mamma well, and not let her die, or anyway send home Auntie Dora."

This was Ben's idea, and it brought a world of comfort, making him ask Johnnie "if it wouldn't be nicer after all to have Auntie than mamma."

"Perhaps it would, if I hadn't been so *sassy* to her that morning, twitting her about not caring for us like Auntie, and telling her to *dry up*. Oh, oh!" and the conscience-smitten boy rolled on the floor in his first real sorrow.

To Ben, looking on in wonder, there came a thought fraught, as he hoped, with comfort to his brother, and pursing up his little mouth, he said:

"Pho! I wouldn't keel over like that 'cause I'd said *dry up*. 'Taint a swear. It's a real nice word, and all the boys in the street say so."

Still Johnnie was not comforted, and in a state of terrible suspense he waited from day to day until the fatal morning when there came a telegram which he spelled out with Burt and Ben sitting on the doorstep beside him, their fat hands on his knee, and their little round dirty faces turned inquiringly towards him as he read:

"SARATOGA, August 31st.

"Your mother died at midnight. We shall be home to-morrow, on the evening train."

There was at first no sudden outburst, but a compressed

quivering of the lip, a paling of the cheek, a hopeless look in the eyes, which closed tightly as Johnnie began to realize the truth. Then, with a loud, wild cry, he threw himself upon the grass, while Ben and Burt laughed gleefully at the contortions of body which they fancied were made for their amusement. At last, however, they too understood it partially, and Ben tried to imitate his brother's method of expressing grief by also rolling in the grass, while Burt, thinking intently for a moment, said, with a sigh of relief:

"I'm plaguy glad Aunty isn't dead too."

And this was all the consolation there was in that home at Beechwood. Dora was not dead. She was coming home and would bring sunshine with her. With a desire to have everything done in accordance with her taste, and also with a view to honor his mother's memory, Johnnie, roused at last, and without a word of consultation with any one, sought the old colored sexton, bidding him toll the bell, and adding with a quivering lip:

"It's for my mother, and if you'll toll it extra for an hour I'll give you half a dollar now, and a bushel of shagbarks in the fall."

It did not occur to the negro that possibly some higher authority than Johnnie's was needful ere he proceeded to toll for a person dead in Saratoga, but love of gain and shag-barks predominated over other feelings, and for a full hour and a quarter the bell from the old church-steeple rang out its solemn tones, tolling till the villagers wondered if it would never stop, and repaired, some of them, to the spot, where Johnnie sat like a second Shylock, holding the sexton's watch and keeping accurate note of time as the old man bent to his task, and tolled that long requiem for Margaret Russell. This done Johnnie wended his way to a dry-goods store, and before night-fall there were streamers of crape hanging from the gate and from every door-knob, while a band of the same was tied around the arms of Ben and Burt, who wore them quietly for a time and then made what they called horse blankets for their velocipede. Poor little babies of four and five, they knew no better, and only acted as other children do when left wholly to themselves. Years hence they will weep for the mother scarcely remembered, but now her death was nothing to them, except as they saw the deep distress of Johnnie, who, long after they were sleeping in their cribs, sobbed passionately upon his pillow, sorrowing most of all for the angry words spoken to the mother who would never know his grief. How long to him were the hours of the next day, when they waited for the dead. It was also a day of peace and quiet, for owing to Johnnie's continual efforts there was only a single fight between the little boys, who otherwise comported themselves with admirable propriety, asking often when Aunt Dora would come, and if Johnnie was sure she was not dead too?

At last the train came screaming in, and shortly after the hearse stopped before the gate, while the coffin was brought slowly up the walk and placed in the darkened parlor. With a great sobbing cry Johnnie sprang towards Dora, but suddenly checked himself, as there flashed upon his mind that to his father belonged the first greeting of sorrow. And who that has passed through such a scene that knows not the comfort there is in the sympathy of a warm-hearted child! Squire Russell felt it keenly, as he held his first-born in his arms and heard his boyish attempts at consolation.

"We'll love each other more, father, now our mother's gone. Poor father, don't cry so hard. If you'll stop I'll try to do so too. We've got Aunt Dora left and all the children. Benny, come and kiss poor father, because mother is dead."

Such were Johnnie's words, and they fell soothingly on the father's heart, making him think he had not lost everything which made his life desirable. He had his children still, and he had Dora too. She was in the nursery now, with Ben and Burt clinging to her neck, and asking why she cried when they were so glad to have her back, asking, too, what made mamma so cold, and why she was sleeping in that long queer box on the parlor table. They did not know what death meant, and continued their questionings until their eyelids closed in slumber, and they forgot the long box on the parlor table, with the mother sleeping in it.

The night was hot and sultry, and as Dora lay tossing restlessly, she fancied she heard a sound from the parlor, which was just beneath her room, and throwing on her dressing-gown she went noiselessly down the stairs to the parlor door, which was open, and saw a little form kneeling by the coffin and talking to the unconscious dead.

"O mother, maybe you can hear me; I'm Johnnie, and I'm so sorry I was ever bad to you, and made your head ache so! Poor mother, I used to think I loved Aunt Dora best, but now I know I didn't! There's nothing like a mother, and I was going to tell you so when you got home, but you're dead and I can't! O mother! mother! will you never know?"

"She does; she did know, Johnnie, for I told her," Dora said, advancing into the room and taking the child in her arms; "I told her you were sorry, and she forgave you freely, sending you messages of love, and bidding me cut her longest, brightest curl for you. I did so, Johnnie; it is in my room, and to-morrow you shall have it."

"Why not to-night?" Johnnie pleaded, and so his aunt brought him the lock of hair cut from Margaret's head, the mother's last memento, which Johnny took with him to his room, sleeping more quietly because of that tress of hair upon his pillow.

It was a long procession which followed Margaret to her grave, and for the sake of Johnnie the sexton again tolled for the dead, until the husband and the sister wished the sad sounds would cease. Sadly they returned to the house, leaving Margaret behind them, and missing her more than one month ago they would have thought it possible. But as the days went by the family gradually resumed its wonted cheerfulness, for Dora was there still: their head, their blessing, and comforter. Many lonely hours Squire Russell experienced, it is true, but there was always a solace in knowing that Dora would welcome him home after a brief and necessary absence; that Dora would preside at his table, and keep his children in order; that Dora, in short, would do everything which the most faithful of sisters could do. The children, too, clung to Dora even more than they were wont to do; and little Daisy, taught by Clem, the nurse-maid, called her *mamma*, a name which Ben and Burt were quick to catch, and which Dora did not like to hear, especially if the father chanced to be present.

At Dora's heart there was a constant dread of some impending evil, and when, three weeks after Margarets' death, she stood one night alone with Dr. West, listening to his farewell, she felt again a longing to throw herself on his protection, and thus she might be saved from danger. But the doctor, though treating her with the utmost tenderness, had never broached the subject of his love since that time at Anna's grave, where she answered him so indifferently. Her foolish words had hurt him more since than they did then, causing him sometimes to wonder if she did really care for him. If not, or if the germ of her affection was as yet very small, it was better not to press the matter, but let it take its course; and so, trusting that absence would do all that he wished done, he only said good-by as he would have said it to a dear sister, and hardly so, for when he would have kissed the sister, he left Dora unkissed, fancying she would be better pleased with such a parting. His caresses had wearied Anna, and he would not err this way again, so he never touched the lips which would have paid him back so gladly, but merely pressed the little hand which trembled in his, as he said to her, "A year is not very long, Dora. It will pass sooner than we think, and you must not forget me." Another pressure of the hand, and he was gone, leaving the maiden far more desolate than he dreamed. Could he have known how fast the tears came, when alone in her room she went over with the parting and said to herself, "He does not love me now. My waywardness has sickened him;" could he have seen her when in the early dawn she watched him as he left the house for the last time, he would have turned back, and by taking her with him, or staying himself with her, would have saved her from the dark storm which would bear her down with its mighty force.

But this he did not know, and he went his way to Morrisville, where his mother waited for him, and where Jessie, just returned from Saratoga, sparkled, and flashed, and flitted around him, asking him to write occasionally to her father, and tell them of California.

"Why not write to *you?*" he replied, and Jessie responded at once:

"To me, then, if you like; I shall be delighted."

Judge Verner, and Bell, and Mattie Randall all heard this conversation, and so there could be no harm in it, Jessie thought, while the others thought the same, knowing that the light-hearted girl was already corresponding with at least ten gentlemen, for not one of whom did she care in the least. She was a merry little creature, and she made the doctor's stay at Morrisville much pleasanter than it would otherwise have been, and after he was fairly on the sea, she wrote to Dora a glowing account of "the perfectly splendid time she had with Doctor West, the best and most agreeable man in the world. We are going to correspond, too," she added in a postscript, "and that will make the eleventh gentleman on my list. I want it an even dozen, and then I'll be satisfied."

Dora knew Jessie was a flirt, but this did not lessen the pang with which she read that Jessie, and not herself, was to be the recipient of the doctor's letters. Never had the autumn seemed so dreary to her before; and when the first wintry snows were falling she shrank, with a nervous dread, from the coming months, with the long, long evenings, when there would be nothing to occupy her time, except, indeed, the children, or the game of chess which she played nightly with her brother.

For one who at first mourned so sorely for the dead, the squire had recovered his spirits wonderfully, and the villagers even hinted that, as is usual with widowers, his dress had undergone a change, being now more youthful and stylish than in former days when Margaret was alive. Young girls blushed when he appeared at any of the social gatherings, while the older ones grew very conscious of themselves, and the mothers were excessively polite and gracious to the squire. He was happier than he used to be, notwithstanding that he went twice a week to Margaret's grave, and always spoke of her as " my dear wife." It soothed his conscience to do this, particularly as he felt how much he enjoyed going home from Margaret's grave, and finding order and quiet and pleasant words, where once there had been confusion and fretful complaints. Dora was very pretty in her mourning-garb, with the simple linen band about her neck and wrists, for she would relieve the sombre aspect of her dress with a show of white, even if it were not the fashion. There was not much color in her cheeks, and her eyes were larger than usual, but to the squire and the children she was very beautiful, moving among them as their household goddess, and always speaking so lovingly and kind.

Once, and only once, there came a letter from Dr. West,—a friendly letter, which any one might read, and which said that he was at Marysville, with his mother, whose health was greatly improved.

"I like the country much," he wrote, "and if I had with me a few of my Eastern friends I should be willing to settle here for life; but, as it is, I find myself looking forward eagerly to the time when I shall return and meet you all again."

This passage Squire John read twice, and then glanced again at the "My Dear Dora" with which the letter commenced.

"The doctor is very affectionate," he said, "calling you 'Dear Dora,' though perhaps he has a right, for I remember thinking he admired you."

Dora was bending over Daisy, whom she was rocking to sleep, and he did not see her blushes as she replied:

"That is a very common way of addressing people, and means nothing at all."

Perhaps the squire believed this, but he was quite absent-minded the remainder of the day, and in the evening was twice checkmated by Dora, when his usual custom had been to checkmate her.

Dora's first intention was to answer the doctor's letter

at once, but sickness among the children prevented her from doing so, and when she was at last free to write, the disposition had in a measure left her, and so the answer for which the doctor waited so anxiously was not sent.

CHAPTER XIV.

IN THE SPRING.

ABOUT the house at Beechwood the May flowers were blooming, and in the maple-trees the birds were building their nests, cooing lovingly to each other as they did so, and seeming all unconscious of the young heart which within the doors felt that never before had there come to it a spring so full of sorrow and harrowing dread. Jessie and Bell Verner were both there now, and Jessie had brought two immense trunks and a hat-box, as if her intention was to spend the entire summer. She was just as merry and hoydenish as of old, romping with the children in the grass and on the nursery floor, herself the veriest child among them, while her ringing laugh woke all the echoes of the place and made even the Squire join in it, and try to act young again.

Both Jessie and Bell noted the change in Dora, and Jessie asked her outright what it was that made her look so frightened, as if constantly in fear of something; but Dora could not tell what she feared, for she had scarcely dared to define to herself the meaning of Squire Russell's manner toward her. A stranger would have perceived no difference in his treatment of her now and when his wife was living, but Dora felt the change, and it almost drove her wild, making her one day sharply rebuke the little Daisy for calling her mamma.

"I am not your mother," she said fiercely. "Your mamma is dead, and I am only Auntie."

The child looked up in surprise, but called her mamma just the same, while Dora's eyelids closed tightly over the hot tears she thus kept from falling. That day when Johnnie came home from school at dinner-time he showed unmistakable marks of having been in a fight, and when questioned by his father as to the cause of his black eye, broke out furiously:

"I've been a *lickin*' Bill Carter, and I'll do it again if he ever tells such stuff about you! Why, he said you're a going to get married to that ill-begotten, shoulder-shotten snap-dragon of a Miss Dutton! I told him 'twas the biggest lie, and then he said it wasn't, that it was true, and she was coming here to be our step-mother; that she would cut off 'Tish's curls, spank Ben and Burt twice a day, shake Daisy into shoe-strings, and make Jim and me toe the mark,—the hateful!"

"She ain't, she shan't,—old nasty Dutton," and fiery Ben shook his tiny fist at an imaginary bugbear who was to spank him twice a day.

Jessie laughed aloud. Bell looked amused, Dora disturbed, and the Squire very red, as he said to his son:

"You should not mind such gossip, or allow yourself to get into a passion. Time enough to rebel when the step-mother comes. Now go to your room and bathe your eye."

Johnnie obeyed, muttering as he went:

"There's only one person I'd have for a step-mother any how, and that's Aunt Dora. Guy, wouldn't I raise hob with anybody else!"

"John, leave instantly!" the Squire said sternly, while his face colored crimson, as did Dora's also, making Bell and Jessie glance curiously at each other, as both thought of the same thing.

In their own room, after dinner, they discussed together the possibility of Dora's becoming what Johnnie wished her to be, Bell scouting the idea as preposterous, and Jessie insisting that a girl might love Squire Russell well enough to take him with all his children.

"Not that I think Dora will do so," she said, "for I fancy he is not as much to her taste, even, as he is to mine; and I guess I'd jump in the creek sooner than marry an old widower with half a dozen children."

What the two sisters were discussing privately in their room was talked openly in the village, some of the people arguing that Dora could not do better, while all agreed that for the Squire it would be a match every way desirable both for his own and his children's sake. To the Squire himself the story was told one day, the teller hinting that the matter was entirely settled, and asking when the marriage would take place.

With some jocose reply, the Squire rode away, going round to Margaret's grave, and thence back to his home, where the evening lights were shining, and where Dora, with Daisy in her arms, sat alone in the back parlor, Bell and Jessie having accepted an invitation which she was obliged to decline on account of a bad headache.

There were strange thoughts stirring in the Squire's breast that night, thoughts which had haunted him for weeks and months, aye, since Margaret died, for he could not forget her words.

"You need not wait long. You and Dora are above people's gossip, and it will be so much better for the children."

This was what Margaret had said to him that night when misapprehending her sister just as she was misapprehended, she had told him:

"I have talked with Dora, and she has promised to take my place."

At first he had been satisfied with matters as they were, and had said that he never could marry and love again. But gradually there had crept into life another feeling, which prompted him to watch Dora constantly as she moved about his house; to miss her when she was away,—to think of her the last at night as well as first in the morning,—to wonder, with a harassing jealousy, if Dr.

West cared for Dora, or if she cared for him. No, she did not, he thought, and made himself believe it, else he had never said to her what he did that night, when, with Daisy in her arms, she sat wholly in his power, and was obliged to listen to what was not unexpected, but which, nevertheless, fell like a thunderbolt upon her, turning her into stone, and making her grow faint and sick, just as she did at Saratoga, when the first suspicion dawned upon her that some day John Russell would speak to her what he was speaking now, with one hand on her shoulder and the other on Daisy's golden head. It was a kind, true, fatherly heart he offered her, and she felt that he meant it all. He cast no reflections upon his departed wife,— he merely said:

"You knew Margaret as well as I. She was not, perhaps, as even-tempered as a more healthy person would have been, but I loved her, remembering always what she was when I took her from her home. You were a little girl, then, Dora, and I never dreamed that I should some time be sueing for your hand just as I had sued for Margaret's."

Then he pleaded for his children, who loved her so much; would she be their mother, just as she had promised Margaret she would? Then Dora roused herself, and the face which met the Squire's view made his heart beat faster as he doubted what it portended.

"I did not think Margaret meant what you ask," Dora

said, her words coming gaspingly. "I thought she meant care for them as I have tried to do, and will do still. I'll stay with you, John. I'll be your housekeeper, but don't ask me to be your wife. I can't; I'm too young for you; I'm,—O John! O Margaret!" and here the voice broke down entirely, while Dora sobbed convulsively.

Margaret, too, had said she could not be his wife when he asked her. She, too, had said she was too young, and cried, but hers was not like Dora's crying, and Squire Russell saw the difference, feeling perplexed, but never suspected the truth. It was natural for girls to cry, he thought, when they received an offer of marriage, and so, with both hands on her shoulder, he pleaded again, but this time for himself, telling her in words which his true love made eloquent, how dear she was to him, dearer, if possible, than his early choice, the beautiful Margaret. And Dora believed him, for she knew he was incapable of deception, and that made her pain harder to bear.

"If I had supposed you cared for any one else," he said, "I should not have sought you, but I did not. Dr. West wrote to you, I know, and I was foolish enough to wish he had not called you his *dear Dora*, but you did not answer him, and of course there is but one conclusion to be drawn from that. You do not care for him, nor he for you?"

He put this to her interrogatively, but Dora could not

speak. Once she thought to tell him what there was be tween her and Dr. West, but something kept her silent, and so in perfect good faith, kind, honest, truthful John kept on until she answered:

"Please leave me now; I must think, and I am so stunned and bewildered. I'll answer another time."

Squire Russell was far too good-natured to stay longer if she did not wish it, and stooping down he kissed his sleeping child, and said:

"Let me kiss baby's auntie, too?"

Dora offered no resistance, and he touched her forehead respectfully, and then quitted the room. He had kissed her many times when Margaret was living, but no kiss had ever burned her as this one did, for she knew it was not a brother's kiss, and with a sensation of loathing she passed her hand over the place, and then wiped it with her handkerchief, just as a rustling sound met her ear, and the next moment there was another pleader kneeling at her feet, Johnnie, who had overheard a part of his father's wooing, and who took it up just where his sire had left it; his stormy, impetuous arguments bearing Dora completely away from herself, so that she hardly knew what she did or said.

"You will be father's wife, Aunt Dora; you will, you must!" Johnnie began. "I've prayed for it every single day since I heard that stuff about old Dutton. I've gone to mother's grave and knelt down there, asking that it might be. Jim and 'Tish pray so, too, for I told 'em to, and I should make Ben and Burt, only I knew they'd tell you; and Auntie, you will! Father's older than you a lot, I s'pose, but he is so good, and was so kind to mother, even when she plagued him. I never told, but once after you went to Morrisville, she got awful, and *lammed* him the wust kind,—told him he was fat, and pussy, and awkward, and she was always ashamed of him at watering-places, and a sight more. At last she left the room, and poor papa put his head right in my lap and cried out loud. I cried too, and said to him:

"'Let's *lick* her: I'll help.'

"But he wouldn't hear a word. Says he:

"'Hush, my boy; she's your mother and my wife. She is not as she used to be. She's sick and nervous.'

"And when I asked the difference between *ugly* and *nervous*, he made me stop, and was just as kind to her at supper-time as ever. Tell me such a man won't make a good husband! He'll be splendid, and he's handsomer than he was,—he has lost that look as if he was afraid something was after him, a henpecked look, Clem called it. Poor father; he has had so little comfort, you must make him happy, Auntie; you will, and you'll make us all so good. You know how like Cain we behave without you, and how we all mind when you tell us what is right. Will you be father's wife and help us grow up good?"

He had her face between his warm hands, and was looking at her so earnestly, that for his sake Dora could almost have answered yes, but thoughts of what being his father's wife involved chilled her through and through, and she answered him:

"Johnnie, I do not believe I can."

For an instant the boy's black eyes blazed fiercely at her, and then he angrily exclaimed, "I'll go to ruin, just as fast as I can go! I'll *smoke* to-morrow, if I live, and teach Jim and Ben to do so too! I'll swear, and when the circus comes next week I'll run away to that, and take 'Tish with me; I'll gamble; I'll drink, and when I'm brought home drunker'n a fool, you'll know it is your work!"

He looked like a young tiger as he stood uttering these terrible threats, and Dora quailed before his flashing eyes, feeling that much he had said was in earnest. She did not fear his swearing, or gambling, or drinking, for the present, at least, but he might not always act his best; he might grow surly and hard and unmanageable, even by her, unless she yielded to his request, and this she couldn't do.

"Johnnie," she began, and something in her voice quieted the excited boy, "would you have me marry your father when I do not love him, and just the thought of being his wife makes me almost sick?"

Johnnie was not old enough to comprehend her

meaning. He only felt that it was not a very bad thing to be the wife of a man as good as his father, and he answered her, " You do love him well enough, or you will, and he so affectionate. Why he used to hug and kiss mother every day, even when she was crosser than fury. Of course then he'll hug you most to death."

" Oh—h," Dora groaned, the tone of her voice so indicative of disgust that even Johnnie caught a new idea, which he afterwards acted upon; but he would not yield his point: Dora should be his mother, and he continued the siege until, wearied out with his arguments, Dora peremptorily bade him leave her while she could think in quiet.

Oh, that long, terrible thinking which brought on so racking a headache that Dora was not seen in the parlor on the day following, but lay upstairs in her own room, where, with the bolted door between her and the world outside, she met and battled with what seemed her destiny! One by one every incident connected with Margaret's death came back to her, and she knew now what the questionings meant, far better than she did then, while she half expected the dead sister to rise before her and reproach her for shrinking from her duty. Then the children came up, a powerful argument swaying her in the direction of Squire Russell. She could do them good; she could train them so much better than another, and John, if she refused him, would assuredly bring another there to rule and govern them. These were the arguments in favor of John's suit, while on the other side a mighty barrier was interposed to keep her from the sacrifice. Her love for Dr. West, and the words spoken to her at Anna's grave; and was she not virtually engaged to him?

"Yes,—oh yes, I am!" she cried, and then there came over her all the doubts which had so tortured her since that time in the Morrisville cemetery.

Had he not spoken hastily and repented afterwards? His continued silence on the subject would seem so; and why did he not write to her just as did he to Jessie, who, since coming to Beechwood, had received a letter from him which contained no mention of her, but was full of the light, bantering matter in which he knew Jessie delighted. Dora had heard Jessie say she was going to answer the letter that very day; and suddenly, like a dawn of hope, there flashed over her the determination that she, too, would write and tell him of Squire Russell's offer; and if he loved her still he would come to save her, or he would write, telling her again how dear she was to him, and that he alone must call her his wife.

"Yes, I'll do it," Dora whispered; "I know he is at San Francisco, for Jessie directs there; I'll write to-day. It shall go in the same mail with hers. I'll wait two months for his reply, and then, if he answers Jessie and ignores me, I'll—"

Dora set her teeth firmly together, and her breath came hurriedly, as she paused a moment ere she added, "I'll marry John."

And so with a throbbing head Dora wrote to Dr. West, telling him of the proposal and asking what he thought of it. This was all she meant the letter to mean, for her maidenly reserve would not suffer her to betray her real motive if she knew it, but it was more like a pleading cry for help, more like a wail of anguish for one she loved to save her from a fate she had not strength to resist alone, than like a mere asking of advice. The letter was finished, and just after dark, when sure no one could see her, Dora stole from the house unobserved, and hastening to the office, dropped into the box the missive of so much importance to her.

"It is sure to go with Jessie's," she said, as she wended her way back, "so if hers is received I shall know that mine was also."

Alas! Jessie's had been written the previous night, after that young lady's return from her visit, and while Dora's letter was lying quietly in the box at Beechwood awaiting the morning mail, Jessie's was miles on its way to New York and the steamer which would take it to California a week in advance of the other. But Dora did not know this, neither did she know that it contained the following paragraph:

"There is no news, except the rumor that Squire

Russell will marry his pretty sister-in-law. Bell won't believe a word of it, but some things look like it. Dora is so queer. I had picked her out for you, and believe now that she likes you, though when your name is mentioned, she bites her words off so short and crisp that I am confounded. She is a splendid girl, and will make a grand wife, to say nothing of step-mother."

Little did Jessie suspect the harm these few comparatively harmless lines would cause, and little did Dora suspect it either, as with a load of pain lifted from her heart and consequently from her head, she sat down by her open window and followed with her mind her letter's course to far-off California, and then imagined the quick response it would bring back, and which would make her so happy.

"Johnnie must be the medium between Squire Russell and me," she said. "I'll tell him to-morrow that his father must wait for my definite reply at least six weeks, and possibly two months. At the end of that time I shall know for sure, and if the doctor does not care, there will be a kind of desperate pleasure in marrying my brother."

CHAPTER XV.

WAITING FOR THE ANSWER.

AS Dora reached this conclusion there came a well-known knock upon the door, and unfastening the bolt she admitted Johnnie, who had been up many times that day, but had not before been permitted to enter.

"O Auntie," he cried, "you are better and I'm glad. I didn't mean what I said about swearing, and drinking, and smoking, and I was so mad at myself that I teased Ben and Burt on purpose till they got hoppin', and then I lay still while both little Arabs pitched into me. My! didn't their feet fly like drumsticks as they kicked and struck, and pulled my hair; but when Ben got the big carving-fork, I concluded I'd been punished enough, and so deserted the field! But, Auntie, I do wish you could love father. He has looked so sorry to-day, kind of white about the mouth, and his hand trembled this noon when he carved the turkey. Won't you, Auntie? I've prayed ten times this afternoon that you might, and I begin to have faith that you will. Dr. West, who used to talk to me so good last summer when I was in his

Sunday-school class, said we must have faith that God would hear us."

Dora drew a long, sad sigh, as she wished she too had been taught of Dr. West to pray differently from what she knew she did. Smoothing back John's soft, dark hair, she said:

"Johnnie, girls cannot make a love in a minute, and this came so suddenly upon me, I must have time to think, —six weeks or two months, and then I will decide. Will you tell your father this for me? Tell him I'm sorry to make him feel badly,—that I like him and always shall, even if I am not his wife—that I know how good, how generous he is,—that he will wait until I know my own mind better, and then if I cannot be his, he must not mind it."

"I'll tell him," Johnnie said, while Dora continued:

"And Johnnie, perhaps it had better be understood that nothing is to be said about it in the mean time,— nothing to me by your father."

"Yes, I know, I see. I'll fix it," Johnnie answered. "I'll go to father now," and stooping down, he kissed his aunt tenderly, then suddenly asked, as he looked into her eyes, "You don't mind my kissing you, do you? That don't make you sick?"

"No, oh no!" she answered, and Johnnie departed on his strange errand.

Squire Russell sat in his office or reading-room, pretending to look over his evening paper, but his thoughts were really upstairs with Dora, whom he had not seen that day, and whose illness troubled him greatly, for he rightly associated it with his proposal of the previous night. Squire Russell loved Dora with a great, warm, sheltering love, which would shield her from all harm, and unselfishly yield to her everything, but he had not the nice, quick perception of Dr. West, and had he been younger he could never have satisfied the wants of her higher nature as could the rival whose existence he did not suspect. But he loved her very much. He must have her. He could not live without her, he thought, and womanish man that he was, a tear was gathering in his eyes when Johnnie entered the room abruptly, and locking the door, came and stood beside him.

"What do you wish, my boy?" the Squire said kindly, for he was never impatient with his children.

Johnnie hesitated, beginning to feel that his father's love affair was a delicate matter for him to meddle with.

"Confound it," he began at last, "I may as well spit it out, and then let you knock me down, or lick me, or anything you like. Father, I heard what you said to Auntie last night, and what she said to you, and after you was gone I took the floor and beat you all to smash. I said she must be my mother,—she should be my mother, and all that, and set you up, I tell you, till you'd hardly know yourself from my description. To-night I've seen her again,--have just come from her room to tell you something she bade me tell."

Squire Russell had turned very white at first, feeling indignant at his son for presuming to interfere, but this feeling had disappeared now, and he listened eagerly while Johnnie continued:

"She says its sudden; that she can't make a love in a minute; that she must have six weeks or two months to decide, and then she will tell you sure, and, father, you'll wait; I know you will, and,—and,—well, I guess I'd hold my tongue,—that is, I wouldn't keep teasing her, nor say a word; just let her go her own gait, and above all I wouldn't act lovin' like, for fear she'd up and vomit. She don't mind me kissing her, because I've no beard, I don't shave, nor carry a cane. I'm a boy, and you are a whiskered old chap. I guess that's the difference between us. Father, you'll wait?"

Squire Russell could not forbear a smile at his son's novel reasoning, but he was not angry, and it made his child seem nearer, now that both shared the same secret, and were interested in the same cause. Yes, he would wait two, three, or four months if Dora liked, and meantime things should continue as usual in the household.

"And afterward, father?" Johnnie asked. "How about that? If auntie says no, she'll mean it, and you won't raise a rumpus, will you? You'll grin and bear it like a man?"

Yes, the Squire would do all his son required, and before Dora retired for the night, a bit of paper was pushed under her door, on which was written :

"The governor is O. K. He'll wait and so will I; and if you must say no, he won't raise hob, but *I* will. I tell you now I'll raise the very roof! Don't say no, Auntie, don't !
   " Yours Very Respectfully and Regretfully,
    "JOHN H. RUSSELL."

It was rather embarrassing next morning at the breakfast table, but Johnnie threw himself into the gap, talking loudly and rapidly to his father of the war meeting to be held that night, wishing he was a man, so he could enlist, and predicting, as did many a foolish one at that period, the spring of '61, that the immense force of 75,000, called for by the President, would subjugate the South at once.

The Squire talked very little, and never once glanced at Dora, who in her heart blessed both Jessie and Johnnie, the latter for engaging his father's attention and the former for talking so constantly to herself and Bell.

Dora was very white and nervous, but this was imputed to her illness of the previous day, and so neither Bell nor Jessie dreamed of what had passed between her and their lost, or how her heart was aching with the terrible fear of what might be in store for her.

It had been arranged that the Misses Verner should remain at Beechwood for a long time, and as Bell thought four weeks came under that definition she began to talk of returning home as early as the first of June; but with a look of terror which startled both the girls, Dora begged of them to stay.

"Don't leave me alone!" she cried, clasping Bell's hand pleadingly. "I shall die if you do! Oh, stay,— you would if you knew—"

She did not say what, and Bell gazed at her wonderingly, but decided at last to stay a few weeks longer. Nothing could please Jessie better, for she did not particularly like Morrisville, and she did like Beechwood very much. She liked the lake view, the hills, and the people, and she liked the six noisy, frolicsome children, with their good-humored sire, who treated her much as he would have treated a playful, teasing child not his own, but a guest. Many were the gambols she had with Ben and Burt, and little Daisy, who loved her almost as much as they loved Dora, while upon the matter-of-fact Squire she played off many a saucy trick, keeping him constantly on the alert with plots and conspiracies, and so making the time seem comparatively short, while he waited for Dora's decision. But to Dora there was nothing which brought comfort or diverted her for a moment from the agonizing suspense which grew more and more dreadful as the days went swiftly by, bringing no answer to the letter sent to Dr. West.

"Is it anything in particular you are expecting?" Johnnie asked one day, when she turned so white and shivered, as he returned from the post-office, with letters for all except herself.

"Yes,—no! Oh, I don't know what I expect," she answered, and leaning her head on Johnnie's shoulder, she wept silently, while the boy tried to comfort her, and became from that moment almost as anxious that she should have a letter as she seemed herself.

Regularly each day at mail-time he was at the office, and if there chanced to be a letter for Dora, as there sometimes was, running to her eagerly, but saying always to himself as the weary, disappointed look remained the same:

"The right one has not come."

No, the right one had not come, and now it was more than seven weeks since the night when Dr. West had been written to.

Bell and Jessie were really going home at last, and their trunks stood in the hall ready for the early morning train. Dora had exhausted every argument for a longer stay, but Bell felt that they must go.

"They would come again in the autumn, perhaps, or Dora should visit them. She would need rest by that time, sure," Bell said, and Dora shuddered as she thought how she might never know rest or happiness again, save as she found them in the discharge of what she was beginning to believe was her imperative duty.

"Letters! letters!" shouted Johnnie, running up the walk, his hand full of documents, one of which he was closely inspecting. Spelling out the place where it was mailed, he exclaimed, as he entered the room, "That's from the doctor, for it says 'San Francisco.'"

Instantly both Jessie and Dora started forward to claim it, the hot blood dyeing the cheeks of the latter, but subsiding instantly, and leaving only a livid hue as Jessie took the letter, saying:

"It is for me."

Sinking back in her chair, Dora pressed her hands tightly together, as Jessie broke the seal and read, partly to herself and partly aloud, that message from Dr. West.

"Is still in San Francisco, at the hotel, which is crowded with guests, and will compare very favorably with the best houses in New York City. Begins to think of coming home in the autumn. Mother's health improved. Was pleased to get my letter," and so on.

This was the substance of what Jessie read, until she reached a point where she stopped suddenly, and seemed to be considering; then turning to Johnnie, she asked him to do for her some trifling service, which would take him from the room. When he was gone, she said to Dora:

"Maybe you'll scold, but it cannot now be helped. In my letter to Dr. West, I said, or hinted, at what everybody is talking about,—that is, you know, about your marrying Squire Russell, and this is the doctor's reply: 'What you wrote of Miss Freeman took me by surprise, but it will be a grand thing for the Squire. Tell her that if she decides to mother those six children, she has my best wishes for her happiness. You say you had picked her out for me. She would probably tell you differently, as she has seemed to dislike rather than like me, and according to your own story, bites her words off crisp and short when I am mentioned.'"

"O Jessie, how could you? What made you tell him that? It was cruel of you, when I do like him," Dora cried, her face for an instant crimsoning with passion and then growing deathly white as she felt her destiny crushing down upon her without a hope of escape.

"Because you do," Jessie retorted, anxious to defend herself. "You are just as spiteful as can be when I tease you about him, and I don't care!"

Jessie was vexed at herself for having told Dr. West what she had, and vexed at Dora for resenting it; but she never dreamed of the terrible pain throbbing in Dora's heart, as with a mighty effort she forced back the piteous, despairing cry rising to her lips, and brought there a smile instead, saying pleasantly:

"Well, never mind it now. It does not matter; only Dr. West has been so kind to us in sickness that I ought to like him, and do. Does he say what time he will be home?"

Jessie was thoroughly deceived, and after ascertaining that he merely spoke of coming in the autumn, went to her room, as there were a few things she must yet do for her morrow's journey.

CHAPTER XVI.

THE ENGAGEMENT.

Extract from Dora's Diary.

IS it *I?* *Is* it I? Oh, IS IT I, sitting here tonight with this pressure on my brain, this tightness about my eyes, this anguish in my heart, this feeling of desperation urging me on to meet anything, everything, even death itself? If he received Jessie's letter, he did mine, of course, for they went together; and why not answer me, instead of sending that cold, mocking message? If people ever die of shame surely I ought to die, for did I not almost beg of him to say again what he said at Anna's grave,—to tell me that he loved me and would save me? Yes, it all comes to me now,—all that I wrote and what it meant. And he does not respond. If he ever cared, he does not now, and he spurns my offered love. He wishes me happiness; aye, and why should I not be happy? Many a woman would gladly be the mother of Margaret's six children; and shall I, her sister, who promised so solemnly, refuse? No, John; no, Johnnie; no, Margaret; I will grant your wish. Dr. West, when he comes home, shall have no reason to believe that Dora Freeman ever thought of him, or spoke of him, except in the 'crisp, cross manner' which Jessie has described. John must wait a year from the time Margaret died, but I can give him my decision now, and I will then go to Bell and Jessie, and ask them to be my bridesmaids."

There was a pause made in the diary, and leaning her aching head upon her hands, Dora thought and thought until the hardness softened, when, resuming her pen, she wrote as follows:

"I believe it is my duty to be John's wife, and the mother of Margaret's children. It is true I did not so understand her, but that was what she meant, and I promised solemnly. I can love John, or at least I can keep myself from hating him, knowing how happy I make him, and I do love his children, especially Johnnie. O Johnnie, I should die if it were not for you!"

The pen dropped from the trembling fingers, and again the face was buried in the hands, while Dora nerved herself to do what she vainly imagined was her duty. Squire Russell she knew was in the library, Bell and Jessie in their room, Johnnie in the street, and the other children in bed. There was nothing in the way, and she would go at once, so that the worst might be over as soon as possible. Without a moment longer in which to consider, she rose, and gliding down the stairs, knocked at the library door.

"Come in," the Squire said, his voice and manner changing at once when he saw who his visitor was.

"O Dora, is it you?" he said, rising to his feet, while his face glowed with pleasure.

"Yes, John," and Dora spoke hurriedly. "It is most seven weeks since I said you must wait for my answer. I can give it now as well as any time. I will be your wife."

Not a muscle changed as she said this, neither did her voice tremble, but rang out clear and decided, and it may be a little sharp and unnatural. Dora was very calm, far more so than the Squire, who, taken by surprise, started, and trembled, and blushed, and stammered like some guilty school-boy. This state of things, however, lasted only for a moment, and then rousing himself, Squire Russell drew the unresisting girl to his side, and kissing her forehead, said tenderly:

"God bless you, Dora. You have made me very happy. I was beginning to think it could not be, and was learning to live without you, but that makes my joy the greater. God bless my Dora, and show me how to make her happy!"

Had the Squire followed the promptings of his nature he would have caressed her lovingly, just as he did Margaret when she stood thus beside him; but remembering Johnnie's warnings, he desisted, and it was well he did, else Dora had hated him. Now she suffered him to wind his arms around her, while he told her again how happy she had made him, and blessed her for it.

"Dora," he said, and now he smoothed her hair, "a man of forty is not called old, and I am only that, but I am fourteen years your senior, while my six children make me seem older still, but my heart is young, and I will try so hard to stay with you till you too are old. I'll go with you wherever you wish to go, do anything you like, and never frown upon the things which I know young girls love. I will not be an ogre guarding my girlish wife, but a proud, happy husband, doing that wife's bidding."

Dora could not repress her tears, he spoke so kindly, so earnestly, and she knew he meant all he was saying, while she was deceiving him. She did not think either that she was doing very wrong in thus deceiving him. It was her duty to be his wife, and it was not her duty to analyze her feelings in his sight, unless he asked her for such analysis, which he was not likely to do, for his was not a mind quick to perceive, while suspicion was something to which he was a total stranger. He had always admired Dora, and latterly he had learned to love her devotedly, feeling now that his affection was in part returned, else she had not deliberately come to him and said, "I will be your wife." It made him very happy to know she had said so, and in his happiness he failed to notice the pallor of her face, the drooping of her swollen eyelids, and her apparent wish to get as far from him as possible. Margaret had never been demonstrative, and he hardly expected Dora to be different, so the poor, deluded man was satisfied, and when Dora, who would have everything settled at once, said to him:

"We will wait a year,—till next autumn," he knew what she meant, and answered readily.

"Yes, if you like, though Margaret said it did not matter how soon, the earlier the better for the children's sake."

"I'd rather it should be a year," was Dora's quiet reply, to which the Squire assented, and then, though he so much wished her to stay, he opened the door for her to pass out, as he saw that she desired it.

Half an hour later and Bell Verner, who was just falling to sleep, was startled by a knock, and Dora asked permission to enter.

"What is it? Who's come?" Jessie asked in a dreamy tone, lifting her curly head from the pillow, just as Bell unlocked the door, and Dora stepped into the room.

She was very calm now and decided. The matter was fixed now beyond recall, and she felt a great deal better. Sitting down upon the foot of the bed, she said to Bell and Jessie:

"I could not let you go home without telling you something which may perhaps surprise you."

"Oh, I know. I can guess. You are going to marry Mr. Russell," Jessie cried, and Dora answered:

"Yes. It was Margaret's wish, expressed to both of us, but that is nothing. I begin to feel old; oh, *so* old," and Dora shuddered as she said it. "John is good and will make me a kind husband. It is true that once, when a very young girl like Jessie, I had in my mind another idea for a husband. All girls do in their teens, I guess, but when we get to be twenty-six we begin to lose the fancy man and look for something solid."

This she said to Bell, as if expecting her concurrence rather than that of madcap Jessie. But the contrary was the fact, for Jessie approved the match far more than her sister. Squire Russell was splendid, she said, and would let a body do just as she had a mind, which was a great deal nicer than a dictatorial, overbearing fellow of twenty-eight. Yes, she'd give her consent, and she began to whistle, "Come haste to the wedding," as she nestled back among the pillows, wondering how she should feel to be engaged to Squire Russell. Bell on the contrary saw things in their true light, and she merely replied:

"I am somewhat surprised, I will acknowledge, but if you love him that is all that is necessary."

She was looking directly at 'Dora, but in the dim moonlight the white, haggard face was not plainly discerned, and Bell continued:

"I did think you liked Dr. West, and was positive he liked you."

"Oh, fie," and Jessie sprang up again, "Dora hates him, while he,—well, I guess he likes all the girls,—that is, likes to talk with and flatter them; any way, he has said a great many complimentary things to me, and I knew he meant nothing. They say his heart is buried in that grave in Morrisville. I picked him out for Dora once, you know, and that's all the good it did. Marry the Squire, and let me be bridesmaid."

"Will you?" Dora asked. "Will you and Bell both officiate?"

Jessie assented eagerly, but Bell hesitated. She could not make it seem real that Dora Freeman was to become the wife of Squire Russell. Something would prevent it. At last, however, as Dora urged a reply, she said:

"Perhaps I will, if when the time arrives you still wish for two."

The clock was striking eleven when Dora quitted the apartment of the Misses Verner, but late as it was Johnnie was waiting for her by her door. He had heard the glad news from his father, and he caught Dora round the neck, exclaiming:

"I know, I've heard,—the governor told me. You are,—you are my mother. I never was so happy in my life, was you?"

They were now in Dora's room, where the gas was

burning, disclosing to Johnnie a face which made him start with fear, it was so unnaturally white.

"Auntie," he exclaimed, bending over her, as, reclining upon the bed, she buried her head in the pillows, "what makes you so white, when I'm so glad, and father, too? I never saw him so pleased. Why, the tears danced in his eyes as he told me, while I blubbered like a calf; and you are crying, too, but not as father did, or I. O my! what is it? This is so different. Auntie, Auntie, you are in a fit!" and Johnnie gazed awe-struck upon the little form which shook convulsively as Dora tried to smother her deep sobs. "I'll go for father," Johnnie continued, and then Dora looked up, telling him to stay there where he was.

"But, Auntie, what is the matter?" he asked. "Do girls always cry so when they are engaged? What makes your tears run so like rivers, and so big? It must hurt awfully to be engaged. O dear, dear! I am crying, too!" and then the excited boy wound both arms around Dora's neck and drew her head upon his shoulder, where it lay, while Dora's tears literally ran in rivers down her cheeks.

But the weeping did her good, and she grew very quiet at last, and listened while Johnnie told her how good he was going to be, and how he would influence the others to be good, too.

"We will all be so happy," he said, "that mother, if

she could look at us, would be so glad. Father will read to us winter nights, or you'll play chess with him and sing to us youngsters, and summers we'll go to lots of places, and you shall have heaps of handsome dresses. You're not so tall as mother, and it won't take so many yards, so you can have more. I mean to buy *one* anyhow, with some money I've laid up. I guess it will be red silk, like Jessie's, and you'll have it made low-neck, like hers, with little short sleeves. You've got nice, pretty arms, whiter than Jessie's."

Remembering how much his mother had thought of dress, Johnnie naturally concluded it to be the *Open Sesame* to every woman's heart, and so talked on until she sent him away, for she would rather be alone with her own tumultuous thoughts.

CHAPTER XVII.

EXTRACT FROM DR. WEST'S JOURNAL.

"SAN FRANCISCO, June.

DO I believe it now, after the first stunning effect is over, and I sit here alone thinking calmly of what came to me in Jessie Verner's letter? Do I believe that Dora will marry her brother-in-law, remembering as I do the expression of her face when she sat by the two graves and I told her of Anna? Can there be jealousy where there is no love? I think not, and she was jealous of my commendations of Jessie. Oh, was I deceived, and did her coldness and ill-nature mean more than I was willing to admit? It is very hard to give her up, loving her as I do, but God knows best what is for my good. When I set Anna above Him He took her away, and now He will take my Dora. It is sheer selfishness, I know, and yet I cannot help feeling that I would rather she were lying by Anna's side than to see her Squire Russell's wife. It is a most unnatural match, for there is no bond of sympathy in their natures. Dora must be unhappy after the novelty is gone. Darling Dora,—it is not wicked to speak thus of her now, as there is no certainty in the case, only a surmise, which, nevertheless, has almost broken my heart, for I feel sure that whether she marry the Squire or not, she is lost to me. She does not care for me. She never did, else why does she grow so cross and crisp when my name is mentioned? Alas! that I should ever have thought otherwise, and built up a beautiful future which only Dora was to share with me. I am afraid to record on paper how dear she is to me, or how constantly she has been in my mind since I parted from her. How anxiously I waited for some reply to my letter, and how disappointed I was in the arrival of every mail. I wonder if I did well to answer Jessie so soon, and send that message to Dora? I am confident now that it was not a right spirit which prompted me to act so hastily. I felt that Dora had broken faith with me,—that she should have waited at least the year,—that in some way she was injuring me, and so vindictive pride dictated the words I sent her. May I be forgiven for the wrong; and if Dora is indeed to be the bride of her sister's husband, may she be happy with him, and never know one iota of the pain and suffering her marriage will bring to me.

"Our stay in California has been very pleasant, even though I have failed thus far in what was the secret motive which led me here, the hope of finding the man to whom that letter was addressed long years ago, Robin's father, and, as I believe, Anna's husband. We have been at this hotel just three weeks to-day, and mother likes it better than the private boarding-house we left. Friends seem to spring up around us wherever we go, and I believe I have nearly as many patients in San Francisco as I ever had at home. For this good fortune, which I did not expect, I thank my Heavenly Father, praying that the means I use may be blessed to the recovery of those who so willingly put their lives in my hands.

"How that poor fellow in the next room groans, and how the sound of his moaning makes me long to hasten to his side and alleviate, if possible, the fever which they say is consuming him. Poor fellow, he was making money so fast, I hear, and hoarding it so carefully for his mother, he told his acquaintance, and now he is dying here alone, far from his mother, who would so gladly smooth his dying pillow. I saw him when they carried him through the hall on his arrival from the mountains, and something in the shape of his head and the way the hair curled around it, made me start, it was so like Robert's. But the name, when I asked it, drove the hope away: *John Maxwell,* or *Max,* as he is generally called by those who know him best. He has been here for years, steadily accumulating money, and winning, as it would seem, scores of friends. Even the head chamber-maid, when she heard "young Max" was ill, and was to be brought here, evinced more womanly interest than I supposed her capable of doing. He must be growing worse, his moanings increase so fast, and there seems to be a consultation going on within his room, while my name is spoken by some one, a friend too it would seem, for he says :

"' I wish you would try him at least. I have great faith in that mode of practice.'

"They are going to send for me; they are coming now to the door; they are saying to me:

"' Dr. West, will you step in and see what you think of poor Max's case?'"

CHAPTER XVIII.

POOR MAX.

THAT was what they called him at the hotel, which had been to him a home for years, and you would know by the intonation of their voices that he was a favorite with all. He was very sick, burning with fever, and talking at intervals of his mother, of Dick, and of another whose name the attendants could not well make out. It was of his sweetheart, the chamber-maid surmised, for in the pocket of his vest, which she hung away, she had found a daguerrotype of a young girl, whose marvellous beauty she had never seen excelled.

"Poor Mr. Max! he must have loved her so much! I wonder where she is to-day?" she said, softly, as she continued to scan the lovely face smiling upon her from the worn, old-fashioned case.

Alas! the original of that picture had for many a year been mouldering back to dust, and poor Max, who had loved and wronged her so much, was whispering her name in vain. He was growing worse, his nurse feared, and so at last she sent for Dr. West, of whose skill she had heard so much, and who in a few minutes stepped into the closely darkened room.

"It seemed as if the light worried him," the nurse said, in a whisper, as she saw the doctor glance towards the curtained windows.

"Very likely; but I should like to see him for once," was the doctor's reply, as he took the hot hand in his.

Max's face, which, within a day or two, had grown very thin and was now purple with fever, was turned away from the doctor, who counted the rapid pulse, while the nurse admitted a ray of light, which shone full upon the sick man's pillow, and made Dr. West start suddenly, and turn whiter even than the broad forehead round which the damp brown hair was curling. Then he bent anxiously over his patient, turning him more to the light, where he could see him distinctly. Did he recognize anything familiar in that sunken face, where the beard was growing so heavily,—anything which carried him back to his Northern home, where in his childhood every pastime had been shared by another, and that other his twin brother? Did he see anything which brought to him thoughts of Anna, dead so long ago, or of Robin, who died when the last summer flowers were blooming? Yes; and kneeling by the bedside he whispered, "Robert, Robert, is it you?"

The bright eyes were open and fixed upon him, but

with a vacant stare, while a second look at the flushed face brought a doubt into the doctor's mind.

"He is like my brother Robert, and yet he is not like him," he thought, as he continued to scrutinize the features which puzzled him so much.

"Mother will know," he said at last; and going to his mother, he said to her hurriedly, "Come with me, and tell if you ever saw this Max before."

He was greatly excited, but not more so than his mother, who felt intuitively the shock awaiting her.

"Open that blind wide, and put back that heavy curtain," the doctor said to the frightened nurse, who quickly obeyed his orders, and then waited to see what would happen next.

Max was talking and counting on his fingers till he came to twenty.

"Yes, twenty, that's it," he said; "that's the way the paper read; just twenty years of age, and Dick and I are six years older. Dick loved her, too; he ought to have married her. Dick was a trump."

"What does he say? What does he say? O Richard, what *does* he say?" Mrs. West almost screamed, as she bent down so low that the hot fever breath lifted her silver hair.

Richard made no answer, nor was there need, for the mother instinct recognized the *boy*, the wayward, wandering *Robert*, mourned for as dead during so many dreary years, while the mother love, forgetting all the past, cried out, " My boy, my boy, my Robert, my child ! God has given you back to me at last ! Praised be His name ! "

For an instant something like reason flashed over the wasted face, but it passed away, and to the mother's continued murmurings of love there came only incoherent mutterings of the mountains, the mines, and stocks which seemed to have been substituted for the thoughts of the twenty years and the trump of a Dick, now ministering to the mother, who had fainted and was carried from the room. But she did not stay away long. Her place was by Robert, she said, and she went back to his side, saying to those around her, "He is my boy: he left me years ago, but I have found him at last."

People gossip in California as well as elsewhere, and the hotel was soon full of surmises and wonder, as people repeated to each other that the man known as Max was Robert West, who had taken another name and come among them, for what reason none could guess. The doctor and his mother knew the people would talk, but they did not heed it during the days when with agonizing suspense they hung over the bed of the prodigal, watching for some token of amendment, and praying that the erring one might not be taken from them now and leave the past a darker mystery than ever. He did not talk a great deal, but when he did it was mostly of home scenes in which Anna and Dick were always associated.

Once when they sat alone and Mrs. West was resting in her room, Richard said to Robert, who had spoken of Anna as of some one there with him, "You mean your wife, Anna West; you know you married her privately."

For an instant the wild eyes flashed in Richard's face, and then the delirious man replied, "Did *she* tell you so?"

"Not exactly, but I inferred as much, for when she lay dying, she said, 'Call my baby for his father,' and when I whispered 'Robert,' she nodded assent. They are both dead now, Anna and little Robin. Your wife, your baby, which never saw its father," Richard continued, wishing to impress some idea upon his brother's mind.

But in vain, for Robert did not take the sense of what he heard, except indeed the word *baby*, which he kept repeating to himself, laughing insanely as he did so, "Anna's baby; very funny,—very queer, when she was only a child herself," he would whisper, and that was all which Richard achieved by speaking of the dead.

But there came a day when the stupor passed from brain and head, leaving the latter free from pain and the former clear and bright. He had been sleeping, and when he woke only Richard was with him, and he was sitting where he did not at first observe the eyes fastened so curiously upon him, as Robert West's heart alternately beat with hope and fear. He could not be mistaken, he said to himself. It was no dream that his brother had been there with him,—aye, was there still, looking older, sadder, but his brother all the same. Dick, the kindest, best brother in the world.

"Richard," he said at last very softly, and Richard started, and bent over the sick man, whose eyes read his face for an instant, and then filled with great hot tears, as, winding his arms around the doctor's neck, he sobbed, "It is my brother, 'tis Dick; and you will forgive me. I've got the money safe, honestly earned, too, every cent; more than enough to pay the debt, which I heard you were paying for me. Dear old Dick, we will be happy yet, but tell me first that you forgive me, tell me second how you found me, and tell me third of mother, and all—"

He did not mention Anna, and Richard, in his reply, only answered the questions directly put.

"Call mother," Robert said, when told that she was there, and in a moment she was weeping on the pillow of her erring, but, as it would seem, deeply repentant child, for he repeated to her what he had said to Richard about the money, adding, "And this fall I was coming home to buy back the dear old place, if possible; I was, mother, I was; I've been so bad and wicked, but you will forgive me now, for since I left New York I have not been guilty of a single dishonorable act. Ask the people here, they know. They will tell you that among them all there is no one more popular than *Max;* I go by that name," and Robert's face crimsoned as he said this last.

In his anxiety that his mother should forgive and think well of him, he grew so much excited that all she and Richard could do was to soothe him into quiet by assurances of forgiveness and love. He was too weak to talk longer, and he lay perfectly still, holding his mother's hand and gazing into the dear face which bent so fondly over him. Once his lips quivered with some deep emotion, and when Richard asked what he would say, he answered:

"Mother has changed so much,—her hair has all turned white. Was it for *me*, mother?"

"Not wholly, Robert; it turned about the time when we lost Anna," was Mrs. West answer.

Instantly the sick man's eyelids closed, and one after another the big tears rolled down his sunken cheeks, leaving a red, shining track, such as bitter, scalding tears always leave, but he made no comment, and Anna was not mentioned again until two days had passed, and he was so much better that he sat up in bed, propped on pillows, with his mother at his side, half supporting him. Then suddenly breaking a silence which had fallen upon them, he exclaimed:

"It was an unfortunate hour that saw me installed as

our great Uncle Jason's book-keeper and confidential clerk. He trusted me so entirely, and there were such large sums of money daily passing through my hands, that the temptation was a great one to a person of my expensive tastes and habits. I cannot tell just when I took the first five dollars, replacing it as soon as possible, and then finding the second sin so much easier than the first. It was not a sin, I said then, as did others of my companions who were in the habit of doing the same thing, and who led me on from bad to worse, while all the time my uncle believed me a pattern of honesty. If I had not heard that a part of Uncle Jason's fortune rightfully belonged to us, I do not believe I should have fallen so low. As it was, I made myself think that what I took was mine, and after I learned to gamble it was ten times worse. There is a fascination about those dens of iniquity which you cannot understand, and it proved my ruin. I played every night, sometimes losing, sometimes winning, and gradually staking more and more, until at last I bet so heavily that forgery was the consequence. I don't know what made me do it, for I knew I could not replace that 20,000 dollars, and when the deed was done there was no alternative but to run away. Assuming the name of John Maxwell, I went to England first, and then to California. Uncle Jason had so much faith in me that you know he believed me murdered, until the fraud was discovered, when it seems he behaved most generously, suppressing the facts, and after an interview with you, my brother, consented to keep the whole thing still, provided the money was in time refunded."

"Who told you this?" both Richard and his mother exclaimed, but Robert only replied:

"I heard it, and resolved, if possible, to earn that money and pay it back myself. The voyage out sobered me into a better man, for, mother, your prayers, said over me when I was a child, rang continually in my ears, until I, too, ventured to whisper each day the words, 'Lead us not into temptation,' saying them at first more from habit than anything else, and afterwards because I learned to have faith in them, learned to believe there was something in that petition which did keep me from falling lower. I was not good as you term goodness, and had I died I should assuredly have been lost; but within a few short months there has been a change, so that what I once was doing for your sakes I now do, I trust, from higher, holier motives; and oh! I had so much need of forgiveness, for had I not wronged everybody, and you, my brother, most of all?"

There was a mutual pressure of hands between the brothers, and then they who listened hoped to hear of Anna next, but of her Robert was still silent, and they suffered him to take his own course, following him with breathless interest as he told of his life in the mines, and how he had been successful beyond his most sanguine hopes,—how friends had sprung up around him, and all things had conspired to make him happy, were it not for the dreadful memories of the past which haunted him continually.

"I should have written when I learned that I was safe from a felon's doom," he said, "but with this information came news of so terrible a nature that I was stunned for many months, so that I cared little what became of me, and when feeling came back again, I said I'll wait until I have the money as a sure peace offering. I had it almost earned once, two years ago, but by a great reverse I lost so much that I was compelled to wait yet longer,—wait, as it seems, till you came here to find me. It is all a dream to me yet that you are here, and that I, perhaps, shall breathe again my native air, and visit the old home. Is it greatly changed?"

"Many would think West Lawn improved," Richard replied, "but to us who loved Anna it can never be the same."

There was another silence, and then Richard, who could no longer restrain himself, exclaimed:

"Robert, if you know aught which can throw a ray of light on Anna's dark face, in pity tell us what it is!

You do know,—you must know!—Was Anna your wife?"

Richard could hear the beatings of his own and his brother's heart as he waited for the answer, which, when it came, was a decided " *Yes*, Anna was my wife!"

CHAPTER XIX.

ANNA.

THE summer moonlight was shining into the sick-room, where, with Richard and his mother beside him, Robert West was summoning nerve and courage to tell the story they were waiting so anxiously to hear. With the assertion that "Anna was my wife," he had fainted, and since then a night and a day had intervened, during which no word of the past had escaped his lips. But now that he was stronger, he had said to his mother and brother, "Sit beside me, and if I can I will tell you of Anna."

They needed no second bidding, but gathered closely to him, and there, in the quiet room, Robert West began the story, in which there was a slight recapitulation of what he had before told, but which will help to enlighten the reader with regard to Robert's past.

"I cannot remember the time when I did not love Anna," he said, fixing his eyes upon the ceiling. "As a boy I made no secret of it, but as I grew older I pretended not to care for her more than for any other, and called her a little doll, you know, but it was mere pretense, for I loved the very air she breathed; and when I heard she was engaged to Dick, I cried as young men of twenty-two seldom cry. You know I had then been in New York two years, and that soon after this I was received into Uncle Jason's employ, and trusted by him with everything. For my father's sake, he trusted me, he used to say, never dreaming how unlike the father was the son.

"After losing Anna I cared little for my self-respect, and then first commenced the process of taking five or ten dollars, as I chanced to need it. This I always replaced, and so conscience was satisfied, particularly after I found that other young men, who stood as well as myself, did the same. I cannot account for it, but I now believe that my apparent indifference to Anna attracted rather than repelled her, for when I was at home I used to try the experiment of being very attentive, just to see how she would brighten with pleasure, but it was not until my last visit, made the August before I ran away, that the idea entered my brain of taking her from Richard. He was gone for two weeks, you will remember, and I improved my time to so good advantage that when I finally left Morrisville, I had won a half promise from Anna that she would talk with him and ask to be released. She did not promise this willingly, for her strong sense of right made her question the justice of such an act, and all my arguments were necessary to wring that promise from her. We were out in the graveyard, Dick on that little bench,—you know where."

"Yes, I know;" and Richard's reply was like a groan, as Anna and Dora came up before him, connected with that rustic bench.

"It was a moonlight night, and we stayed there a long, long time, mother thinking we were at some neighbor's house, while you, my brother, were away, never dreaming how falsely I was dealing with you. But Anna thought of you, pleading most for you, even while she confessed her love for me, and saying that daily interviews with you made you more like her brother. And there I had the advantage; I was comparatively a stranger, while the city air and manner I had studied to acquire were not without their effect on Anna. She was almost an angel, but human still, and so the old story was again repeated. The city fop, with sin enough upon his soul to have driven that pure young girl from his sight forever, could she have known it, was preferred to the country boy. But it was hard work, and more than once I gave up in despair, as, wringing her little hands, she cried:

"'O Robert, don't tempt me so. I do love Richard, or I did before you came, and he is so good, so noble. God will never forgive me if I deceive him so dreadfully. Please, Robert, don't tempt me any more.'

"You can imagine how I answered her. There were

kisses and caresses, and assurances that you would rather give her up than take her when her heart was not your own, and so the victory was won, and I acted a most cowardly part. I made Anna promise not to speak of me when talking with you, Richard, or hint in any way that I was the cause of her changed feelings toward you. I then returned to New York, while she asked to be released from her engagement. She wrote to me once, bitterly condemning herself for her deception, as she termed it, and earnestly begging permission to tell you all, but I refused, and held her to her promise; and so matters stood when you decided upon sending her to Boston. You know she came first to New York to Uncle Jason's, whose wife is both deaf and half blind, so she was not in my way at all. After you returned home, Dick, I was there every night, and as Uncle Jason nodded over his paper in his study, while Aunt Eliza nodded over her knitting in the parlor, I had every opportunity for pressing my suit, rejoicing when I saw how I could sway Anna at my will. She was easily influenced by those she loved and trusted—"

Here Robert's voice trembled, and he paused a moment ere he resumed:

"She believed that I was good, and this belief, more than anything I could say, lead her to listen to me. She was to leave on Monday for Boston, and on Saturday I took her for a drive through the city, and when she returned at night she was my wife. How I accomplished it I can hardly tell, for at first Anna refused outright, but she was finally persuaded, and at the house of a clergyman whom I knew by reputation the ceremony was performed. It was the original plan that when her visit was over I should accompany her home and announce our marriage, after which she should return with me to New York, but subsequent events made this impossible. My uncle had commissioned me to telegraph to the friends in Boston that I would be there on Monday with Anna, and he kindly gave me permission to remain a few days, or even longer if I liked. This I professed to have done, but it was a lie I told my uncle, who, believing Anna to be Dick's betrothed, had no suspicion that I cared for her in the least except as my sister. After leaving her at his door on Saturday night, I purposely did not see her again until Monday, when, according to arrangement, I went ostensibly to accompany her to Boston. Anna knew nothing of my real intentions, and it was some time before she understood that we were going to Albany instead of New Haven. In much surprise she questioned me, turning very white and bursting into tears when the truth dawned upon her, and she saw how she was becoming more entangled in the deception. We stayed in Albany at the City Hotel until Thursday morning, and in those three days I was, I believe, as perfectly happy as is possible for mortal man to be. And Anna was happy too,

In her love for me she forgot all else, and I tasted fully of the bliss it was to call that lovely, gentle creature wife. I remained in Boston one night, but Friday found me again in New York, while one week from the next Saturday night,—O, mother! if I could only blot out that Saturday night from the past, but I cannot, and I must tell you how low your boy fell. Knowing how good and pure Anna was I resolved that henceforth my life should be such as she could approve, and to this end I would avoid all my old associates, I said, and never again frequent their haunts or come in contact with them. Chief among these associates was a Stanley, who had first taught me to play, and who had constantly hovered near me as my evil genius. On Saturday, he came into my office, and told me of a rare specimen from Cincinnati who was terribly conceited, but whom *I* could beat so easily. 'He has heaps of money,' he said, 'and if you choose you can make a fortune in an hour. Come to-night, and you are sure to win.'

"Instantly there flashed over me the thought 'if Anna could only dress and live like the ladies of Madison Square,' but with it came the knowledge of how she would disapprove, and I hesitated. The temptation was a strong one, and as I continued to listen I felt my good resolutions giving way. Just for once, and that should be the last, I said, consenting to join my comrade, who evidently believed all he said of the stranger. Ten o'clock found me at Stanley's rooms, opposite my antagonist, whom I at once pronounced a fool. Eleven found me the winner of a considerable amount. Twelve o'clock, my lucky star was still in the ascendant, but when two o'clock of that Sunday morning struck, I was ruined, and my opponent held my note for $20,000.

" Desperate, distracted, what could I do but forge my uncle's name for the amount, taking the precaution to draw from three or four banks where he had funds deposited, and this I did without a thought of the consequences; but when I woke to the peril of my situation I was mad with fear, and determined to run away. But first I wrote to Anna, telling her I was going, but withheld the reason why. After the letter was sent I was seized with a terror lest she by some means should betray me, and so I be brought to justice. My love for her was strong, but dread of a prison life was stronger. Of Uncle Jason I asked and received permission to visit Morrisville for a week, and when I left him he thought I was going home, but I went instead to Boston, reaching there in the night, and next morning hiring a boy to take a note to Anna. She was alone when it was delivered, as the family were out on some shopping expedition. In much alarm she came to the Revere, where I was to meet her, and there the horrible truth was revealed that she was the wife of a felon. She had not received my letter, and what I told her was wholly unexpected. She did not faint, nor scream, nor even reproach me with my sin. She merely sank upon her knees and prayed that I might be forgiven, while into her eyes and face there stole a look which I know now to have been the germ of insanity which afterwards came upon her.

"'Anna,' I said, when her prayer was ended and she sat with her face upon the table, 'I am going to England in a vessel which sails to-night, and from there to California, assuming the name of John Maxwell, and you must not betray me.'

"'Betray you! O Robert!'" and the face she lifted up looked as grieved as if I had struck her.

"'I know you will not do it voluntarily,' I said, 'but you must not make yourself liable to be questioned. No one knows I am here. No one knows you are my wife, and no one must know it. Not yet, at least not till it is settled somehow, and I come back to claim you, or send for you to join me.'

"Again she looked wistfully at me, and I continued: 'If Uncle Jason knew you were my wife, he would question and cross-question you until he frightened it out of you, and I should be captured. I deserve to go to prison, I know, but Anna, darling, think how terrible for one so young to be shut out from this world, wearing my life away. Promise, Anna, and I will be a better man; I will earn enough to pay it back. Promise, if, indeed, you love me.'

"I was kneeling at her feet, sueing almost for my life. I was her husband, and she loved me, erring as I was, and she promised at last to keep her marriage a secret until I said she might tell. I ought to have been satisfied with her word, but each moment the dread of arrest grew greater, and taking the Bible which lay upon the table, I said, 'Swear with your hand on this.'

"Then she hesitated, but I carried my point, and with her hand on the book she loved so much, she took an oath not to tell, and fell fainting to the floor. I restored her as soon as possible, and led her through obscure streets back to Mr. Haverleigh's dwelling. I dared not kiss her as I parted with her at the gate, for it was broad day, but I shall never forget the look in her eyes as they rested on my face, while she said, 'Good-by, Robert. Ask God daily to forgive you as I shall do.'

"I wrung her cold, damp hand, and hurried away, seeing the Haverleigh carriage drive up the street just as I turned into another, and knew that Anna must have been safe in her room when the family returned."

"Poor Anna," sobbed Mrs. West. "That was the time when Rosa Haverleigh found her upon the floor totally unconscious. She was never herself after that, and as they could not rouse her to an interest in anything, they sent her back to us, a white-faced, frightened, half crazed creature even then. O Robert, my son, how much sorrow you have wrought," and the poor mother wept piteously as she remembered the young girl whom she in thought had wronged, and who she now knew had died for the erring Robert, and kept silence even when to do so was to bring disgrace and death upon herself.

"Truly Anna died a martyr's death," Richard murmured, feeling now how glad he was that he had held her in his arms and kissed her quivering lips with the kiss of forgiveness, when all else stood aloof as from a sinful thing.

"Yes, a martyr's death," Robert repeated sadly; "and some time you will tell me how she died and about her child, but now I hasten on with the part which concerns myself. I went to England and then to California, working in the gold mines like a dog, and literally starving myself for the sake of gain. I *would* pay that debt, I said, and I would yet be worthy of Anna. It was some time in October that I stumbled upon a Boston paper in which was a notice of Anna's death, put in by the Haverleighs, I presume, as they were greatly attached to her. I knew it was my Anna, and that I had killed her, and for a time reason and life forsook me. I was sick for weeks, and when I came back to life, *Stanley*, the man who first taught me to sin, was taking care of me. He, too, had come to the land of gold, finding me by mere chance, and knowing at once that I was not John Maxwell, as I had given out. But he betrayed no secrets, and since then has proved the old adage that there is honor even among thieves. By some means he had ascertained that in consideration of a sum of money paid by you, together with your promise of the whole, Uncle Jason had concluded to say nothing of my forgery. He had also heard that West Lawn was sold, and I knew well what prompted this sacrifice, and cursed myself for the sinful wretch I was. Stanley did not remain in California longer than spring, but returned to New York, from which place he has occasionally written and given me tidings of home. At my request he has at four different times been to Morrisville, and reported to me what he learned. In this way I heard of *Robin*, and I know that thoughts of him have helped to make me a better man.

"By some strange chance Stanley was there when Robin died, and mingling with those who followed my child to the grave, he saw you, mother, and Dick, and a young lady was with you, he said, a fair young girl, whom Dick called Dora. Is she to be your wife?" and he turned towards Richard, who, with a half moan, replied, "I hoped so once, but I have lost her now."

Robert pressed the hands of his brother in token of sympathy, and then continued: "I never saw my boy, but I wept bitterly when I heard he was dead, while my desire to return was materially lessened; but this feeling wore away, and I came again to look eagerly forward to the time when with the gold in my hand I could go back and pay the heavy debt I owe you."

"Did you never hear directly from Anna?" Richard asked, remembering the letter sent to California.

"Yes, once; and it made me for a time almost as mad as my darling. I was up in the mountains when I read it, and the livelong night I lay upon the ground, crying as men are not apt to cry. I have that letter now. It is in my wallet. Would you like to see it?"

A moment after Dr. West held in his hand a worn, yellow paper, on which were traced the last words ever written by the unfortunate Anna, words which made the doctor's chest heave with anguish as he read them, while his mother sobbed hysterically. A part of this letter we transcribe for the reader :

* * * "I am in a mad-house, darling, where are so many, many crazy people, and they say that I am crazy too. It's only the secret in my head and heart which makes them burn so cruelly. Richard and mother brought me here. Poor Richard looks so white and sorry, and speaks so kindly of you, wondering where you are, that once I bit my tongue until it bled, to keep from telling what I knew. If I had not promised with my hand upon the Bible, I am sure I should tell, but that oath haunts me day and night, and I dare not break it, so now I never talk, and I was glad when they brought me here, for it was safer so. It was dreadful at first, and sometimes I most wished I could die, but God is here just as He is in Morrisville, and at last I prayed to Him as I used to do. You see I forgot to pray for a while, it was so terrible, and I thought I was lost forever, but I've found God again, and I don't mind the dreadful place. Everybody is kind to me, everybody says 'poor girl,' and you need not worry because I am here. I pray for you every minute, and God will hear and save you, because He has promised, and God never lies. Dear, darling Robert, if I dared tell you something, it might perhaps bring you home to spare me from the shame which is surely coming, unless I tell, and that I've sworn not to do. It makes me blush to write it, and so I guess I won't; but just imagine, if I was your wife before all the world, and we were living somewhere alone, and Richard did not love me, as I know he does, and folks called me Mrs. West instead of poor Anna, and you always hurried home at night to see me, wouldn't it be nice if we had a little baby between us to love, you because it was Anna's, and I because it was Robert's! But now, O Robert, what shall I do, with you away, and that Bible oath in my heart. God will help me, I hope, and perhaps take me home to him, where they know I am innocent. Poor Richard, I pity him most when he comes to know it, but God will care for him, and when I am gone he will find some other one more worthy than I for him to love.

"There came a young girl here yesterday, not to stay, for her brains all were sound, but with some more to look at us, and as they reached my door I heard the attendant whisper something of me, while the stranger came up to me and said:

"'Poor girl, does your head ache very hard?' and she put her hand so gently on my hair; but I would not look up, and she went on with her companion, who called her Dora. I don't know why her voice made me think of Richard, but it did, it was so soft and pitiful, just like his when he speaks to me. It made me cry, and I prayed carefully to myself, 'God send to Richard another love, with a voice and manner like Dora.'" * * *

Richard could read no farther, but dropping the letter upon the bed, he buried his face in his hands and moaned:

"Darling Anna, your prayer will never be answered, but I thank you for it all the same, and I am so glad that I never forsook nor quite lost faith in you. O Anna! O Dora! Dora!"

The last name was wrung from him inadvertently, but Robert caught it up and said:

"Was the Dora who was with you at Robin's grave the same of whom Anna speaks?"

"I think so,—yes, I am sure, for she once told me of a visit made to the asylum, and related an incident similar to this which Anna mentions."

"Then Dick," and Robert spoke reverently but decidedly, "then she will be yours. Anna prayed for it once, and I have implicit faith in Anna's prayers. They followed me over land and sea, bringing me at last to the fountain of all peace."

Richard made no reply to this, but asked reproachfully why his brother did not hasten home after receiving that touching message from Anna.

"The letter was a long time coming," Robert said. "And as I was not expecting it, I never inquired at the post-office until I saw it advertised. It was then the first of September, and Anna was already dead, but this I did not know, and I was making up my mind to brave even a prison for her sake, when I saw that paper which told me of her death. The rest you know, except, indeed, the debt of gratitude I owe to you and mother for all your kindness to my wife and boy, and for the love with which you have ever cherished me. If I get well, I trust my life will show that a wretch like me can reform. I have money enough to pay the debt with interest, and, Richard, it is all yours, earned for you, and hoarded as carefully as miser ever hoarded his gains. But now tell me of Anna at the last. Did no one suspect she was my wife?"

"No one but myself, and I did not till she was dying," Richard replied. "No one dreamed of questioning her of you, and so she was spared that pain."

And then he told Robert the sad story which our readers already know, the story of Anna's death, of Robin's birth, and his short life, while Robert, listening to it, atoned for all the wrong by the anguish he endured and the tears he shed, as the narrative proceeded. At last, when it was finished, he sank back upon his pillow, wholly exhausted with excitement and fatigue.

For weeks after that he hovered so near the verge of death that even the mother despaired, and looked each day to see the life go out from her child, who in his boyhood had never been so dear to her as now. But youth and a strong constitution triumphed, and again the fever abated, leaving the sick man as weak and helpless as a child, but anxious for the day when he would be able to make the homeward voyage.

CHAPTER XX.

RICHARD.

SO absorbed was Mrs. West in Robert that she seldom noticed Richard, and so she paid no heed when he one day came into the sick-room, looking whiter even than his brother, by whose side he sat down as usual, doing for him the many offices he had been accustomed to perform, and except for his suffering face, giving no token of the terrible pain which wrung his heart when he that morning read in Jessie's letter that the worst he had feared was true, and that Dora was to be married in September.

"For a person just engaged she acts very strangely," Jessie wrote, "and Bell will insist that she does not love her future lord, but is marrying him from some mistaken sense of duty. What do you think?"

Dr. West could not tell what he thought, he only knew that his brain grew giddy, and his soul faint and sick as he realized that Dora was lost to him forever. Never even when Anna died had he suffered so keen a pang as now, when in the solitude of his chamber he tried to pray, while the words he would utter died away in unmeaning sounds. But God, who readeth the inmost secrets of the heart, knew what his poor sorrowing child would ask, and the needed strength to bear was given all the same.

It was very tedious now, waiting in that sick-room, for there crept into Richard's mind the half conviction that if he would see Dora for only one brief moment, he could save her from the sacrifice. But Robert's improvement was slow, and day after day went by, until at last there came a morning when there was put into Richard's hand a soiled, worn-looking letter, whose superscription made his heart for an instant stop its beatings, for he recognized Dora's handwriting, and involuntarily pressed the missive to his lips ere he broke the seal. It had been weeks and weeks upon the road, lying for a long time in another office, but it had come to him at last; he had torn the envelope open; he was reading Dora's cry for help, written so long ago, a cry to which he gave a far different interpretation from what she had intended.

"Oh, why did I not speak to her again!" he exclaimed; "why was I permitted to form so wrong an estimate of woman's character? But it is not yet too late. The wedding is to be the 15th of September, Jessie wrote. A steamer sails from here in a few days, and Robert must be able by that time to leave California, or if he is not I shall leave him behind with mother and fly to Dora. Oh if I could go to-day!"

An hour later, and Robert knew all there was to know

of Dora as connected with his brother, and warmly approved the plan of sailing in the Raritan. I shall grow stronger on the sea, he said, and the result proved that he was right, for when at last the Raritan was loosened from her moorings and gliding swiftly over the blue waters of the Pacific, he lay on her deck, drinking in new strength and vigor with each freshening breeze. But with Richard it was different. Now that they were really off, and Robert needed comparatively little of his help, he sank beneath the load of anxiety and excitement, and taking to his berth, scarcely lifted his head from the pillow while the ship went gliding on towards home and Dora Freeman.

CHAPTER XXI.

THE NIGHT BEFORE THE WEDDING.

NEVER had a summer passed so slowly to Dora Freeman as had the last, and yet now that it was gone, it seemed to her scarcely more than a week since the night she had said words from which resulted all the busy preparations going on around her: the bridal dresses packed away in heavy travelling trunks, for they were going to Europe too,—the perfect happiness of Johnnie, who, twenty times each day, kissed her tenderly, whispering, "I am so glad that you are to be my mother"—the noisy demonstrations of the younger ones, and the great joy which beamed all over the Squire's honest face each time he looked at his bride-elect and thought how soon she would be his. Gradually the pressure about Dora's heart and brain had loosened, and she did not feel just as she had done when she first promised to be Squire Russell's wife. She had accustomed herself to the idea, until each thought did not bring a throb of pain, while the excitement of getting ready, and the anticipated tour to places she had never expected to see, had afforded her some little satisfaction. She knew that the world generally looked at her in wonder, while Bell and Mattie totally disapproved, both framing some excuse for not being present at the wedding. But as is usually the case opposition only helped the matter by making her more determined to do what she really believed to be her duty. Besides this she was strengthened and upheld by Johnnie, who was to be the companion of her travels, and who always came between her and every sharp, rough point, smoothing the latter down and making all so bright and easy that she blessed him as her good angel. Owing to his constant vigilance, his father was not often very demonstrative of his affection, except by looks and deeds done for her gratification, but still there were times when, Johnnie being off guard, the father acted the fond lover to the pale, shrinking girl, who, shutting her teeth firmly together, suffered his caresses because she must, but gave him back no answering token of affection. Sometimes this quiet coldness troubled him, particularly as Letitia and Jimmie both asked him at different times why Auntie cried so much,—" did everybody just before they were married? Did mother?"

After Jessie came, Dora felt a great deal better, for Jessie made the future anything but gloomy. Jessie was like a brilliant diamond, flashing and sparkling, and singing and dancing and whistling until the house seemed like a different place, and even Squire Russell wished he could keep her there forever.

And now it was the day before the bridal. Every trunk was packed, and everything was ready for the ceremony, which was to occur at an early hour in the morning, as the bridal pair were to take the first train for New York. Jessie upon the grassy lawn was romping with the children, and occasionally addressing some saucy, teasing remark to the bridegroom-elect, who was smoking his cigar demurely beneath the trees, and wishing Dora would join them. But Dora was differently employed. With the quiet which had suddenly fallen upon the household, a terrible reaction had come to her, and as if waking from some horrid nightmare, she began to realize her position, to feel that only a few hours lay between herself and a living death. Vaguely, too, she began to see how, with every morning mail, there had come a shadowy hope that something might be received from Dr. West, that in some way he would yet save her from Squire Russell. But for months no news had been received of him by any one, and now the last lingering hope had died, leaving only a feeling of despair. She could not even write a line in her journal, and once she thought to burn it, but something stayed the act, and 'mid a rain of tears, she laid it away, resolving never to open its lids again until her heart ached less than it was aching now.

"I shall get over it, I know," she moaned, as she seated herself by the window. "If I thought I should not, I would go to Squire Russell before the whole world, and on my knees would beg to be released; but I am tired now, and excited, and everything looks so dark,—even my pleasant chamber is so close that I can scarcely breathe. I wonder if the breeze from the lake would not revive me. I'll try it,—I'll go there. I'll sit where Richard and I once sat. I'll listen to the music of the waves just as I listened then, and if this does not quiet me, if the horror is still with me,—perhaps—"

There was a hard, terrible look in Dora's eyes as the evil thought first flashed upon her, a look which grew more and more desperate as she began to wonder how deep the waters were near the shore, and if the verdict would be " accidental drowning, " and if Dr. West would care.

Alas for Dora! the tempter was whispering horrible things to her, and she, poor, half-crazed girl, was listening to him as she stole from the back door, and took her way across the fields to where the waters of the lake lay sparkling in the September sun now low in the western horizon.

CHAPTER XXII.

DOWN BY THE LAKE SHORE.

HE shadowy woods which skirt the lake shore tell no tales of what they see, neither do the mossy rocks, nor yet the plashing waves kissing the pebbly beach, and so Dora was free to pour out her griefs, knowing there was no listening human ear, and forgetting for a time that there was an eye which kept watch over her, as with her face upon the yielding sand she moaned so piteously. She could not sit where she and Richard sat, and so she chose the projecting trunk of a fallen tree, and sat where her feet could touch the water below if she should wish it so, as once she did, dipping the tip of her thin slipper, and holding it there till it was wet through to see what the feeling was!

Dora did not try to pray. She never thought of that, but only remembered how desolate, how miserable she was, vainly imagining that to rest beneath the waters lying so calmly at her feet was to end all the pain, the misery, and woe.

The sun was going down the west now very fast, and

out upon the bosom of the lake, at some distance from the shore, it cast a gleam like burnished gold, and Dora, gazing wistfully upon it, fancied that if she could but reach that spot, and sink into that golden glory, it would be well with her. No thoughts of the hereafter crossed her disordered mind, and so she sat and watched the shining spot, until there came to her a memory of the night when Robin died, and the time when the sunshine round Anna's picture looked like the bed of fire upon the lake.

"They are in heaven," she said; adding mournfully, "and where is that heaven?"

"Not where they go who take their lives in their own hands," seemed whispered in her ear, and with a shudder she woke to the great peril of her position.

"Save me, O God!" she sobbed, as she moved cautiously back from her seat upon the tree, breathing freer when she knew that beneath her there was no dark, cold water into which she could dip her feet at pleasure.

She had dipped them there until both hose and slippers were dripping wet, but this she did not heed, and once off from the tree, she sat down where Richard sat, and tried to look the present calmly in the face,—to see if there were not some bright, happy spots, if she would but accept them. With her head bowed down, she did not hear the footstep coming through the woods, and drawing near to her; but when a strange voice said interrogatively, "Miss Freeman?" she started and uttered a nervous cry, for the face she saw was the face of a stranger. And yet it was so like to Dr. West, that she looked again to reassure herself.

"I am Robert West," the man began, abruptly. "I am Richard's brother. He sent me here,—he sent me to *his Dora*, and you are she."

For an instant a tumultuous throb of joy shot through Dora's heart, but it quickly passed, as she answered Robert:

"You are mistaken, sir. I am to be Squire Russell's wife to-morrow."

Sitting down beside her, Robert repeated rapidly a part of what the reader already knows, telling her of Anna, of his own sin, and exonerating Richard from all blame. Then he told her of the meeting in California, of his long illness,—of Richard's anguish when he heard that she was to be married,—of the reaction when that letter so long in coming was received,—of his haste to embark for home, and his illness during the voyage,—illness which made him so weak that he was brought from New York on pillows, and partly in his brother's arms.

"But he has reached here in safety," Robert continued. "He arrived perhaps an hour ago. He is at his old boarding-place, Miss Markham's, and mother is there with him. He knows you are not married yet, and would have come to you himself, but for his illness, which made it impossible, and so he sent me to say that even as he loves you, so he believes that you love him, and to beg of you not to sacrifice your happiness to a mistaken sense of duty. You could not be found when I inquired for you, but a servant said she saw you going towards the lake, and as she pointed me the way, I came on until I found you. Miss Freeman, you know my brother, and know that there lives no better, more upright man, or one who will make you happier as your husband. You have heard my errand, and now what word shall I take back to Richard, or will you go yourself and see him?"

Dora had sat like one stunned as Robert told his story; hope, joy, and despair alternately succeeding each other in her heart as she listened. At a glance, too, she took in all the difficulties of her position, and saw how impossible it was for her to overcome them. This was in her mind when Robert asked if she would go to Richard, and with a bitter moan she answered:

"No, no; oh no! he has come too late. I cannot break my word to John, and he trusting me so fully. Tell Richard it might have been, but cannot be now."

Again Robert West pleaded for his brother, and for the poor heart-broken girl beside him, but her answer was just the same:

"It might have been, but cannot be now."

At last as it grew darker around them, and the night dew made Dora shiver, Robert gave up the contest, and said:

"You must go home, Miss Freeman. It is imprudent to stay here longer in the damp night air. I am satisfied that you do not know what you are saying, and so I shall see Squire Russell, and acquaint him with the whole."

In an instant Dora was on her knees, begging that her betrothed might be spared this pain.

"Think of the sorrow, the disappointment, the disgrace,—for to-morrow morning early is the wedding, and everybody knows. Why, our passage to Europe is secured, and we must go."

"Not if I have the power to prevent it," was Robert's reply, as he led her across the fields, still insisting that he should see Squire Russell.

At last, when she saw how much in earnest he was, she said, "I will tell him myself; I can do it more gently, and it will not hurt so much. Don't go to him, but leave it with me."

"Will you tell him all and ask to be released?" Robert said, making her stand still while she replied, "I'll tell him all, how I love Richard best; but I shall not ask to be released."

Robert was satisfied, for from what he had heard of

Squire Russell he believed he would never require of Dora so great a sacrifice.

"I shall be here with the early dawn," he said, as he left her at the gate.

Dora did not reply, but stood with her eyes riveted upon the house across the street, where she knew was Dr. West. There was a light shining from the windows of the upper room, while the figure of a woman wearing a widow's cap was occasionally seen passing to and fro.

"That is Richard's room," she whispered, feeling an intense desire to fly at once to his side and assert her right to stay there.

Then, remembering her promise to Robert, she walked slowly to the house, meeting in the door with Johnnie, who, wild with excitement, exclaimed, "Hurrah, guess who has come! Dr. West,—and I have been in to see him. He's whiter than a ghost, and what is funny, his chin fairly shook when I told him I was to have a new mother to-morrow, and what do you think, that woman, his mother, put me out of the room and said too much talking hurt him. Did you know he was here?"

"Yes, I knew, Johnnie; where's your father?" Dora asked, feeling that if she waited longer her courage would give way.

"Father's in the library, and he's ordered us youngsters to keep out. I guess he's expecting you, for he asked lots of times where you was, and nobody knew,

Jessie's over there," and Johnnie jerked his shoulder in the direction of the doctor's window.

Very slowly, as if going to her grave, Dora walked on till she came to the library door. It was shut, and as she stood there trembling, she caught the sound of a voice praying within, a voice which trembled with happiness and gratitude as John Russell thanked the God who had given to him Dora.

"I can't; oh, I can't," Dora sighed, as, faint and sick, she leaned against the wall, while that prayer proceeded.

Then, when it was finished, still feeling that she could not talk with him that night, she went up to her room, and in the garments all damp and stained with night dew, and the slippers wet with the waters of the lake, she sat down by the open window and watched the light across the way, until she heard Jessie coming and knew that Robert was with her. They were talking, too, of her, for she heard her name coupled with Dr. West's, while Jessie said, " It's dreadful, and I do so pity Squire Russell,--he is such a nice, good man."

And Jessie did pity him and Dora, too, hardly knowing what was best, or what she 'ought to advise. She had been present when Robert returned from his interview with Dora, and as Richard could not wait till she was gone she came to know the whole, expressing great surprise, and wounding Richard cruelly by saying, " It has gone so far that I do not believe it can be prevented."

But Robert thought differently, and repeated Dora's promise to talk with Squire Russell that night.

"Then he will give her up," Jessie exclaimed, "he is so generous and so wholly unselfish. Oh, how I do pity him!" and in the heat of her great pity Jessie would almost have been Dora's substitute, if by that means she could have saved the Squire from pain.

She did admire and like him, and appreciated his kind, affable, pleasant ways, all the more because they were so exactly the opposite of her father's quick, brusque, nervous manner. The door of the library was open now, and she saw him sitting there as she passed, and longed so much to go and comfort him if the blow had fallen, or prepare him for it if it had not. I'll see Dora first, she thought, and she hastened up to Dora's door, but it was locked, while to her whispered question, "Have you told him yet?" Dora answered, "No, no, not yet; I can't to-night. Please leave me, Jessie; I want to be alone."

It was the queerest thing she ever heard of, Jessie thought, as she turned away,—queerer than a novel ten times over. Then, as she spied Johnnie in the parlor, the little meddlesome lady felt a great desire to see if he suspected anything; but Johnnie did not, and only talked of Europe and the grand things he should see. Not a hint or insinuation, however broad, would he take, and mentally styling him stupid and dull, Jessie left him in disgust, and walked boldly into the library, apologizing for her call by saying she had been to see Dr. West, and thought the Squire might wish to hear directly from him. The Squire was very glad to hear, and glad also to see Jessie, who amused and interested him.

"I have been thinking of calling myself, with Dora, but have not seen her this evening. Where is she?" he said.

"Locked in her room," Jessie replied, as she took the chair he offered her, and continued: "Dora acts queerly, but I suppose that is the way I shall do the night before I am married. Wouldn't I feel so funny, though! Do you know you and Dora seem to me just like a novel, in which I am a side character; but to keep up the romance some tall, handsome knight ought at the last minute to appear and carry her off."

"And so make a tragedy so far as I am concerned," the Squire said, playfully, as he smoothed the little black curly head moving so restlessly.

"Oh, I guess you would not die," Jessie replied; "not if Dora loved the knight the best. You would rather she should have him, and some time you would find another Dora who loved you best of all."

Jessie was growing very earnest, very sympathetic, very sorry for the unsuspecting bridegroom, and as his hand still continued to smooth her curls, she suddenly caught it between her own, and giving it a squeeze darted from the room, leaving the Squire to wonder at her manner, and to style her mentally "a nice little girl, whom it would not be hard for any man to love."

CHAPTER XXIII.

THE BRIDAL DAY.

THE morning was breaking in the east,—a bright, rosy morning, such as is usual in early September,—a morning when the birds sang as gayly among the trees as in the summer-time, and when the dew-drops glittered on the flowers just as they had done in the mornings of the past. All night the gas had burned dimly in the sick-room across the street, and all the night the sick man had prayed that he might be prepared for what the future had in store, whether of joy or sorrow. All night Jessie and Johnnie had slept uneasily, dreaming, one of the Roman Forum, where he repeated the speech made at his last exhibition, and the other that she, instead of Dora, wore the bridal wreath and stood at John Russell's side, and found it not so very terrible after all. All night Squire Russell had lain awake, with a strange, half sad, half delicious feeling of unrest, which drove slumber from his pillow, but brought no shadow of the storm gathering round his head. All night, too, Dora,—but over the scene of agony, contrition, remorse, terror, hope, and despair which her chamber witnessed, we draw a veil, and speak only of the results.

With the dawn the household was astir, for the elaborate breakfast was to be served before the ceremony, which was to take place at half past seven. In the children's room there was first the opening of sleepy little eyes, as Clem called out, "Come, come, wake up. This is your father's wedding-day." Then there was a scampering across the floor, a patter of tiny feet, a chorus of birdlike voices, mingled occasionally with wrathful exclamations as Ben's antagonistic propensities clashed with those of Burt, who declared that "Aunt Dora was going to be father's mother, too, as well as theirs." Then there were louder tones, and finally a fight, which was quelled by Jessie, who appeared in dressing-gown, with her brush in hand, and seemed in no hurry to finish a toilet which she intuitively felt would be made for naught.

Across the yard came Squire John from visiting Margaret's grave, where he had left a tear and a bouquet of flowers. Up the walk, from the front gate, came Robert West, a look of determination on his handsome face, which boded no good to the bridegroom-elect, who, guessing at once that he was the doctor's brother, greeted him cordially and bade him sit down till the breakfast was announced. Up the same gravel walk came the woman who was to dress the bride, and just as Robert West was stammering some apology for being there unbidden, she asked if Miss Freeman had come down.

Nobody had seen her yet; nobody had heard her either, though Jessie had been three times to her door, while Clem had been once, but neither could get an answer.

"Would she be apt to sleep so soundly on this morning?" Squire John asked, just as Jessie, who had again tried the door, came running to the head of the stairs, her brush in her hands, and her dressing-gown flying back as she breathlessly explained to the anxious group in the hall below how she was positive she had heard a moan as if Dora was in distress.

"Burst the door," the Squire ordered, his face white as ashes, as he hurried up the stairs, followed by Robert West.

Yes, there was a moan, a faint, wailing sound, which met the ears of all, and half crazy with fear Squire John pressed heavily against the bolted door until it gave way, when he stood modestly back while Jessie, stooping under his arm, darted into the room, exclaiming:

"Dora, O Dora! what's the matter? What makes her so sick?" and she cast an appealing glance at her companions, who stood appalled at the change a few hours had wrought in Dora, the bride of that morning.

In her soiled garments, damp and wet, she had sat or

lain the entire night, but the burning fever had dried them and stained her face with a purplish red, while her eyes, bloodshot and heavy, had in them no ray of intelligence. She was lying now upon the bed, her hands pressed to her forehead, as if the pain was there, while she moaned faintly, and occasionally talked of the light on the wall which had troubled her so much.

"It would not go out," she said to Jessie, who gently lifted up the aching head and held it against her bosom. "It was there all the night, and I know it burned for him. Does he know how sick I am?"

A glance of intelligence passed between Robert West and Jessie, for they knew that the light from Richard's room had shone into Dora's through the darkness, and this it was which troubled her. Squire John had no such suspicions, and when she asked, "Does *he* know how sick I am?" he bent over her tenderly, and smoothing her brown hair, said, "Poor child, poor darling, I do know, and I am so sorry. Is the pain very hard?"

At the sound of his voice Dora started, while there came into her face a rational expression, and as he continued to caress her, her lip quivered, her eyes filled with tears, and she said, pleadingly, as a child would beg forgiveness of an injured parent:

"Dear John, don't be angry, I could not help it. I tried to come to you last night when everybody was asleep and the clock was striking twelve. I tried to come, but I could not find the way for the light on the wall. I can't, I can't. The trunks are all packed too, and the people are coming. Tell them I can't."

"Poor little girl, never mind. I know you can't, and it don't make one bit of difference, for I can wait, and I will tell the folks how sick my Dora is," John said, kissing her softly. Then in an aside to Jessie, he added, "She thinks I'll be disappointed because the wedding is deferred, and it troubles her. There's the door-bell now. I must go down to explain," and he hurried away to meet the guests, who were arriving rapidly, and who, as they turned their steps homeward, seemed more disappointed than the bridegroom himself.

Blessed Squire John! He was wholly unselfish, and as in his handsome wedding-suit he stood bowing out his departing guests, he was not thinking of himself, but of Dora and how she might be served.

"Margaret believed fully in homœopathy," he said to the last lady, who asked what doctor he would call; "but Dr. West is sick, and what can I do?"

"He might prescribe," returned the lady, who was also one of Dr. West's adherents. "You can tell him her symptoms, and he can order medicine."

"Thank you; I never thought of that. I'll go at once," John said; and bareheaded as he was, he crossed the street, and was soon knocking at Mrs. Markham's door.

"The doctor's worse," she said, in reply to his inquiry.

"He seems terribly excited, and acts as if he was possessed."

"But I must see him," Squire John continued. "Miss Freeman is very sick, and he must prescribe."

"Ain't there no wedding after all? Wall, if that don't beat me!" was Mrs. Markham's response, as she carried to Dr. West the message which roused him from the hopeless, despairing mood into which he had fallen.

He had insisted upon sitting up by the window, where he could watch the proceedings across the street, and as Robert did not return, while one after another the invited guests went up the walk into the house, he gave up all as lost, and sick with the crushing belief, went back to his bed, whispering sadly :

"Dora is not for me. But God knows best!"

He did not see the bridegroom coming to his door, but when the message was delivered it diffused new life at once.

"Yes, show him up; I must talk with him," he said, and a moment after Squire John stood before his rival, his honest face full of anxiety, and almost bedewed with tears as he stated all he knew of Dora's case. "If I could see her I could do so much better," Richard said; "but that is impossible to-day, so I must send," and with hands which shook as they had never shaken before, he gave out the medicine which he hoped might save Dora's life.

"If you were able to go," the Squire said, as he stood

in the doorway, "I would carry you myself; but perhaps it is not prudent."

He looked anxiously at the doctor, who replied:

"If she gets no better, I'll come."

And then as the door closed upon the Squire, he gave a great pitying groan as he thought how trustful and unsuspicious he was.

Holding fast to the medicine, and repeating the direction, Squire Russell hastened back to the house, finding that Dora had been divested of her soiled garments, and placed in bed, where she already seemed more comfortable, though she kept talking incessantly of the light on the wall which would not let her sleep.

"It's perfectly dreadful, isn't it?" Jessie said to Robert, who, ere going home, stepped to the door of Dora's room. "I'm sure I don't know what to do. I wish Bell was here."

Dora heard the name, and said:

"Yes, Bell; she knows, she understands,—she said I ought not to do it. Send for Bell."

Accordingly Robert was furnished with the necessary directions, and left the house for the telegraph office, just as the Squire entered.

Johnnie was nearly frantic. At first he had seemed to consider that his trip to Europe was prevented, and, boy-like, only was greatly disappointed; but when he was admitted into the room and saw Dora's burning cheeks and bright, rolling eyes, he forgot everything in his great distress for her.

"Auntie must not die! Oh, she must not die!" he sobbed, feeling a keener pang than any he had known when they brought home his dead mother. Intuitively he seemed to feel that his father's grief was greater than his own, and keeping close to his side he held his hand, looking up into his face, and whispering occasionally:

"Poor father, I hope she won't die!"

The father hoped so too, but as the hours wore on and the fever increased, those who saw her, shook their heads doubtingly, saying with one accord:

"She must have help soon, or it will come too late."

"Help from where? Tell me. Whom shall I get? Where shall I go?" John asked, and the answer was always the same. "If *Dr. West* could come, but I suppose he can't!"

"He *can!* he *shall!!*" Johnnie exclaimed, as the house seemed filled with Dora's delirious ravings. "Father and that Mr. West can bring him in a chair! He shall!" and Johnnie rushed across the street, nearly upsetting Mrs. West in his headlong haste, and bursting upon Richard with the exclamation, "She'll die! she is dying, and you shall go! You must,—you will! We'll take you in this big chair!" and Johnnie wound his arm around the doctor's neck, while he begged of him to go and save Aunt Dora.

At first the doctor hesitated, but when his brother also joined in the boy's request, he said, " I'll go."

CHAPTER XXIV.

THE SHADOWS OF DEATH.

IT was a novel sight to see the little procession which half an hour later left Mrs. Markham's house and moved across the street. Wrapped in a blanket and reclining in the huge arm-chair which Squire John, his coachman, and Robert West were carrying was Dr. West, while behind him walked his mother, with Johnnie and Jim and Burt and Ben bringing up the rear.

"I think I had better go in alone. Too many may disturb her," Richard suggested, as, supported by his brother and the Squire, he reached the upper hall and turned towards Dora's chamber.

All saw the propriety of this, and so only Jessie was present when Richard first sat down by Dora's side, and taking her hot hand pressed it between his own, calling her by name and asking if she knew him.

"Yes, Richard, and you have come to save me; I am so glad, and the night was so long, with the light on the wall," Dora replied, and over her cheeks the tears fell refreshingly.

"You have done her good already," Jessie whispered

to the doctor, who, repressing his intense desire to hug the sick girl to his bosom, proceeded carefully to examine every symptom and then to prescribe.

She was very sick, he said, and the utmost quiet was necessary; only a few must be allowed to see her, and no one should be admitted whose presence disturbed her in the least. This was virtually keeping Squire Russell away, for his presence did disturb her, as had been apparent all the day, for she grew restless and talkative and feverish the moment he appeared. It smote the doctor cruelly to see how meekly he received the order.

"Save her, doctor," he said, "save my Dora and I will not mind giving you all I'm worth."

But the power to save was not vested in Dr. West. He could only use the means, and then with agony of soul pray that they might be blessed, that Dora might live even though she should never be his. It was unnecessary for him to return to Mrs. Markham's, and yielding to what seemed best for all, he remained at Squire Russell's during the dreadful days of suspense when Dora's life hung on a thread, when Bell and Mattie, both of whom came in answer to Robert's telegram, bent over her pillow, always turning away with the feeling that she must die, when Jessie, yielding her place as nurse to more experienced hands, took the children to the farthest part of the building, where she kept them quiet, stifling her tears while she sang to them childish songs, or told them fairy stories; and when Squire Russell, banished from the sick-room, sat in the hall all the day long watching Dora's door with a wistful, beseeching look, which touched the hearts of those who saw it, and who knew of the blow in store for him even if Dora lived. It was no secret now, to five at least, that Dora could never be Squire Russell's wife. Mrs. West, Bell, Mattie, Jessie, and Robert all knew it, and while four approved most heartily, *Jessie* in her great pity hardly knew what she should advise. She was so sorry for him sitting so patiently by the hall window, and she wanted so much to comfort him. Sometimes, as she passed near him, she did stop, and smoothing his hair, tell him how sorry she was, while beneath the touch of those snowy fingers, his heart throbbed with a feeling which prompted him to think much of Jessie, even while he kept that tireless watch near Dora.

It was strange how the doctor bore up, appearing better than when he first came to Dora. It was excitement, he knew, and he was glad of the artificial strength which kept him at her side, noting every change with minuteness which went far toward effecting the cure for which he prayed.

Two weeks had passed away, and then one night, just as the autumn twilight was stealing into the room, Dora woke from a long, heavy sleep, which Richard had watched breathlessly, for on its issue hung her life or death. It was over now, and the hand Richard held was wet with perspiration. Dora was saved, and burying his head upon her pillow, the doctor said aloud:

"I thank thee, O my Father, for giving me back my darling."

Richard was alone, for Bell and Mattie had both left the room to take their supper, and there was no one present to see the look of unutterable joy which crept into his face, when, in response to his thanksgiving, a faint voice said:

"Kiss me once, Richard, for the sake of what might have been, then let me die,—here, just as I am, alone with you."

He kissed her more than once, more than twice, while he said to her:

"You will not die; the crisis is past; my darling will live."

Neither thought of Squire Russell then, so full, so perfect was that moment of bliss in which each acknowledged the deep love filling their hearts with joy. Dora was the first to remember, and with a moan she turned her face to the wall while the doctor still held and caressed the little wasted hand which did not withdraw itself from his grasp. There was joy in the household that night, for the glad news that Dora was better spread rapidly, while smiles and tears of happiness took the place of sorrow. Squire Russell was gone; business which required attention had taken him away for several hours, and when he returned it was too late to visit the sick-room; but he heard from Johnnie that Dora would live, and from his room there went up a prayer of thanksgiving to Heaven, who had not taken away one so dear as Dora.

CHAPTER XXV.

BREAKING THE ENGAGEMENT.

"POOR Squire Russell," Jessie kept repeating to herself, as she saw him next morning going up to Dora, who would far rather not have seen him until some one had told him what she knew now must be.

But there was no longer a reason why he should not be admitted to her presence, and so he came, his kind face bathed in tears, and glowing all over with delight as he stooped to kiss "his lily," as he called her, asking how she felt, and whispering to her of his joy that she was better.

"I knew the doctor would help you," he said, rubbing his hands complacently. "You would have died but for him. We will always like Dr. West, Dora, for he saved your life."

"I guess I would not talk any more now,—it tires her," Jessie said, in a perfect tremor of distress; and taking his arm, she lead him away; then, closing the door upon him, she went back to Dora, who was weeping silently.

"It seems dreadful to deceive him any longer," Jessie

said, and as Dr. West just then came in she appealed to him to know if it were not a shame for that nice man to be kept so in the dark. "If you and Dora love each other, as I suppose you do, why, you'll have each other of course, and Squire Russell must console himself as best he can. For my part, I pity him," and Jessie flounced out of the room, leaving Dr. West alone with Dora.

For a long time they talked, Dora weeping softly while the doctor soothed and comforted, and told her of the love cherished so many years for the little brown-eyed girl, who now confessed how dear he was to her, but cried mournfully when she spoke of Squire Russell. It was cruel when he trusted and loved her so much. Perhaps, too, it was wrong, she said. It might be her imperative duty to take charge of those children, and then she startled the doctor by saying:

"You know how much I love you. I am not ashamed to confess it, but I am most afraid that when the time comes to talk with John, I shall tell him that I will marry him."

"*Not by a jug full!* I'll tend to that myself. I know now what has been the matter!" was almost screamed in the ears of Dr. West and Dora, as Johnnie rushed into the room.

He had started to come before, he said, but had been arrested at the door by something Dora was saying to the doctor.

"I know it's paltry mean to listen," he continued, "but I could not help it, and so I stood stiller than a mouse, and heard all you had to say. That's why Aunt Dora has looked so white and cried so much, and didn't want father to kiss her. I understand. She didn't like him, but she's pesky willing to have *you* slobber over her as much as you want to," and the boy turned fiercely toward the doctor. "I counted, and while I stood there you kissed her *fourteen* times! It was smack, smack, till I was fairly sick, and sort of mad with all the rest. I know auntie always *has* done right, and so I s'pose she is right now, but somehow I can't help feeling as if the governor was abused, and *me* too! How, I'd like to know, am I ever going to Europe if you don't have father? O Auntie, think again before you quit entirely!" and overmastered with tears, Johnnie buried his face in the bed-clothes, begging of Dora "to think again, and not give poor father the mitten!"

"You are making her worse! You had better go out!" the doctor said kindly, laying a hand on Johnnie's shoulder; but the boy shook it off, savagely exclaiming:

"You let me *be*, old Dr. West. I shall stay if I have a mind to!" But when Dora said:

"Johnnie, Johnnie, please don't," he melted at once, and sobbed aloud.

"I was mad, Auntie; and I guess I'm mad yet, but I do love you. O Auntie, poor father! I'm going right off to tell him. He shan't be fooled any longer!" and the excited child darted from the room ere Dora had time to stop him.

Rushing down the stairs and entering the library, he called loudly for his father, but he was not there. He had gone into the village, Jessie said, asking if it was anything in particular which he wanted. "Yes, of course. I want to tell him how it's all day with him and Auntie. She don't like him, and she does like Dr. West. Poor father! was there ever anything so mean?"

Here at last was one who in part expressed her own sentiments, and the impulsive Jessie replied:

"It is mean, I think, and I am so sorry for your father. Of course Dora intends to do right, and likes the doctor best, because he is not so old as your father; but young as I am, I should not think it so awful to marry a man of forty. Why, I think it would be rather jolly, for I could do just as I pleased with him. Yes, I blame Dora some—"

"I won't have Aunt Dora blamed," Johnnie roared, a reaction taking place the moment any one presumed to censure her. "No, I won't have her blamed, so you just hush up. If she don't want father she shan't have him, and I'll lick the first one who says she shall."

Here Johnnie broke down entirely, and with a howling cry fled away into the garden, leaving Jessie perfectly amazed as she thought "how very unsatisfactory it was to meddle with a love-affair."

Meanwhile Johnnie had seated himself beneath a tree in a sunny, quiet spot, where he was crying bitterly, and feeling almost as much grieved as when his mother died. Indeed, he fancied that he felt worse, for then there was hope in the future, and now there was none. Hearing the sound of the gate, and thinking his father had returned, he rose at last, and drying his eyes, repaired to the house, finding his conjecture true, for Squire Russell had come, and was reading his paper in the library. With his face all flushed with excitement, and his eyes red with weeping, Johnnie went to him at once, and bolting the door, began impetuously, "I would not mind it a bit, father. I'd keep a stiff upper lip, just as if I did not care."

"What do you mean?" the Squire asked, in surprise, and Johnnie continued: "I mean that you and Aunt Dora have *played out*, and you may as well hang up your fiddle, for she don't want you, and she does want Dr. West, and that's why she has grown poor as a shark and white as chalk. I just found it out, standing by the door and hearing the greatest lot of stuff,—how he asked her to marry him once, and she got into a tantrum and wouldn't say yes, though she wanted to all the time. What makes girls act so, I wonder?"

Squire Russell was too deeply interested to offer any

explanation with regard to girls' actions, and Johnnie went on:

"Then he went off to California, and didn't write, as she hoped he would, and you and I asked her to have you, and she did not want to, but thought it was her duty, and wrote to ask the doctor, and he didn't get the letter for weeks and weeks, and when he did he was most distracted, and cut stick for home; and Aunt Dora didn't know it, and went off to the Lake, and sat with both feet in the water, and Mr. Robert West found her there and told her, and got her home, and she most had a fit, and, O thunder! what a muss they have kicked up!"

Here Johnnie stopped for breath, while his father grasped the table with both hands, as if he thus would steady himself, while he said slowly, with long breaths between the words, "How—was it—my son? Tell me —again. I—I do not—think—I understand."

Briefly then Johnnie recapitulated, telling how he happened to find it out, and adding, "Such kissing I never heard! *Fourteen* smashers, for I counted; and don't you know, father, how, if you even touched her hand or her hair, she would wiggle and squirm as if it hurt her? Well, I peeked through the crack of the door, and instead of wigglin' she snugged up to him as if she liked it, and I know she did, for her eyes fairly shone, they were so bright, when she looked at him. But, father, she talked real good about you, and said that if you insisted she should marry you just the same; but you won't father, will you?"

"No, my son, no. O Dora!"

The words were a groan, while the Squire laid his face upon the table. Instantly Johnnie was at his side comforting him as well as he was able, and trying manfully to keep down his own choking sorrow.

"Never mind, father, never mind; we will get along, you and I. And I'll tell you now what folks say, and that is, that no chap has a right to marry his wife's sister, which I guess is so. Don't cry, father, don't. Somebody will have you, if Aunt Dora won't. There,—there," and Johnnie tried in vain to hush the grief becoming rather demonstrative as the Squire began to realize what he had lost.

Noisy grief is never so deep as the calm, quiet sorrow which can find no outlet for its tears, and so Squire Russell was the more sure to outlive this bitter trial; but that did not help him now, or make the future seem one whit less desolate. It was an hour before Johnnie left him, and went into the hall, where he encountered Jessie, to whom he said, " I've told him and he'll do the handsome thing, but it almost kills him. Maybe you, being a girl, can talk to him better than I," and Johnnie went on up to Dora's chamber, while Jessie, after hesitating a moment, glided quietly into the library, where Squire Russell still sat with his head upon the table.

Jessie was a nice little comforter, and so the Squire found her as she stood over him, just as she did when Margaret died, smoothing his hair, her favorite method of expressing sympathy, and saying to him so softly, "I pity you, and I think you so good to give her up."

He could talk to Jessie ; and bidding her to sit down, he asked what she knew of Dora's love-affair with the doctor, thereby learning some things which Johnnie had not told him.

"It is well," he said at last; "I see that Dora is not for me; I give her to Dr. West; and, Miss Verner,— Jessie,—I thank, you for your sympathy with both of us. I am glad you are here."

Jessie was glad, too, for if there was anything she especially enjoyed, it was the whirl and the excitement going on around her. Bowing, she too quitted the library, and went up to corroborate what Johnnie had already told to Dora.

After that Squire Russell sat no more in the upper hall watching Dora's door, but stayed downstairs with his little children, to whom he attached himself continually, as if he felt that he must be to them father and mother both. Now that the crisis was past, the doctor thought it advisable to go back to Mrs. Markham's, his boarding-place, but he met Squire Russell first, and heard from his own lips a confirmation of what Johnnie had said. There was no malice in John Russell's nature, and he treated the doctor as cordially and kindly as if he had not been his rival.

"God bless you both," he said; "I blame no one,— harbor no ill-feeling towards any one. If Dora had told me frankly at first it might have saved some pain, some mortification, but I do not lay it up against her. She meant for the best. It is natural she should love you more than me. God bless her; and doctor, if you like, marry her at once, but don't take her away from here yet; wait a little till I am more settled,—for the children's sake, you know."

Dr. West could not understand the feeling which prompted Squire Russell to want Dora to stay there, but he recognized the great unselfishness of the man whose sunshine he had darkened, and with a trembling lip he, too, said, "God bless you," as he grasped the hand most cordially offered, and then hurried away. It was a week before the Squire could command sufficient courage to have an interview with Dora, as she had repeatedly asked that he might do. With a faltering step he approached her door, hesitating upon the threshold, until Jessie, coming suddenly upon him, said to him, cheerily, "It will soon be over, never mind it; go in."

So he went in, and stayed a long, long time, but as they were alone, no one ever knew all that had passed between them. The Squire was very white when he came out, but his face shone with a look of one who felt that he had done right, and after that the expression did not change except that it gradually deepened into one of content and even cheerfulness, as the days went by, and people not only came to know that the wedding between himself and Dora would never be, but also to approve the arrangement, and to treat him as a hero who had achieved a famous victory. As for Dora, Jessie and Bell found her after the interview weeping bitterly over what she called her own wicked selfishness and John's great generous goodness in giving her up so kindly, and making her feel while he was talking to her that it really was no matter about him. He was not injured so very much, although he had loved her dearly. He still had his children, and with them he should be happy.

"Oh, he is the best man!" Dora said; "the very best man that ever lived, and I wish he might find some suitable wife, whom he could love better than he did me, and who would make him happy."

"So do I! I guess I do!" retorted Jessie, industriously cutting a sheet of note-paper in little slips and scattering them on the floor. "I've thought of everybody that would be at all suitable, for I suppose he must be married on account of the children; but there is nobody good enough except—" and Jessie held the scissors and paper still a moment, while she added, "except Bell. I think she would answer nicely. She is twenty-nine,—almost that awful thirty,—which no unmarried woman ever reaches, they say; and I'd like to be aunt to six children right well, only I believe I should thrash Jim and Letitia, —who, by the way, is not very bright. Did you ever discover it, Dora?"

Dora had sometimes thought Letitia a little dull, she said, and then she turned to Bell to see how she fancied the idea of being step-mother to all those dreadful children; but Bell did not fancy it at all, as was plainly indicated by the haughty toss of her head as she replied that:

"Thirty had no terrors for her, but was infinitely preferable to a widower with six children."

Jessie whistled, while Dora smiled softly as she caught the sound of a well-known step upon the stairs, and knew her physician was coming.

Bell and Jessie always left her alone with him, and when they were gone he kissed her pale cheek, which flushed with happiness, while her sunny eyes looked volumes of love into the eyes meeting them so fondly.

"My darling has been crying," the doctor said. "Will she tell me why?"

And then came the story of her interview with John, who had proved himself so noble and good.

"Yes, I know; he came from you to me!" the doctor replied, and into Dora's eyes there crept a bashful, frightened look, as she wondered if John had said to Richard what he did to her.

He had in part, viz., that he wished matters to proceed just as if he had never thought of marrying Dora; that as soon as she was able he would like to see her the doctor's wife, and then if there were no objections on the part of either, he would like to have her remain at Beechwood awhile, at least until he could make some other arrangement for his children.

"I told him you might," Richard said, as he imprisoned the hand which was raised to remonstrate. "I said I knew you would be willing to stay, and that I should like my new boarding-place very much; and now nothing remains but for you to get well as fast as possible, for the moment the doctor pronounces you convalescent you are to be his wife. Do you understand?"

He did not tell her then of the plan which was maturing, and for the furtherance of which Robert was sent away, viz., the purchase of the homestead whose loss Dora had so much deplored.

There was an opening in the town for a new physician, the doctor had ascertained; and though he would dislike to leave his many friends in Beechwood, still, for Dora's sake, he could do so, and he had sent Robert to open negotiations with the present proprietor of the place once owned by Colonel Freeman, and for which there was ample means to pay in the sum brought by the prodigal from the mines of California.

But this was a secret until something definite was

known, and Richard willingly acceded to the Squire's proposition that he and Dora should remain there until something was devised for the children.

Of this Dora was not much inclined to talk, and as she was tired and excited, the doctor left her at last, stopping on his way from the house to look at little Daisy, whom Jessie held in her lap, and who seemed feverish and sick. The doctor did not then say what he feared, but when later in the day he came again, the child's symptoms had developed so rapidly, that he had no hesitancy in pronouncing it the scarlet fever, then prevailing to an alarming extent in an adjoining town.

Squire Russell had thought his cup full to overflowing, but in his anxiety for Daisy, he forgot his recent disappointment, and, as a father and mother both, nursed his suffering child, assisted by Jessie, whose services there, as elsewhere, were invaluable. It was indeed a house of mourning, and for weeks a dark cloud brooded over it as one after another, Ben and Burt, Letitia and Jim, were prostrate with the disease which Daisy had been the first to take, and from which she slowly recovered. When Letitia was smitten down Jessie was filled with remorse, for she remembered what she had said of the quiet child, and with a sister's tenderness she nursed the little girl, who would take her medicine from no one else From the first Ben and Burt were not very ill, but for a time it seemed doubtful which would gain the mastery, life or death, in the cases of Letitia and Jim. With regard to Letitia that question was soon settled, and one October morning Jessie put gently back upon the pillow the child who had died in her lap, kissing her the last of all ere she went the dark road already trodden by the mother, who in life would have chosen anybody else than Jessie Verner to have soothed the last moments of her little girl.

But Jessie's work was not yet done, and while the sad procession went on its way to the village graveyard, where Margaret was lying, she sat by Jimmie's side fanning his feverish cheeks, and carefully administering the medicines which were no longer of avail.

Two days after Jimmie, too, died in Jessie's lap, and as she gave him into his father's arms the weeping man blessed her silently for all she had been to him and his, and felt how doubly desolate he should be without her.

CHAPTER XXVI.

GIVING IN MARRIAGE.

THERE were two little graves now by Margaret's, and in the house two vacant chairs, and two voices hushed, while Squire Russell counted four children where he had numbered six, and yet the unselfish man would hear of no delay to Dora's marriage.

"Let it go on the same," he said. "It will make me feel better to know that there are around me some perfectly happy ones."

And so the day was appointed, and Bell and Mattie were summoned again from Morrisville, whither the latter had gone during the children's illness. Judge Verner was lonely with both of his daughters absent, and as of the two he was most accustomed to Bell, he would have been quite content with having her back again if she had not told him how Jessie had turned nurse to Squire Russell's children, and was consequently in danger of taking the disease. This roused him, and in a characteristic letter to Jessie he bade her "not make a fool of herself any longer by tending children with canker-rash and feeding them with sweetened water, but to pack up her traps and come home."

To this the saucy Jessie replied that "she should not come home till she was ready; that the Judge could shut up, and what he called sweetened water was quite as strong as the medicine which once cured his colic so soon." Then, in the coaxing tone the Judge could never resist, she added, "You know I'm just in fun, father, when I talk like that, but really I must stay till after Dora is married, and you must let me, that's a dear, good old soul," and so the "good old soul" was cajoled into writing that Jessie might stay, adding in postscript, "Bell tells me you say all sorts of extravagant things about that widower, and this is well enough as long as they mean nothing, but for thunder's sake don't go to offering yourself to him in a streak of pity. A nice wife you would make for a widower with six children,—you who don't know how to darn a pair of stockings, nor make a bed so that the one who sleeps the back side won't roll out of the front. Mind, now, don't be a fool."

"I wonder what put that idea into father's head," Jessie said, as she read the letter. "I would not have Squire Russell, let alone offering myself to him. And I do know how to darn socks. Any way, I can pull the holes together, which is just as well as to put in a ball and peek and poke and weave back and forth, and make lace-work of it just as Bell does. It's a real old-maidish trick, and I won't be an old maid anyhow, if I have to marry Squire Russell," and crushing the letter into her pocket Jessie went dancing down the stairs, whistling softly for fear of disturbing the sick children.

That afternoon Dora found her, with her face very red and anxious, bending over a basket of stockings and socks, which she was trying to darn after the method most approved by Bell. "Clem had so much to do that day," she said, "that she had offered to help by taking the darning off her hands." But it was a greater task than Jessie had anticipated, and Johnnie's aid was called in before it was finished, the boy proving quite as efficient as the girl, and as Clem secretly thought, succeeding even better. This was before Letitia and Jimmie died, and since their death the Judge had made no effort to call her home, but suffered her to take her own course, which she did by remaining in Beechwood, where they would have missed her so much, and where, if she could not darn socks neatly, she made herself generally useful as the day for the wedding approached. It was arranged to take place on Christmas Eve, and it was Jessie who first suggested that the house should be trimmed even more elaborately than the little church upon the common, where the ceremony was to be performed. With Johnnie as her prime minister, Jessie could accomplish almost anything, and when their work was done, every one joined heartily in praise of the green festoons and wreaths, on which were twined the scarlet berries of the mountain ash, with here and there a blossom of purest white, purloined from the costly flowers which Squire Russell ordered in such profusion from the nearest hothouse. Dora took but little part in the preparations. She was very happy, but her joy was of that quiet kind, which made her content to be still and rest, after the turmoil and wretchedness through which she had passed. The doctor was with her constantly, and to Jessie, who saw the look of perfect peace upon his face and Dora's, they seemed the impersonation of bliss, while even Bertie noted the change in Dora, saying to her once as she sat with the doctor:

"You don't look now, Auntie, as you did when you was married to pa."

Dora could only blush, while the doctor laughingly tossed the little fellow upon his shoulder and carried him off to the office. If Squire Russell suffered, it was not perceptible, and Jessie thought he had recovered wonderfully, while Dora, too, hoped the wound had not been so deep as even to leave a scar. He was very kind and thoughtful, remembering everything that was needful to be done, and treating Dora as if she had been his daughter. He wished her to forget the past; wished to forget it himself; and by the cheerful, active course he took, he bade fair to do so. He should give the bride away, he said, and when Mattie Randall, to whom he was a study, asked kindly if he was sure he was equal to it, he answered, "O yes, wholly so. I see now that Dora would never have been happy with me. I should have laid her by Madge in less than a year. I am glad it has all happened as it has."

He did seem to be glad, and when, on the night of the 24th, the little bridal party stood waiting in the parlor for the carriages which were to take them to the church, his face was as serene and placid as if he had never hoped to occupy the place the doctor occupied. Through much sorrow he had been tried and purified, until now in his heart, always unselfish and kind, there was room for the holier, gentler feelings which only the peace of God can give. Not in vain had he in the solitude of his chamber writhed and groaned over the crushing pang with which he gave Dora up, while the tears wept over his dead children were to him a holier baptism than any received before, washing him clean and making him a noble-minded Christian man. Margaret's grave had during those autumn months witnessed many an earnest prayer for the strength and peace which were found at last, and were the secret of his composure. Just before the sun-setting of Dora's bridal day, he had gone alone to the three lonely graves and laid upon the longest the exquisite cross of evergreen and white wax berries which Jessie's fingers had fashioned for this very purpose, Jessie's brain having been the first to conceive the plan. There was also a bouquet of buds for each of the smaller graves, and Squire Russell placed them carefully upon the sod, which he watered with his tears; then, with a whispered prayer, he went back across the fields to where Dora, in her bridal dress, was waiting, but not for him. He was not the bridegroom, and he stood aside as the doctor bounded up the stairs, in obedience to Jessie's call that he should come and see if ever anybody looked so sweetly as his bride, but charging him not to touch her lest some band, or braid, or fold, or flower should give way.

"It won't be always so," he said, standing off as Jessie directed. "By and by she will be all my own, and then I can hug her,—*so!*" and in spite of Jessie's screams, he wound his arms around Dora's neck, giving her a most emphatic kiss as his farewell to Dora Freeman. "When I kiss you again you will be Dora West," he whispered, as he drew the blushing girl's arm in his, and led her down the stairs.

The church was crowded to its utmost capacity, and it was with some difficulty that the colored sexton had kept a space cleared for the bridal party, which passed slowly up the aisle, while the soft notes of the organ floated on the air. Then the music ceased, and only the rector's voice was heard, uttering the solemn words, "I require and charge you both," etc.; but there was no need for this appeal, there was no impediment, no reason why these two hearts, throbbing so lovingly, should not be joined together, and so the rite went on, while amid the gay throng only one heart was heavy and sad. Robert West, leaning against a pillar, could not forget another ceremony, where he was one of the principal actors, while the other was Anna, beautiful Anna, over whose head the snows of many a wintry eve had fallen, and who but for him might have been now among the living. He had visited her grave and Robin's, had knelt on the turf which covered them, and sued so earnestly for pardon, had whispered to the winds words of deepest love and contrition, as if the injured dead could hear, and then he had gone away to seek the man whom he had so wronged, and who for the brother's-sake had kept his sin a secret. Uncle Jason had forgiven him, had said that all was right, that every trace of his error was destroyed, and Robert had mingled fearlessly again among his fellow-men, who, only guessing in part his guilt, and feeling intuitively that he had changed, received him gladly into their midst.

Summoned by his brother's letters, he had returned to Beechwood, and now formed one of the party, who, when the rite was over, went back to the brightly illuminated house, where the Christmas garlands, the box, and the pine, and the fir were hung, and where the marriage festivities proceeded rationally, quietly, save as Jessie's bird-like voice pealed through the house, as she played off her jokes, first upon one and then another, adroitly trying to coax Bell and the young clergyman, Mr. Kelly, under the mistletoe bough, and then screaming with delight as her father and Mrs. David West were the first to pass within the charmed circle. Jessie was alive with fun and frolic, and making Bell sit down at the piano, she declared that somebody should dance at Dora's wedding if she had to dance alone.

"Take Johnnie," Dora said, and the two were soon whirling through the rooms, the boy's head coming far above the black curls of the merry little maiden, who flashed, and gleamed, and sparkled among the assembled guests till more than one heart beat faster as it caught the influence of her exhilarating presence.

Robert West dreamed of her that night; so did Mr. Kelly, the rector; and so did Squire Russell; but the two first forgot her again next morning, as each said good-by to the handsome, stately Bell,—a far more fitting match for either than the black-eyed sprite who for a moment had made their pulses quicken. But not so with the Squire. To him the house was very desolate when he returned to it, after having accompanied the bride, and groom, and guests to the cars, which all took for Morrisville, whither they were going. It was Dora he missed, the servants said, pitying him, he looked so sad, while he too believed it was Dora; and still as he knelt that day in church, there was beside him another face than Dora's, —a saucy, laughing, face, which we recognize as belong.

ing to Jessie,—who, at that very moment, while keeping her companions in a constant turmoil and her father in a constant scold, was thinking of him and saying mentally:

"Poor Squire Russell! how I pity him,—left there all alone! and how I wonder if he misses me!"

CHAPTER XXVII.

MORE OF MARRIAGE.

THE homestead where Dora's childhood had been passed "could not be bought for love nor money;" so Robert, the negotiator, had reported to his brother on the morning following the latter's marriage, and so Richard reported to Dora, as he sat with her at Mattie Randall's, up in the chamber which Dora called hers, and where Anna had died. Mattie had wished to give the bridal pair another room, but Dora would take no other; and as Richard was satisfied, they occupied the one whose walls had witnessed so much sorrow in the days gone by. But there was no grief there now, nothing but perfect bliss, as Richard held his darling to his heart and told her for the thousandth time how dear she was to him, and how he thanked the Father of all good for giving her to him at last. In all his joy he never forgot his God, or placed Him second to Dora, who listened and smiled and returned his fond caresses until he told her of his plan to buy the homestead, and how that plan had been defeated by the refusal of the present proprietor. Then Dora hid her face in his bosom and wept softly to the memory of her old home, which Richard had tried so hard to buy back for her.

"You are so good, so kind," she said, as he asked her why she cried, and pitied what he thought was her disappointment. "It is not that," she continued, as she dried her tears. "It is your thoughtful love for me. I should be very happy at the old place, but, Richard, I am not sure that I should not be happier in Beechwood, where I have lived so long, and where you have so many friends. There John's children would be nearer me, and I must care for them."

And so it was arranged that Richard should buy the fine building spot to the right of Squire Russell's, and that until the house he would erect should be completed, Dora should remain at home and care for the children.

This plan, when submitted to the Squire, met his hearty approval, and made the future look less dreary than before. He should not be left alone entirely, for Dora would be near to counsel and advise, and his face was very bright and cheerful as he welcomed the travellers back from their long trip, which lasted until February.

Towards the latter part of April, Jessie accepted of Dora's cordial invitation to visit them again, and came to Beechwood, the same bright, laughing, gleeful creature as ever, the sunshiny being in whom, the moment he saw her seated again by his fireside, Squire Russell recognized the want he had felt ever since she left him the winter previous. He was so glad to have her back,—his eldest child he called her,—and treated her much as if he had been her father, notwithstanding that she made ludicrous attempts at dignity, on the strength of being twenty her next birthday, which was in June. Jessie was very pretty this spring, Squire Russell thought when he thought of her at all, and so thought the Rector of St. Luke's, Mr. Kelly, who came nearly every day, ostensibly to talk with Mrs. Dr. West about some new plan for advancing the interests of the Sunday-school, but really to catch a glimpse of Jessie's sparkling beauty, or hear some of her saucy sayings. But always, when he left the house and went back to his bachelor rooms, he said to himself, " It would never do. She is a frolicsome, pretty little plaything, who would amuse and rest me vastly, but she would shock my parishioners out of all the good I could ever instill into their minds. No, it won't do."

Robert West, too, whose pulse had beaten a little faster at the sight of Jessie Verner, had given himself to his country, so there was no one to contest the prize with Squire Russell, into whose brain the idea that he could win it never entered until Johnnie put it there. To Johnnie it came suddenly, making him start quickly from the book he was reading, and hurry off to Dr. West, asking if Deacon Bowles was not a great deal older than Mrs. Bowles, whom the villagers still called Amy, making her seem so youthful. The doctor thought he was, but could not tell just how many years, and as this was the point about which Johnnie was anxious, he conceived the bold plan of calling on Mrs. Amy to ascertain, if possible, her exact age, and also that of her husband. He found her rocking her baby to sleep and looking very pretty and girlish in her short hair, which she had taken a fancy to have cut off. Amy was fond of Johnnie, and she smiled pleasantly upon him, speaking in a whisper and keeping up a constant "sh-sh-sh" as she moved the cradle back and forth.

"What a nice baby," Johnnie began, as if he had never seen it before; "but it seems funny to see you with a baby, when you look so like a girl. You can't be very old."

"Turned thirty. Sh-sh—" was the reply.

A gratified blush mounting Amy's cheek, while Johnnie continued:

"Mother was thirty-two, and father was thirty-nine. He is most forty-one now. Is the deacon older than that?"

"Going on fifty-one. Sh-sh—" Amy replied, her "sh-sh's" being more decided as baby showed signs of waking.

Johnnie had learned what he wished to know, and bidding Mrs. Bowles good morning, he ran home, repeating to himself:

"Turned thirty,—going on fifty-one. Ought from one is one, three from five is two. That makes twenty-one. Most twenty,—most forty-one. Ought from one is one, two from four is two. *That* makes twenty-one. Jemima! It'll do, it'll do!" and Johnnie ran on with all his might till he reached home, where he found Jessie, whom he astonished with a hug which almost strangled her.

"It will do! it will do!" he exclaimed, as he kissed her, and when she asked what would do, he answered, "I know, I know, but I shan't tell!" and he darted off, big with the important thing which he knew and should not tell.

That night, as Squire Russell sat in his library, Johnnie came in and startled him with the question:

"Father, who will take care of us when Aunt Dora is gone? Her new house will be done in September."

"I don't know, my son;" and the Squire laid down his paper, for the question which Johnnie asked had also been troubling him.

There was silence a moment, during which Johnnie almost twisted a button from his jacket, and then he broke out abruptly:

"Why don't you get married?"

"Married! To whom?" the Squire exclaimed; and Johnnie replied:

"You know. The nicest girl in all creation after Aunt Dora. She isn't too young, neither. Amy Bowles is twenty-one years younger than the deacon, and Jessie ain't any more."

"Jessie! Jessie Verner!" the squire gasped, and Johnnie continued:

"Yes, Jessie Verner; I most know she'll have you. Any way, I'll make her. You break the ice, and I'll pitch in! Will you, father? Will you have Jessie?"

"It would be better to ask first if she'll have me," the father replied, rubbing his head, which seemed a little numb with the sudden shock.

"I hear her. I'll send her in! You ask her, father!" Johnnie exclaimed, darting to the door, as he heard Jessie in the upper hall whistling " three hundred thousand more."

As he reached the threshold he paused, while he added:

"I guess Jessie will stand a huggin' better than Aunt Dora, so you might come that game on her!" and Johnnie rushed after Jessie ere his father had time to recover his breath.

Jessie could not at once be found, and as Johnnie would not tell her what his father wanted of her, she was in no particular hurry to answer the summons, so that Squire Russell had time to collect his thoughts, and to discover that little Jessie Verner was very dear to him, and that though he had never entertained an idea of making her his wife till Johnnie suggested it, the idea was by no means distasteful, and if she were willing, why of course he was. But would she come? Yes, she was coming, for he heard her in the hall calling back to Johnnie:

"Mind, now, if you have played me a trick you will be sorry. I don't believe he wants me."

"Yes he does; you ask him," was Johnnie's reply, and advancing into the library, Jessie began innocently:

"Johnnie said you wanted me. Do you, Squire Russell!"

"Yes, Jessie, I do want you very much. Sit down while I tell you."

He drew her chair near to himself, and wholly unsuspicious, Jessie sat down to listen, while he told her how he wanted her.

CHAPTER XXVIII.

DORA'S DIARY.

MAY 31st, 1863.—I did not think when last I closed this book, that I could ever be as happy as I am now,—happy in everything, happy in Richard's love, happy in the love of God, for my precious husband has been the means of leading me to the source of all happiness. He says I was a Christian before, but I cannot believe it. At least, it was a cold, tame kind of Christian, such as I never wish to be again! Dear Richard, how good and true he is, and how he tries to make me happy. Every day I see some new virtue in him, and the tears often come as I wonder why God should have blessed me above the generality of womankind. I know I have the kindest, and best, and dearest husband in the world. He has gone for a few days to Fortress Monroe, where Robert is at present with his men, while Mother West has gone into the hospital as nurse. She felt it was her duty, and we did not oppose her, knowing how much good she would do to the poor, suffering soldiers. My heart bleeds for them, and yet I cannot feel it the doctor's duty to go. Somebody must stay at home, and when I see how his patients cling to him, and how useful he is here, I think it is his place to stay. If I am wrong and selfish, may I be forgiven.

"In the autumn our new house will be completed, and then I shall leave Margaret's family, but not alone, for Jessie is actually coming to be John's wife, and is now at home making her preparations. Does Margaret know? If so, she surely feels kindly now toward the little girl, who will make the best of mothers to the children.

"It was very strange, and though Richard and I had laughed together over the possibility, it took me wholly by surprise. I was sitting in my room one night last April, waiting for Richard, when Jessie came rushing in, her eyes red with weeping, and her frame quivering with emotion. I was startled, particularly as she threw herself on the floor beside me, and exclaimed:

"'O Dora, I've done the silliest thing, and father will scold, I know, and call me a fool, and say *I* proposed, when I didn't, though I am afraid I said yes too quick! Do you think I did? Tell me, do.'

"Then I managed to get from her that she was engaged to Squire Russell; that Johnnie inveigled her in by saying his father wanted her; that she asked if he did, and he told her, 'Yes, he wanted her for his little wife; wanted to keep her always!' and she was so frightened.

"'Oh, you don't know anything about it!' she said.

'I felt just as I did once when I took chloroform to have a tooth out, and acted just so, too, foolish like, for I talked everything and told him everything; how I was a little bit of a body who did not know anything, who had never learned anything, but had always done as I pleased and always wanted to; how I could not be sober if I tried, and would not if I could; how I was more fit to be Johnnie's wife than his; how father was not as rich as some thought, but had two apoplectic fits ever so long ago, and might have another any time and die, while Bell and I would have to take care of ourselves,—go out governesses, or something; and, maybe, if he knew that he would not want me, but if he didn't, and I ever had to be a governess, perhaps he would let me come here to teach his children, and that was so silly for me to say, and I knew it all the time, just like chloroform. And then, O Dora, how ridiculous the next thing was. He only laughed at the governess, and held me tighter, and I guess,—I am most sure,—he kissed me; and I am awfully afraid I kissed him back! Do you think I did?'

"I thought it quite likely, I said, and with a groan Jessie continued:

"'The very silliest thing of all was my telling him I could not darn his socks, nor make his shirts, and he would have to wear big holes in them or go without; and,—oh, do you believe, he laughed real loud, and said he would go without? Do you think he meant it?'

"'Yes, Jessie, undoubtedly he meant it,' and Richard's merry laugh broke in upon us.

"So absorbed had I been in Jessie that I had not heard the doctor, who entered in time to hear the last of Jessie's confession, and who at the recital of John's magnanimity could restrain himself no longer, but laughed long and loud, while Jessie wept silently. At last, however, we managed to draw from her that in spite of all her faults, every one of which she acknowledged, even to the fact that sometimes when going to parties she powdered her arms, and that four of her teeth were filled, John had persisted in saying that he loved her, and could not live without her; that as to powder, Margaret always used it; that he knew a place on Broadway where he could get the very best article in use; that most everybody's teeth were either false or filled by the time they were twenty, and he guessed she was quite as genuine as any of the feminine genus.

"'Did you tell him about the cotton?' Richard asked, wickedly, but Jessie innocently replied:

"'I don't know what you mean, but if it's the sheets and pillow-cases I am expected to furnish, Bell bought four pieces just before the rise, and I know she will let me have some. Any way, I shall not ask Squire Russell to buy them,' and thus Richard was foiled and I was glad.

"'And so it is finally settled, and you are to be my little sister?' Richard said, and Jessie replied:

"'Yes; that is I told him to ask my father, and please, Dr. West, will you write too and tell him how I did not do the courting, or ever think of such a thing? Father will scold, I know, and maybe swear. He always does, but I don't care, I—'

"There was a call for Dr. West, who went out leaving us alone; and then winding my arm around Jessie, I said:

"'And are you sure you love Squire Russell well enough to be his wife?'

This question threw Jessie into another impetuous outburst, and she exclaimed:

"'That is just what he asked me, too; and if I had not loved him before I should have done so when he said, "I wish you to be certain, Jessie, so there need be no after-repentance. I have borne one disappointment," and he looked so white and sad. "A second would kill me. If I take you now, and then have to give you up, my life will go with you. Can you truly say you love me, Jessie, and are perfectly willing to be mine?"

"'I was foolish then, Dora, for I told him straight out how it was very sudden; but the knowing he loved me brought into life a feeling which kept growing and growing so fast, that even in a few minutes it seemed as if I had loved him all my life. He is so good and kind, and will let me do just as I please. Don't you believe he will?"

"I had no doubt of it, and I smoothed her short curls while she told me how sorry she was that she ever thought Letitia stupid, or Jimmie less interesting than the others.

"'It seems as if they died just to be out of my way, and I do so wish they were back.'

"Then she said that the wedding was to be the 25th of June, her twentieth birthday, that is, if her father consented; that John had promised to take her to Europe some time, but not this year, and they were going instead to the White Mountains, to Newport, and lots of places, and Johnnie was going with them. Then she settled her bridal *trousseau*, even to the style of her gaiters, declaring she would not have those horrid square toes, if they were fashionable, for they made one's foot so clumsy, and she put up her fairy little feet, which looked almost as small as Daisy's. Dear little Jessie, of whom I once was jealous! What a child she is, and what a task she is taking upon herself! But her heart is in it, and that makes it very easy. Had I loved John one half as well as she seems to love him, I should not now be Richard's wife, waiting for him by the window as I wait for him many nights, knowing that though he chides me for sitting up so late, he is usually pleased to find me so, and kisses me so tenderly as he calls me a naughty girl, and bids me hurry to bed.

"June 28th.—The house is very still these days, for John and Johnnie are gone, and with them all the bustle, the stir, and the excitement which has characterized our home for the last few weeks. I invited Bell to return with me from the wedding, but her father said no, he could not spare both his daughters; and so she stayed, her tears falling so fast as she said to me at parting: 'You cannot guess how lonely I am, knowing Jessie will never come home to us again, just as she used to come.'

"Poor Bell, I pity her; but amid her tears I saw, as I thought, a rainbow of promise. As the clergyman at Morrisville chanced to be absent, Mr. Kelly went down with us to perform the ceremony, and if I am not mistaken he will go again and again until he brings Bell away with him. The wedding was a quiet affair, save as Jessie and Johnnie laughed and sported and played. The bride and groom were, however, perfectly happy, I know, which was more than could be said for the Judge. At first he had, as Jessie predicted, said all kinds of harsh things about the match, but Bell and Jessie won him over, until he was ready to receive his son-in-law with the utmost kindness, which he did, acting the polite, urbane host to perfection, and only breaking down when Jessie came to say good-by. Then he showed how much he loved his baby, as he called her, commending her so touchingly to her husband's patient care, because 'she was a wee, helpless thing,' that we all cried, Richard and all, while the Squire could not resist giving his fairy bride a most substantial hug, right before us all, as he promised to care for her as tenderly as if she were his little Daisy instead of his little wife. I have no fears for them. It is a great responsibility which Jessie has assumed, but her sunny nature, which sees only the brightest side, and the mighty love which her husband and Johnnie have given her, will interpose between her and all that otherwise might be hard to bear. God bless her. God keep her in all her pleasant journeyings, and bring her safely back to us, who wait and watch for her as for the refreshing rain.

"DECEMBER 24th, 1863—CHRISTMAS EVE.—Just one year I have been Richard's wife, and in that time I cannot recall a single moment of sadness, or a time when Richard's voice and manner were not just as kind and loving as at first. My noble husband, how earnestly I pray that I may be worthy of him, and make him as happy as he makes me. We are in our new home now, and I cannot think of a single wish ungratified. Everything is as I like it. The furniture is of my own and Richard's selecting, and is as good as our means would afford,—not grand and costly like Mattie's and Jessie's, but plain and nice, such as the furniture of a village doctor's wife ought to be. And Richard's mother is with us now, resting from the toils of life as nurse in the hospital. We would like so much to keep her, but she says 'No, not till the war is over ; then if my life is spared, I will come back to live and die with my children.'

"Captain Robert is coming to-night and to-morrow all take their Christmas dinner with me; I said all, meaning John and Jessie, with their four children, and Mr. Kelly, with his bride, Isabel. She has been here just a week in the parsonage, which the people bought and fitted up when they heard their clergyman was to bring his wife among them. Judge Verner, too, is there, or rather at Squire Russell's, where the children call him grandpa, and where he seems very fond of staying. He will divide his time between his daughters, and if that apoplectic fit of which Jessie spoke ever does make its appearance, Richard will be near to attend him, for the Judge will have no other physician. 'Homœopathy is all a humbug,' he says, 'but hanged if he will take any other medicine.' He has great pride now in Mrs. Squire Russell, who certainly has developed into a wonderfully domestic woman, so that Richard even cites her for my example. Perfectly happy at home, she seldom cares to leave it, but stays contentedly with the children, to whom she is a mother and a sister both. Johnnie calls her Jessie, but to the others she is mamma to all intents and purposes, and could Margaret know, she would surely bless the whistling, hoydenish girl, who is all the world now to husband and children both.

"Dear Jessie! I might write volumes in her praise, but this is the very last page of my journal, kept for so many years. The book is filled; whatever there was of romance in my girl history is within its pages, and here at its close I write myself a happy, happy woman. From the church-tower on the common the clock is striking twelve, and Richard, coming in from his long cold ride across the snow-clad hills, bids me a merry Christmas; then glancing at what I have written, he says, 'Yes, darling, God has been very good to us. Let us love Him through the coming year more than ever we have done before.'

"With a full heart I say Amen, and so the story is done."

THE END.

THE RECTOR OF ST. MARK'S.

THE RECTOR OF ST. MARK'S.

CHAPTER I.

FRIDAY AFTERNOON.

THE Sunday sermon was finished, and the young rector of St. Mark's turned gladly from his study-table to the pleasant south window where the June roses were peeping in, and abandoned himself for a few moments to the feeling of relief he always experienced when his week's work was done. To say that no secular thoughts had intruded themselves upon the rector's mind, as he planned and wrote his sermon, would not be true, for, though morbidly conscientious on many points and earnestly striving to be a faithful shepherd of the souls committed to his care, Arthur Leighton had all a man's capacity to love and to be loved, and though he fought and prayed against it, he had seldom brought a sermon to the people of St. Mark's in which there was not a thought of Anna Ruthven's soft, brown eyes, and the way they would look at him across the heads of the congregation. Anna led the village choir, and the rector was painfully conscious that far too much of earth was mingled with his devotional feelings during the moments when, the singing over, he walked from his chair to the pulpit, and heard the rustle of the crimson curtain in the organ-loft as it was drawn back, disclosing to view five heads, of which Anna's was the centre. It was very wrong he knew, and on the day when our story opens he had prayed earnestly for pardon, when, after choosing his text, "Simon, Simon, lovest thou me?" instead of plunging at once into his subject, he had, without a thought of what he was doing, idly written upon a scrap of paper lying near, " Anna, Anna, lovest thou me more than these?" the these referring to the wealthy Thornton Hastings, his old classmate in college, who was going to Saratoga this very summer for the purpose of meeting Anna Ruthven, and deciding if she would do to become Mrs. Thornton Hastings, and mistress of the house on Madison Square. With a bitter groan for the enormity of his sin, and a fervent prayer for forgiveness, the rector had torn the slips of paper in shreds and given himself so completely to his work, that his sermon was done a full hour earlier than usual, and he was free to indulge in reveries of Anna for as long a time as he pleased.

"I wonder if Mrs. Meredith has come," he thought, as, with his feet upon the window-sill, he sat looking across the meadow to where the chimneys and gable roof of Captain Humphreys' house were visible, for Captain Humphreys was Anna Ruthven's grandfather, and it was there she had lived since she was three years old.

As if thoughts of Mrs. Meredith reminded him of something else, the rector took from the drawer of his writing-table a letter received the previous day, and opening to the second page, read as follows :

"Are you going anywhere this summer? Of course not, for so long as there is an unbaptized child, or a bedridden old woman in the parish, you must stay at home, even if you do grow as rusty as did Professor Cobden's coat before we boys made him a present of a new one. I say, Arthur, there was a capital fellow spoiled when you took to the ministry, with your splendid talents, and rare gift for making people like and believe in you.

"Now, I suppose you will reply that for this denial of self you look for your reward in heaven, and I suppose you are right; but as I have no reason to think I have stock in that region, I go in for a good time here, and this summer I take Saratoga, where I expect to meet one of your lambs. I hear you have in your flock forty in all, their ages varying from sixteen to fifty. But this particular lamb, Miss Anna Ruthven, is, I think, the fairest of them all, and as I used to make you my father confessor in the days when I was rusticated out in Winsted, and fell so desperately in love with the six Miss Larkins, each old enough to be my mother, so now I confide to you the programme as marked out by Mrs.

Julia Meredith, the general who brings the lovely Anna in the field.

"We, that is, Mrs. Meredith and myself, are on the best of terms. I lunch with her, dine with her, lounge in her parlors, drive her to the park, take her to operas, concerts, and plays, and compliment her good looks, which are wonderfully well-preserved for a woman of forty-five. I am twenty-six, you know, and so no one ever associates us together in any kind of gossip. She is the very quintessence of fashion, and I am one of the danglers whose own light is made brighter by the reflection of her rays. Do you see the point? Well, then, in return for my attentions, she takes a very sisterly interest in my future wife, and has adroitly managed to let me know of her niece, a certain Anna Ruthven, who, inasmuch as I am tired of city belles, will undoubtedly suit my fancy, said Anna being very fresh, very artless, and very beautiful withal. She is also niece to Mrs. Meredith, whose only brother married very far beneath him, when he took to wife the daughter of a certain old-fashioned Captain Humphreys, a pillar, no doubt, in your church. This young Ruthven was drowned, or hung, or something, and the sister considers it as another proof of his wife's lack of refinement and discretion, that at her death, which happened when Anna was three years old, she left her child to the charge of her parents, Captain Humphreys and spouse, rather than to Mrs. Meredith's care, and that, too, in the very face of the lady's having stood as sponsor for the infant, an act which you will acknowledge as very unnatural and ungrateful in Mrs. Ruthven, to say the least of it.

"You see I am telling you all this, just as if you did not know Miss Anna's antecedents even better than myself; but possibly you do not know that, having arrived at a suitable age, she is this summer to be introduced into society at Saratoga, while I am expected to fall in love with her at once, and make her Mrs. Hastings before another winter. Now, in your straightforward way of putting things, don't imagine that Mrs. Meredith has deliberately told me all this, for she has not; but I understand her perfectly, and know exactly what she expects me to do. Whether I do it or not depends partly upon how I like Miss Anna, partly upon how she likes me, and partly upon yourself.

"You know I was always famous for presentiments or fancies, as you termed them, and the latest of these is that you like Anna Ruthven. Do you? Tell me, honor bright, and by the memory of the many scrapes you got me out of, and the many more you kept me from getting into, I will treat Miss Anna as gingerly and brotherly as if she were already your wife. I like her picture, which I have seen, and believe I shall like the girl, but if you say that by looking at her with longing eyes I shall be guilty of breaking some one of the ten commandments,—I don't know which,—why, then, hands off at once. That's fair, and will prove to you that, although not a parson like yourself, there is still a spark of honor, if not of goodness, in the breast of

"Yours truly,
"THORNTON HASTINGS.

"If you were here this afternoon, I'd take you to drive after a pair of bays, which are to sweep the stakes at Saratoga this summer, and I'd treat you to a finer cigar than often finds its way to Hanover. Shall I send you out a box, or would your people pull down the church about the ears of a minister wicked enough to smoke. Again adieu.

"T. H."

There was a half-amused smile on the face of the rector as he finished the letter, so like its thoughtless, light-hearted writer, and wondered what the Widow Rider, across the way, would say of a clergyman who smoked cigars, and rode after a race-horse with such a gay scapegrace as Thornton Hastings. Then the amused look passed away, and was succeeded by a shadow of pain, as the rector remembered the real import of Thornton's letter, and felt that he had no right to say, "I have a claim on Anna Ruthven; you must not interfere." For he had no claim on her, though half his parishioners had long ago given her to him, while he had loved her, as only natures like his can love, since that week before Christmas, when their hands had met with a strange, tremulous flutter, as together they fastened the wreaths of evergreen upon the wall, he holding them up, and she driving the refractory tacks, which would keep falling, so that his hand went often from the carpet or basin to hers, and once accidentally closed almost entirely over the little soft white thing, which felt so warm to his touch.

How prettily Anna had looked to him during those memorable days, so much prettier than the other young girls of his flock, whose hair was tumbled ere the day's work was done, and whose dresses were soiled and disordered; while hers was always so tidy and neat, and the braids of her chestnut hair were always so smooth and bright. How well, too, he remembered that brief ten minutes, when, in the dusky twilight which had crept so early into the church, he stood alone with her and talked, he did not know of what, only that he heard her voice replying to him, and saw the changeful color on her cheek as she looked modestly into his face. That was a week of delicious happiness, and the rector had lived it over many times, wondering if, when the next Christmas came, it would find him any nearer to Anna Ruthven than the last had left him.

"It must," he suddenly exclaimed. "The matter shall be settled before she leaves Hanover with Mrs.

Meredith. My claim is superior to Thornton's, and he shall not take her from me. I'll write what I lack the courage to tell her, and to-morrow I will call and deliver it myself."

An hour later, and there was lying in the rector's desk a letter, in which he had told Anna Ruthven how much he loved her, and had asked her to be his wife. Something whispered that she would not refuse him, and with this hope to buoy him up, his two miles' walk that warm afternoon was neither warm nor tiresome, and the old lady by whose bedside he read and prayed was surprised to hear him as he left her door, whistling an old love-tune which she, too, had known and sang fifty years before.

CHAPTER II.

SATURDAY AFTERNOON.

MRS. JULIA MEREDITH had arrived, and the brown farm-house was in a state of unusual excitement; not that Captain Humphreys or his good wife, Aunt Ruth, respected very highly the great lady who so seldom honored them with her presence, and who always tried to impress them with a sense of her superiority, and the mighty favor she conferred upon them by occasionally condescending to bring her aristocratic presence into their quiet, plain household, and turn it topsy-turvy. Still she was Anna's aunt, and then it was a distinction which Aunt Ruth rather enjoyed,—that of having a fashionable city woman for her guest,—and so she submitted with a good grace to the breaking in upon all her customs, and uttered no word of complaint when the breakfast-table waited till eight, and sometimes nine o'clock, and the freshest eggs were taken from the nest, and the cream all skimmed from the pans to gratify the lady who came very charming and pretty in her handsome cambric wrapper, with rosebuds in her hair. She had arrived the previous night, and while the rector was penning his letter, she was running her eye rapidly over Anna's face and form, making an inventory of her charms, and calculating their value.

"A very graceful figure, neither too short nor too tall. This she gets from the Ruthvens. Splendid eyes and magnificent hair, when Valencia has once taken it in hand. Complexion a little too brilliant, but a few weeks of dissipation will cure that. Fine teeth, and features tolerably regular, except that the mouth is too wide and the forehead too low, which defects she takes from the Humphreys. Small feet and rather pretty hands, except that they seem to have grown wide since I saw her before. Can it be these horrid people have set her to milking the cows?"

These were Mrs. Meredith's thoughts that first evening after her arrival at the farm-house, and she had not materially changed her mind when the next afternoon she went with Anna down to the Glen, for which she affected a great fondness, because she thought it was romantic and girlish to do so, and she was far from having passed the period when women cease caring for youth and its appurtenances. She had criticised Anna's taste in dress,—had said that the belt she selected did not harmonize with the color of the muslin she wore, and suggested that a frill of lace about the neck would be softer and more becoming than the stiff white linen collar.

"But in the country it does not matter," she added. "Wait till I get you to New York, under Madam Blank's supervision, and then we shall see a transformation such as will astonish the Hanoverians."

This was up in Anna's room; and when the Glen was reached Mrs. Meredith continued the conversation, telling Anna of her plans for taking her first to New York, where she was to pass through a reformatory process with regard to dress. Then they were going to Saratoga, where she expected her niece to reign supreme, both as a beauty and a belle.

"Whatever I have at my death I shall leave to you," she said; "consequently you will pass as an heiress expectant, and I confidently expect you to make a brilliant match before the winter season closes, if, indeed, you do not before we leave Saratoga."

"O aunt," Anna exclaimed, her eyes flashing with unwonted brilliancy, and the rich color mantling her cheek. "You surely are not taking me to Saratoga on such a shameful errand as that?"

"Shameful errand as what?" Mrs. Meredith asked, looking quickly up, while Anna replied:

"Trying to find a husband. I cannot go if you are, much as I have anticipated it. I should despise and hate myself forever. No, aunt, I cannot go."

"Nonsense, child. You don't know what you are saying," Mrs. Meredith retorted, feeling intuitively that she must change her tactics and keep her real intentions concealed if she would lead her niece into the snare laid for her.

Cunningly and carefully for the next half hour she talked, telling Anna that she was not to be thrust upon the notice of any one,—that she herself had no patience with those intriguing mammas who push their bold daughters forward, but that as a good marriage was the *ultima thule* of a woman's hopes, it was but natural that she, as Anna's aunt, should wish to see her well settled in life, and settled, too, near herself, where they could see each other every day.

"Of course there is no one in Hanover whom you, as a Ruthven, would stoop to marry," she said, fixing her eyes inquiringly upon Anna, who was pulling to pieces the wild flowers she had gathered, and thinking of that twilight hour when she had talked with their young clergyman as she never talked before. Of the many times, too, when they had met in the cottages of the poor, and he had walked slowly home with her, lingering by the gate as if loth to say good-by, she thought, and the life she had lived since he first came to Hanover, and she learned to blush when she met the glance of his eye, looked fairer far than the life her aunt marked out as the proper one for a Ruthven.

"You have not told me yet. Is there any one in Hanover whom you think worthy of you?" Mrs. Meredith asked, just as a footstep was heard, and the rector of St. Mark's came round the rock where they were sitting.

He had called at the farm-house, bringing the letter, and with it a book of poetry, of which Anna had asked the loan.

Taking advantage of her guest's absence, Grandma Humphreys had gone to a neighbor's after a receipt for making a certain kind of cake, of which Mrs. Meredith was very fond, and only Esther, the servant, and Valencia, the smart waiting-maid, without whom Mrs. Meredith never travelled, were left in charge.

"Miss Anna's down in the Glen with Mrs. Meredith. Will you be pleased to wait while I call them?" Esther said, in reply to the rector's inquiries for Miss Ruthven.

"No, I will find them myself," Mr. Leighton rejoined. Then, as he thought how impossible it would be to give the letter to Anna in the presence of her aunt, he slipped it into the book, which he bade Esther take to Miss Ruthven's room.

Knowing how honest and faithful Esther was, the rector felt that he could trust her without a fear for the safety of his letter, and went to the Glen, where the tell-tale blushes which burned on Anna's cheek at sight of him more than compensated for the coolness with which Mrs. Meredith greeted him. She, too, had detected Anna's embarrassment, and when the stranger was presented to her as "Mr. Leighton, our clergyman," the secret was out.

"Why is it that since the beginning of time girls have run wild after young ministers?" was her mental comment, as she bowed to Mr. Leighton, and then quietly inspected his *personnel*.

There was nothing about Arthur Leighton's appearance with which she could find fault. He was even finer-looking than Thornton Hastings, her *beau ideal* of a man, and as he stood a moment by Anna's side, looking down upon her, the woman of the world acknowledged to herself that they were a well-assorted pair, and as across the chasm of twenty years there came to her an episode in her life, when, on just such a day as this, she had answered "no" to one as young and worthy as Arthur Leighton, while all the time the heart was clinging to him, she softened for a moment, and by the memory of the weary years passed with the rich old man whose name she bore, she was tempted to leave alone the couple standing there before her, and looking into each other's eyes with a look which she could not mistake. But when she remembered that Arthur was only a poor clergyman, and thought of that house on Madison Square which Thornton Hastings owned, the softened mood was changed, and Arthur Leighton's chance with her was gone.

Awhile they talked together in the Glen, and then

walked back to the farm-house, where the rector bade them good-evening, after casually saying to Anna:

"I brought the book you spoke of when I was here last. You will find it in your room, where I asked Esther to take it."

That Mr. Leighton should bring her niece a book did not seem strange at all, but that he should be so very thoughtful as to tell Esther to take it to her room struck Mrs. Meredith as rather odd, and as the practised warhorse scents the battle from afar, so she at once suspected something wrong, and felt a curiosity to know what the book could be.

It was lying on Anna's table as she reached the door on her way to her own room, and pausing for a moment, she entered the chamber, took it in her hands, read the title page, and then opened it where the letter lay.

"Miss Anna Ruthven," she said. "He writes a fair hand;" and then, as the thought, which at first was scarce a thought, kept growing in her mind, she turned it over, and found that, owing to some defect, it had become unsealed, and the lid of the envelope lay temptingly open before her. "I would never break a seal," she said, "but surely, as her protector, and almost mother, I may read what this minister has written to my niece."

And so she read what he had written, while a scowl of disapprobation marred the smoothness of her brow.

"It is as I feared. Once let her see this, and Thornton

Hastings may woo in vain. But it shall not be. It is my duty, as the sister of her dead father, to interfere, and not let her throw herself away."

Perhaps Mrs. Meredith really felt that she was doing her duty. At all events she did not give herself much time to reason upon the matter, for, startled by a slight movement in the room directly opposite, the door of which was ajar, she thrust the letter into her pocket, and turned to see—Valencia, standing with her back to her, and arranging her hair in a mirror which hung upon the wall.

"She could not have seen me; and, even if she did, she would not suspect the truth," was the guilty woman's thought, as with the stolen missive in her pocket she went down to the parlor, and tried, by petting Anna more than her wont, to still the voice of conscience, which clamored loudly of the wrong, and urged a restoration of the letter to the place whence it was taken.

But the golden moment fled, and when, later in the evening, Anna went up to her chamber, and opened the book which the rector had brought, she never suspected how near she had been to the great happiness she had sometimes dared to hope for, or dreamed how fervently Arthur Leighton prayed that night, that if it were possible, God would grant the boon he craved above all others, —the priceless gift of Anna Ruthven's love.

CHAPTER III.

SUNDAY.

HERE was an unnatural flush on the rector's face, and his lips were very white, when he came before his people that Sunday morning, for he felt that he was approaching the crisis of his fate; that he had only to look across the row of heads, up to where Anna sat, and he should know the truth. Such thoughts savored far too much of the world which he had renounced, he knew, and he had striven to banish them from his mind; but they were there still, and would be there until he had glanced once at Anna, who was occupying her accustomed seat, and quietly turning to the chant she was so soon to sing: "Oh, come, let us sing unto the Lord; let us heartily rejoice in the strength of His salvation." The words echoed through the house, filling it with rare melody, for Anna was in perfect tone that morning, and the rector, listening to her with hands folded upon his prayer-book, felt that she could not thus "heartily rejoice," meaning all the while to darken his whole life, as she surely would if she told him "no." He was looking at her now, and she met his eyes at last, but

quickly dropped her own, while he was sure that the roses burned a little brighter on her cheek, and that her voice trembled just enough to give him hope, and help him in his fierce struggle to cast her from his mind, and think only of the solemn services in which he was engaging. He could not guess that the proud woman who had sailed so majestically into church, and followed so reverently every prescribed form, bowing in the creed far lower than ever bow was made before in Hanover, had played him false, and was the dark shadow in his path.

That day was a trying one for Arthur, for, just as the chant was ended, and the psalter was beginning, a handsome carriage dashed up to the door, and had he been wholly blind, he would have known, by the sudden sound of turning heads, and the suppressed hush which ensued, that a perfect hailstorm of dignity was entering St. Mark's.

It was the Hethertons, from Prospect Hill, whose arrival in town had been so long expected. There was Mrs. Hetherton, who, more years ago than she cared to remember, was born in Hanover, but who had lived most of her life either in Paris, New York, or New Orleans, and who this year had decided to fit up her father's old place, and honor it with her presence for a few weeks at least; also, Fanny Hetherton, a brilliant brunette, into whose intensely black eyes no one could long look, they were so bright, so piercing, and seemed so thoroughly to read one's inmost thoughts; also, Colonel Hetherton, who had served in the Mexican war, and retiring on the glory of having once led a forlorn hope, now spent his time in acting as attendant on his fashionable wife and daughter; also, young Simon Bellamy, who, while obedient to the flashing of Miss Fanny's black eyes, still found stolen opportunities for glancing at the fifth and last remaining member of the party, filing up the aisle to the large, square pew, where old Judge Howard used to sit, and which was still owned by his daughter. Mrs. Hetherton liked being late at church, and, notwithstanding that the colonel had worked himself into a tempest of excitement, had tied and untied her bonnet-strings half a dozen times, changed her rich basquine for a thread lace mantilla, and then, just as the bell from St. Mark's gave forth its last note, and her husband's impatience was oozing out in sundry little oaths, sworn under his breath, she produced and fitted on her fat, white hands a new pair of Alexanders, keeping herself as cool, and quiet, and ladylike as if outside upon the gravelled walk there was no wrathful husband threatening to drive off and leave her, if she did not "quit her cussed vanity, and come along."

Such was the Hetherton party, and they created quite as great a sensation as Mrs. Hetherton could desire, first upon the people nearest the door, who rented the cheaper pews; then upon those farther up the aisle, and then upon Mrs. Meredith, who, attracted by the rustling of heavy silk and the perfume emanating from Mrs. Hetherton's handkerchief, slightly turned her head at first, and as the party swept by, stopped her reading entirely, and involuntarily started forward, while a smile of pleasure flitted across her face as Fanny's black, saucy eyes took her, with, others, within their range of vision, and Fanny's black head nodded a quick nod of recognition. The Hethertons and Mrs. Meredith were evidently friends, and in her wonder at seeing them there, in stupid Hanover, the great lady forgot for a while to read, but kept her eyes upon them all, especially upon the fifth and last-mentioned member of the party, the graceful little blonde, whose eyes might have caught their hue from the deep blue of the summer sky, and whose long silken curls fell in a golden shower beneath the fanciful French hat. She was a beautiful young creature, and even Anna Ruthven leaned forward to look at her as she shook out her airy muslin and dropped into her seat. For a moment the little coquettish head bowed reverently, but at the first sound of the rector's voice it lifted itself up quickly, and Anna saw the bright color which rushed into her cheeks, and the eager joy which danced in the blue eyes, fixed so earnestly upon the rector, who, at sight of her, started suddenly, and paused an instant in his reading. Who was she, and what was she to Arthur Leighton, Anna asked herself, while, by the fierce pang which shot through her heart as she watched the stranger and the clergyman, she knew that *she* loved the rector of St. Mark's, even if she had doubted it before.

Anna was not an ill-tempered girl, but the sight of those gay city people annoyed her, and when, as she sang the Jubilate Deo, she saw the soft blue orbs of the blonde and the coal-black eyes of the brunette turned wonderingly towards her, she was conscious of returning their glance with as much of scorn as it was possible for her to show. Anna tried to ask forgiveness for that feeling in the prayers which followed; but when the services were over, and she saw a little figure in blue and white flitting up the aisle to where Arthur, still in his robes, stood waiting for her, an expression upon his face which she could not define she felt that she had prayed in vain; and with a bitterness she had never before experienced, she watched the meeting between them, growing more and more bitter as she saw the upturned face, the wreathing of the rose-bud lips into the sweetest of smiles, and the tiny white hand, which Arthur took and held while he spoke words she would have given much to hear.

" Why do I care ? It's nothing to me," she thought, and, with a proud step, she was leaving the church, when her aunt, who was shaking hands with the Herthertons, signed for her to join her.

The blonde was now coming down the aisle with Mr. Leighton, and joined the group just as Anna was introduced as " **My niece, Miss Anna Ruthven.**"

"Oh, you are the Anna of whom I have heard so much from Ada Fuller. You were at school together in Troy," Miss Fanny said, her searching eyes taking in every point as if she were deciding how far her new acquaintance was entitled to the praise she had heard bestowed upon her.

"I knew Miss Fuller,—yes;" and Anna bowed haughily, turning next to the blonde, Miss Lucy Harcourt, who was telling Colonel Hetherton how she had met Mr. Leighton first among the Alps, and afterwards travelled with him until their party returned to Paris, where he left them for America.

"I was never so surprised in my life as I was to find him here. Why, it actually took my breath for a moment," she went on, "and I greatly fear that, instead of listening to his sermon, I have been roaming amid that Alpine scenery, and basking again in the soft moonlight of Venice. I heard you singing, though," she said, when Anna was presented to her, "and it helped to keep up the illusion, it was so like the music heard from a gondola that night when Mr. Leighton and myself made a voyage through the streets of Venice. Oh, it was so beautiful," and the blue eyes turned to Mr. Leighton for confirmation of what the lips had uttered.

"Which was beautiful?—Miss Ruthven's singing or that moonlight night in Venice?" young Bellamy asked, smiling down upon the little lady, who still held Anna's hand, and who laughingly replied:

"Both, of course, though the singing is just now freshest in my memory, I liked it so much. You must have had splendid teachers," and she turned again to Anna, whose face was suffused with blushes as she met the rector's eyes, for to his suggestions and criticisms and teachings she owed much of that cultivation which had so pleased and surprised the stranger.

"Oh, yes, I see it was *Arthur*. He tried to train me once, and told me I had a squeak in my voice. Don't you remember?—those frightfully rainy days in Rome?" Miss Harcourt said, the *Arthur* dropping from her lips as readily as if they had always been accustomed to speak it.

She was a talkative, coquettish little lady, but there was something about her so genuine and cordial, that Anna felt the ice thawing around her heart, and even returned the pressure of the fingers which had twined themselves around her, as Lucy rattled on until the whole party left the church. It had been decided that Mrs. Meredith should call at Prospect Hill as early as Tuesday, at least; and, still holding Anna's hand, Miss Harcourt whispered to her the pleasure it would be to see her again.

"I know I am going to like you. I can tell directly I see a person,—can't I, Arthur?" and kissing her hand to Mrs. Meredith, Anna, and the rector, too, she sprang into the carriage, and was whirled rapidly away.

"Who is she?" Anna asked, and Mr. Leighton replied:

"She is an orphan niece of Colonel Hetherton's and a great heiress, I believe, though I never paid much attention to the absurd stories told concerning her wealth."

"You met in Europe," Mrs. Meredith said, and he replied:

"Yes, she has been quite an invalid, and has spent four years abroad, where I accidently met her. It was a very pleasant party, and I was induced to join it, though I was with them in all not more than four months."

He told this very rapidly, and an acute observer would have seen that he did not care particularly to talk of Lucy Harcourt, with Anna for an auditor. She was walking very demurely at his side, pondering in her mind the circumstances which could have brought the rector and Lucy Harcourt in such familiar relations as to warrant her calling him Arthur, and appearing so delighted to see him.

"Can it be there was anything between them?" she thought, and her heart began to harden against the innocent Lucy, at that very moment chatting so pleasantly of her and of Arthur, too, replying to Mrs. Hetherton, who suggested that *Mr. Leighton* would be more appropriate for a clergyman:

"I shall say Arthur, for he told me I might when we were in Rome. I could not like him as well if I called him Mr. Leighton. Isn't he splendid though in his gown, and wasn't his sermon grand?"

"What was the text?" asked Mr. Bellamy mischievously, and with a toss of her golden curls and a merry twinkle of her eyes, Lucy replied, "Simon, Simon, lovest thou me?"

Quick as a flash of lightning the hot blood mounted to his face, while Fanny cast upon him a searching glance as if she would read him through. Fanny Hetherton would have given much to know the answer which Mr. Simon Bellamy mentally gave to that question, put by one whom he had known but little more than three months. It was not fair for Lucy to steal away all Fanny's beaux, as she surely had been doing ever since her feet touched the soil of the New World, and truth to tell Fanny had borne it very well, until young Mr. Bellamy showed signs of desertion. Then the spirit of resistance was roused, and she watched her lover narrowly, gnashing her teeth sometimes when she saw his ill-concealed admiration for her sprightly little cousin, who could say and and do with perfect impunity so many things which in another would have been improper to the last degree. She was a tolerably correct reader of human nature, and from the moment she witnessed the meeting between Lucy and the rector of St. Mark's she took courage, for she readily guessed the channel in which her cousin's preference ran. The rector, however, she could not read so well; but few men she knew could withstand the fascinations of her cousin, backed as they were by the glamour of half a million; and though her mother, and possibly her father too, would be shocked at the *mesalliance* and throw obstacles in its way, she was capable of removing them all, and she would do it, too, sooner than lose the only man she had ever cared for. These were Fanny's thoughts as she rode home from church that Sunday afternoon, and by the time Prospect Hill was reached Lucy Harcourt could not have desired a more powerful ally than she possessed in the person of her resolute, strong-willed cousin.

CHAPTER IV.

BLUE MONDAY.

IT was to all intents and purposes "blue Monday" with the rector of St. Mark's, for aside from the weariness and exhaustion which always followed his two services on Sunday, and his care of the Sunday-school, there was a feeling of disquiet and depression, occasioned partly by that *rencontre* with pretty Lucy Harcourt, and partly by the uncertainty as to what Anna's answer might be. He had seen the look of displeasure on her face as she stood watching him and Lucy, and though to many this would have given hope, it only added to his nervous fears lest his suit should be denied. He was sorry that Lucy Harcourt was in the neighborhood, and sorrier still for her tenacious memory, which had evidently treasured up every incident which he could wish forgotten. With Anna Ruthven absorbing every thought and feeling of his heart, it was not pleasant to remember what had been a genuine flirtation between himself and the sparkling belle he had met among the Alps.

It was nothing but a flirtation he knew, for in his inmost soul he absolved himself from ever having had a thought of matrimony connected with Lucy Harcourt. He had admired her greatly and loved to wander with her amid the Alpine scenery, listening to her wild bursts of enthusiasm, and watching the kindling light in her blue eyes, and the color coming to her thin, pale cheeks, as she gazed upon some scene of grandeur, and clung close to him as for protection, when the path was fraught with peril.

Afterwards in Venice, beneath the influence of those glorious moonlight nights, he had been conscious of a deeper feeling, which, had he tarried longer at the syren's side, might have ripened into love. But he left her just in time to escape what he felt would have been a most unfortunate affair for him, for sweet and beautiful as she was, Lucy was not the wife for a clergyman to choose. She was not like Anna Ruthven, whom both young and old had said was so suitable for him.

"And just because she is suitable, I may not win her, perhaps," he thought, as he paced up and down his library, wondering when she would answer his letter, and wondering next how he could persuade Lucy Harcourt that between the young theological student, sailing in a gondola through the streets of Venice, and the rector of St. Mark's, there was a vast difference; that while the former might be Arthur with perfect propriety, the latter should be Mr. Leighton, in Anna's presence, at least.

And yet the rector of St. Mark's was conscious of a pleasurable emotion, even now, as he recalled the time when she had, at his request, first called him Arthur, her birdlike voice hesitating just a little, and her soft eyes looking coyly up to him, as she said:

"I am afraid that Arthur is hardly the name by which to call a clergyman."

"I am not in orders yet, so let me be Arthur to you. I love to hear you call me so, and you to me shall be Lucy," was his reply.

A mutual clasp of hands had sealed the compact, and that was the nearest to a love-making of anything which had passed between them, if we except the time when he had said good-by, and wiped away the tear which came unbidden to her eye as she told him how lonely she should be without him.

Hers was a nature as transparent as glass, and the young man, who for days had paced the ship's deck so moodily, was fighting back the thoughts which whispered that in his intercourse with her he had not been all guileless, and that if in her girlish heart there was feeling for him stronger than that of friendship, he had helped to give it life.

Time and absence and Anna Ruthven had obliterated all such thoughts till now, when Lucy herself had brought them back again with her winsome ways, and her evident intention to begin just where they had left off.

"Let Anna tell me yes, and I will at once proclaim our engagement, which will relieve me from all embarrassments in that quarter," the clergymen was thinking, just as his housekeeper came up, bringing him two notes, one in a strange handwriting, and the other in the graceful running hand which he recognized as Lucy Harcourt's.

This he opened first, reading as follows:

"PROSPECT HILL, June —."

"MR. LEIGHTON.—DEAR SIR:—Cousin Fanny is to have a picnic down in the west woods to-morrow afternoon, and she requests the pleasure of your presence. Mrs. Meredith and Miss Ruthven are to be invited. Do come. "Yours truly,
"LUCY."

Yes, he would go, and if Anna's answer did not come before, he would ask her for it. There would be plenty of opportunities down in those deep woods. On the whole, it would be pleasanter to hear the words from her own lips, and see the blushes on her cheeks when he tried to look into her eyes.

The imaginative rector could almost see those eyes,

and feel the touch of her hand as he took the other note, which Mrs. Meredith had shut herself in her room to write, and sent slyly by Valencia, who was to tell no one where she had been.

A gleam of intelligence had shone in Valencia's eyes as she took the note and carried it safely to the parsonage, never yielding to the temptation to read it as she had read the one found in her mistress's pocket, while the family were at church.

Mrs. Meredith's note was as follows:

"MY DEAR MR. LEIGHTON:—It is my niece's wish that I answer the letter you were so kind as to enclose in the book left for her last Saturday. She desires me to say that though she has a very great regard for you as her clergyman and friend, she cannot be your wife, and she regrets exceedingly if she has in any way led you to construe the interest she has always manifested in you into a deeper feeling.

"She begs me to say that it gives her great pain to refuse one as noble and good as she knows you to be, and she only does it because she cannot find in her heart the love without which no marriage can be happy.

"She is really very wretched about it, because she fears she may lose your friendship, which she prizes so much; and, as a proof that she will not, she asks that the subject may never, in any way, be alluded to; that when you meet it may be exactly as heretofore, without a word or sign on your part that you ever offered her the highest honor a man can offer a woman.

"And I am sure, my dear Mr. Leighton, that you will accede to her wishes. I am very sorry it has occurred, sorry for you both, and especially sorry for you; but believe me, you will get over it in time, and come to see that my niece is not a proper person to be a clergyman's wife.

"Come and see us as usual. You will find Anna appearing very natural.

"Yours cordially and sincerely,
"JULIE MEREDITH."

This was the letter which the cruel woman had written, and it dropped from the rector's fingers, as, with a groan, he bent his head upon the back of a chair, and tried to realize the magnitude of the blow which had fallen so suddenly upon him. Not till now did he realize how, amid all his doubts, he had still been sure of winning her, and the shock was terrible.

He had staked his all on Anna, and lost it; the world, which before had been so bright, looked very dreary now, while he felt that he could never again come before his people weighed down with so great a load of pain and humiliation; for it touched the young man's pride that, not content to refuse him, Anna had chosen another than herself as the medium through which her refusal must be conveyed to him. He did not fancy Mrs. Meredith. He would rather she did not possess his secret, and it hurt him to know that she did.

It was a bitter hour for the clergyman, for strong and clear as was his faith in God, he lost sight of it for a time, and poor, weak human nature cried :

" It's more than I can bear."

But as the mother does not forget her child, even though she passes from its sight, so God had not forgotten, and the darkness broke at last and the lips could pray again for strength to bear and faith to do all that God might require.

"Though He slay me I will trust Him," came like a ray of sunlight into the rector's mind ; and ere the day was over he could say with a full heart, " Thy will be done."

He was very pale, and his lip quivered occasionally as he thought of all he had lost, while a blinding headache, induced by strong excitement, drove him nearly wild with pain. He had been subject to headaches all his life, but he had never suffered as he was suffering now but once, and that on a rainy day in Rome, when, boasting of her mesmeric power, Lucy had stood by him, and passed her hands soothingly across his throbbing temples.

How soft and cool they were,—but they had not thrilled him as the touch of Anna's did when they hung the Christmas wreaths and she wore that bunch of scarlet berries in her hair.

That time seemed very far away, farther even than Rome and the moonlight nights of Venice. He did not like to think of it, for the bright hopes which were budding then were blighted now, and dead; and with a moan, he laid his aching head upon his pillow, and tried to forget all he had ever hoped or longed for in the future.

"She will marry Thornton Hastings. He is a more eligible match than a poor clergyman," he said, and then, as he remembered Thornton's letter, and that his man Thomas would be coming soon to ask if there were letters to be taken to the office, he arose, and going to the study table, wrote hastily:

"DEAR THORNE:—I am suffering from one of those horrid headaches which used to make me as weak and helpless as a woman, but I will write just enough to say that I have no claim on Anna Ruthven, and you are free to press your suit as urgently as you please. She is a noble girl, worthy even to be Mrs. Thornton Hastings, and if I cannot have her, I would rather give her to you than any one I know. Only don't ask me to perform the ceremony.

"There, I've let the secret out, but no matter, I have always confided in you, and so I may as well confess that I have offered myself and been refused.

"Yours truly,
"ARTHUR LEIGHTON."

The rector felt better after that letter was written. He had told his grievance to some one, and it seemed to have lightened half the load.

"Thorne is a good fellow," he said, as he directed the letter. "A little fast, it's true, but a splendid fellow after all. He will sympathize with me in his way, and I would rather give Anna to him than any other living man."

Arthur was serious in what he said, for, wholly unlike as they were, there was between him and Thornton Hastings one of those strong friendships which sometimes exist between two men, but rarely between two women, of so widely different temperaments. They had roomed together four years in college, and countless were the difficulties from which the sober Arthur had extricated the luckless Thorne, while many a time the rather slender means of Arthur had been increased in a way so delicate that expostulation was next to impossible.

Arthur was better off now in worldly goods, for by the death of an uncle he had come in possession of a few thousand dollars, which had enabled him to travel in Europe for a year, and left a surplus, from which he fed the poor and needy with no sparing hand

St. Mark's was his first parish, and though he could have chosen one nearer to New York, where the society was more congenial to his taste, he had accepted of what God offered to him, and had been very happy there since

Anna Ruthven came home from Troy and made such havoc with his heart. He did not believe he should ever be quite so happy again, but he would try to do his work, and take thankfully whatever of good might come to him.

This was his final decision, and when at last he laid down to rest, the wound, though deep and sore, and bleeding yet, was not quite as hard to bear as it had been earlier in the day, when it was fresh and raw, and faith and hope seemed swept away.

CHAPTER V.

TUESDAY.

THAT open grassy spot in the dense shadow of the west woods was just the place for a picnic, and it looked very bright and pleasant that warm June afternoon, with the rustic table so fancifully arranged, the camp-stools scattered over the lawn, and the bouquets of flowers depending from the trees.

Fanny Hetherton had given it her whole care, aided and abetted by Mr. Bellamy, what time he could spare from Lucy, who, endued with a mortal fear of insects, seemed this day to gather scores of bugs and worms upon her dress and hair, screaming with every worm, and bringing Simon obediently to her aid.

"I'd stay at home, I think, if I was silly enough to be afraid of a harmless caterpillar like that," Fanny had said, as with her own hands she took from Lucy's curls and threw away a thousand-legged thing, the very sight of which made poor Lucy shiver, but did not send her to the house.

She was too much interested and too eagerly expectant of what the afternoon would bring, and so she perched herself upon the fence where nothing but ants could molest her, and finished the bouquets which Fanny hung upon the trees until the lower limbs seemed one mass of blossoms and the air was filled with the sweet perfume.

Lucy was bewitchingly beautiful that afternoon in her dress of white, with her curls tied up with a blue ribbon, and her fair arms bare nearly to the shoulders. Fanny, whose arms were neither plump nor white, had expostulated with her cousin upon this style of dress, suggesting that one as delicate as she could not fail to take a heavy cold when the dews began to fall; but Lucy would not listen. Arthur Leighton had told her once that he liked her with bare arms, and bare they should be. She was bending every energy to please and captivate him, and a cold was of no consequence provided she succeeded. So like some little fairy, she danced and flitted about, making fearful havoc with Mr. Bellamy's wits, and greatly vexing Fanny, who hailed with delight the arrival of Mrs. Meredith and Anna. The latter was very pretty and very becomingly attired in a light, airy dress of blue, finished at the throat and wrists with an edge of soft, fine lace. She, too, had thought of Arthur in the making of her toilet, and it was for him that the white rose-buds were placed in her heavy braids of hair, and fastened on her belt. She was very sorry that she had allowed herself to be vexed with Lucy Harcourt for her familiarity with Mr. Leighton, very hopeful that he had not observed it, and very certain now of his preference for herself. She would be very gracious that afternoon, she thought, and not one bit jealous of Lucy, though she called him Arthur a hundred times.

Thus it was in the most amiable of moods that Anna appeared upon the lawn, where she was warmly welcomed by Lucy, who, seizing both her hands, led her away to see their arrangements, chatting gayly all the time, and casting rapid glances up the lane as if in quest of some one.

"I'm so glad you've come. I've thought of you so much. Do you know it seems to me there must be some bond of sympathy between us, or I should not like you so well at once. I drove by the rectory early this morning, the dearest little place, with such a lovely garden. Arthur was working in it, and I made him give me some roses. See, I have one in my curls. Then, when he brought them to the carriage, I kept him there while I asked numberless questions about you, and heard from him just how good you are, and how you help him in the Sunday-school and everywhere, visiting the poor, picking up ragged children, and doing things I never thought of doing; but I am not going to be so useless any longer, and the next time you visit some of the very miserablest, I want you to take me with you.

"Do you ever meet Arthur there? Oh, here he

comes," and with a bound, Lucy darted away from Anna towards the spot where the rector stood receiving Mrs. and Miss Hetherton's greeting.

As Lucy had said, she had driven by the rectory, with no earthly object but the hope of seeing the rector, and had hurt him cruelly with her questionings of Anna, and annoyed him a little with her anxious inquiries as to the cause of his pallid face and sunken eyes; but she was so bewitchingly pretty, and so thoroughly kind withal, that he could not be annoyed long, and he felt better for having seen her bright, coquettish face, and listened to her childish prattle. It was a great trial for him to attend the picnic that afternoon, but he met it bravely, and schooled himself to appear as if there were no such things in the world as aching hearts and cruel disappointments. His face was very pale, but his recent headache would account for that, and he acted his part successfully, shivering a little, it is true, when Anna expressed her sorrow that he should suffer so often from these attacks, and suggested that he take a short vacation and go with them to Saratoga.

"I should so much like to have you," she said, and her clear honest eyes looked him straight in the face, as she asked why he could not.

"What does she mean?" the rector thought. "Is she trying to tantalize me? I expected her to be *natural*, as her aunt laid great stress on that, but she need not overdo the matter by showing me how little she cares for having hurt me so."

Then, as a flash of pride came to his aid, he thought, "I will at least be even with her. She shall not have the satisfaction of guessing how much I suffer," and as Lucy then called to him from the opposite side of the lawn, he asked Anna to accompany him thither, just as he would have done a week before. Once that afternoon he found himself alone with her in a quiet part of the woods, where the long branches of a great oak came nearly to the ground, and formed a little bower which looked so inviting that Anna sat down upon the gnarled roots of the tree, and tossing her hat upon the grass, exclaimed, "How nice and pleasant it is in here. Come sit down, too, while I tell you again about my class in Sunday-school, and that poor Mrs. Hobbs across the mill-stream. You won't forget her, will you? I told her you would visit her the oftener when I was gone. Do you know she cried because I was going? It made me feel so badly that I doubted if it was right for me to go," and pulling down a handful of the oak-leaves above her head, Anna began weaving a chaplet, while the rector stood watching her with a puzzled expression upon his face. She did not act as if she ever could have dictated that letter, but he had no suspicion of the truth, and answered rather coldly, "I did not suppose you cared how much we might miss you at home."

Something in his tone made Anna look up into his face, and her eyes immediately filled with tears, for she knew that in some way she had displeased him.

"Then you mistake me," she replied, the tears still glittering on her long eyelashes, and her fingers trembling among the oaken leaves. "I do care whether I am missed or not."

"Missed by whom?" the rector asked, and Anna impetuously replied, "Missed by the parish poor, and by you, too, Mr. Leighton. You don't know how often I shall think of you, or how sorry I am that—"

She did not finish the sentence, for the rector had leaped madly at a conclusion, and was down in the grass at her side with both her hands in his.

"Anna, O Anna," he began so pleadingly, "have you repented of your decision? Tell me that you have and it will make me so happy. I have been so wretched ever since."

She thought he meant her decision about going to Saratoga, and she replied, "I have not repented, Mr. Leighton. Aunt Meredith thinks it's best, and so do I, though I am sorry for you, if you really do care so much."

Anna was talking blindly, her thoughts upon one subject, while the rector's were upon another, and matters were getting somewhat mixed when, "Arthur, Arthur, where are you?" came ringing through the woods, and Lucy Harcourt appeared, telling them that the refreshments were ready. "We are only waiting for you two, wondering where you had gone, but never dreaming that you had stolen away to make love," she said playfully, adding more earnestly as she saw the traces of agitation visible in Anna's face, "and I do believe you were. If so, I beg pardon for my intrusion."

She spoke a little sharply, and glanced inquiringly at Mr. Leighton, who, feeling that he had virtually been repulsed a second time by Anna, answered her, "On the contrary, I am very glad you came, and so I am sure is Miss Anna. I am ready to join you at the table. Come, Anna, they are waiting," and he offered his arm to the bewildered girl, who replied, "Not just now, please. Leave me for a moment. I won't be long."

Very curiously Lucy looked at Anna, and then at Mr. Leighton, who, fully appreciating the feelings of the latter, said, by way of explanation, "You see she has not quite finished that chaplet which I suspect is intended for you. I think we had better leave her," and drawing Lucy's arm under his own, he walked away, leaving Anna more stunned and pained than she had ever been before. Surely if *love* had ever spoken in voice and manner, it had spoken when Mr. Leighton was kneeling on the grass, holding her hands in his. "Anna, O Anna;" how she had thrilled at the sound of those words and waited for what might follow next. Why had his manner changed so suddenly, and why had he been so glad to be interrupted. Had he really no intention of making love to her ; and if so, why did he rouse her hopes so suddenly and then cruelly dash them to the ground? Was it that he loved Lucy best, and that the sight of her froze the words upon his lips ?

" Let him take her, then. He is welcome for all of me," she thought; and as a keen pang of shame and disappointment swept over her, she laid her head for a moment upon the grass and wept bitterly. " He must have seen what I expected, and I care most for that," she sobbed, resolving henceforth to guard herself at every point, and do all that lay in her power to further Lucy's interests. " He will thus see how little I really care," she said, and lifting up her head she tore in fragments the wreath she had been making but which she could not now place on the head of her rival.

Mr. Leighton was flirting terribly with Lucy when she joined the party assembled around the table, and he never once looked at Anna, though he saw that her plate was well supplied with the best of everything, and when at one draught she drained her glass of ice-water, he quietly placed another within her reach, standing a little before her and trying evidently to shield her from too critical observation. There were two at least who were glad when the picnic was over, and various were the private opinions of the company with regard to the entertainment. Mr. Bellamy, who had been repeatedly foiled in his attempts to be especially attentive to Lucy Harcourt, pronounced the whole thing "a bore," Fanny, who had been highly displeased with his deportment, came to the conclusion that the enjoyment did not compensate for all the trouble; and while the rector thought he had never spent a more thoroughly wretched day, and Anna would have given worlds if she had stayed at home, Lucy declared that never in her life had she had so perfectly delightful a time, always excepting, of course, " that moon light sail in Venice."

CHAPTER VI.

WEDNESDAY.

THERE was a heavy shower the night succeeding the picnic, and the morning following was as balmy and bright as June mornings are wont to be after a fall of rain. They were always early risers at the farmhouse, but this morning Anna, who had slept but little, arose earlier than usual, and leaning from the window to inhale the bracing air and gather a bunch of roses fresh with the glittering rain-drops, felt her spirits grow lighter, and wondered at her discomposure of the previous day. Particularly was she grieved that she should have harbored a feeling of bitterness towards Lucy Harcourt, who was not to blame for having won the love she had been foolish enough to covet.

"He knew her first," she said, "and if he has since been pleased with me, the sight of her has won him back to his allegiance, and it is right. She is a pretty creature, but strangely unsuited, I fear, to be his wife," and then, as she remembered Lucy's wish to go with her when next she visited the poor, she said :

"I'll take her to see the Widow Hobbs. That will

give her some idea of the duties which will devolve upon her as a rector's wife. I can go directly there from Prospect Hill, where, I suppose, I must call with Aunt Meredith."

Anna made herself believe that in doing this she was acting only from a magnanimous desire to fit Lucy for her work, if, indeed, she was to be Arthur's wife,—that in taking the mantle from her own shoulders, and wrapping it around her rival, she was doing a most amiable deed, when down in her inmost heart, where the tempter had put it, there was an unrecognized wish to see how the little dainty girl would shrink from the miserable abode, and recoil from the touch of the dirty hands, which were sure to be laid upon her dress if the children were at home, and she waited impatiently to start on her errand of mercy.

It was four o'clock when, with her aunt, she arrived at Colonel Hetherton's, and found the family assembled upon the broad piazza,—Mr. Bellamy dutifully holding the skein of worsted from which Miss Fanny was crocheting, and Lucy playing with a kitten, whose movements were scarcely more graceful than her own, as she sprang up and ran to welcome Anna.

"Oh yes; I shall be delighted to go with you. Pray let us start at once," she exclaimed, when after a few moments' conversation Anna told where she was going.

Lucy was very gayly dressed, and Anna smiled to her

self as she imagined the startling effect the white muslin and bright ribbons would have upon the inmates of the shanty where they were going. There was a remonstrance from Mrs. Hetherton against her niece walking so far, and Mrs. Meredith suggested that they should ride, but to this Lucy objected. She meant to take Anna's place among the poor when she was gone, she said, and how was she ever to do it if she could not walk so little ways as that. Anna, too, was averse to the riding, and felt a kind of grim satisfaction when, after a time, the little figure, which at first had skipped along with all the airiness of a bird, began to lag, and even pant for breath, as the way grew steeper and the path more stony and rough. Anna's evil spirit was in the ascendant that afternoon, steeling her heart against Lucy's doleful exclamations, as one after another her delicate slippers were torn, and the sharp thistles, of which the path was full, penetrated to her soft flesh. Straight and unbending as a young Indian, Anna walked on, shutting her ears against the sighs of weariness which reached them from time to time. But when there came a half-sobbing cry of actual pain, she stopped suddenly and turned towards Lucy, whose breath came gaspingly, and whose cheeks were almost purple with the exertions she had made.

"I cannot go any farther until I rest," she said, sinking down exhausted upon a large flat rock beneath a walnut-tree.

Touched with pity at the sight of the heated face, from which the sweat was dripping, Anna too sat down beside her, and laying the curly head in her lap, she hated herself cordially, as Lucy said :

"You've walked so fast I could not keep up. You do not know, perhaps, how weak I am, and how little it takes to tire me. They say my heart is diseased, and an unusual excitement might kill me."

"No, oh no!" Anna answered with a shudder, as she thought of what might have been the result of her rashness, and then she smoothed the wet hair, which, dried by the warm sunbeams, coiled itself up in golden masses, which her fingers softly threaded.

"I did not know it until that time in Venice when Arthur talked to me so good, trying to make me feel that it was not hard to die, even if I was so young and the world so full of beauty," Lucy went on, her voice sounding very low, and her bright shoulder-knots of ribbon trembling with the rapid beating of her heart. "When he was talking to me I could be almost willing to die, but the moment he was gone the doubts and fears came back, and death was terrible again. I was always better with Arthur. Everybody is, and I think your seeing so much of him is one reason why you are so good."

"No, no, I am not good," and Anna's hands pressed hard upon the girlish head lying in her lap. "I am wicked beyond what you can guess. I led you this rough way when I might have chosen a smooth though longer road, and walked so fast on purpose to worry you."

"To worry *me*. Why should you wish to do that?" and lifting up her head, Lucy looked wonderingly at the conscience-stricken Anna, who could not confess to the jealousy, but who in all other respects answered truthfully : "I think an evil spirit possessed me for a time, and I wanted to show you that it was not so nice to visit the poor as you seemed to think, but I am sorry, oh so sorry, and you'll forgive me, won't you?"

A loving kiss was pressed upon her lips and a warm cheek was laid against her own, as Lucy said, "Of course I'll forgive you, though I do not quite understand why you should wish to discourage me or tease me either, when I liked you so much from the first moment I heard your voice, and saw you in the choir. You don't dislike me, do you?"

"No, oh no. I love you very dearly," Anna replied, her tears falling like rain upon the slight form she hugged so passionately to her, and which she would willingly have borne in her arms the remainder of the way, as a kind of penance for her past misdeeds; but Lucy was much better, and so the two, between whom there was now a bond of love which nothing could sever, went on together to the low dismal house where the Widow Hobbs lived.

The gate was off the hinges, and Lucy's muslin was

torn upon a nail as she passed through, while the long fringe of her fleecy shawl was caught in the tall tufts of thistle growing by the path. In a muddy pool of water, a few rods from the house, a flock of ducks were swimming, pelted occasionally by the group of dirty, ragged children playing on the grass, and who, at sight of the strangers and the basket Anna carried, sprang up like a flock of pigeons, and came trooping towards her. It was not the sweet, pastoral scene which Lucy had pictured to herself, with Arthur for the background, and her ardor was greatly dampened even before the threshold was crossed, and she stood in the low, close room where the sick woman lay, her eyes unnaturally bright, and turned wistfully upon them as she entered. There were ashes upon the hearth and ashes upon the floor, a hair-brush upon the table and an empty plate upon the chair, with swarms of flies sipping the few drops of molasses and feeding upon the crumbs of bread left there by the elfish-looking child now in the bed beside its mother. There was nothing but poverty,—squalid, disgusting poverty, visible everywhere, and Lucy grew sick and faint at the, to her, unusual sight.

"They have not lived here long. We only found them three weeks ago; they will look better by and by," Anna whispered, feeling that some apology was necessary for the destitution and filth visible everywhere.

Daintily removing the plate to the table, and carefully

tucking up her skirts, Lucy sat down upon the wooden chair and looked dubiously on while Anna made the sick woman more tidy in appearance, and then fed her from the basket of provisions which Grandma Humphreys had sent.

"I never could do that," Lucy thought, as shoving off the little dirty hand fingering her shoulder-knots she watched Anna washing the poor woman's face, and bending over her pillow as unhesitatingly as if it had been covered with ruffled linen like those at Prospect Hill, instead of the coarse soiled rag which hardly deserved the name of pillow-case. "No, I never could do that," and the possible life with Arthur which the maiden had more than once imagined began to look very dreary, when suddenly a shadow darkened the door, and Lucy knew before she turned her head that the rector was standing at her back, and the blood tingled through her veins with a delicious feeling; as, laying both his hands upon her shoulders, and bending over her so that she felt his breath upon her brow, he said:

"What, my lady Lucy here? I hardly expected to find two ministering angels, though I was almost sure of one," and his eye rested on Anna with a wistful look of tenderness, which neither she nor Lucy saw.

"Then you knew she was coming," Lucy said, an uneasy thought flashing across her mind as she remembered the picnic, and the scene she had stumbled upon.

But Arthur's reply, "I did not know she was coming; I only knew it was like her," reassured her for a time, making her resolve to emulate the virtues which Arthur seemed to prize so highly. What a difference his presence made in that wretched room. She did not mind the poverty now, or care if her dress was stained with the molasses left in the chair, and the inquisitive child with tattered gown and bare, brown legs was welcome to examine and admire the bright plaid ribbons as much as she chose.

Lucy had no thought for anything but Arthur, and the subdued expression of his face, as kneeling by the sick woman's bedside he said the prayers she had hungered for more than for the contents of Anna's basket, which were now purloined by the children crouched upon the hearth and fighting over the last bit of gingerbread.

"Hush-sh, little one," and Lucy's hand rested on the head of the principal belligerent, who, awed by the beauty of her face and the authoritative tone of her voice, kept quiet till the prayer was over and Arthur had risen from his knees.

"Thank you, Lucy; I think I must constitute you my deaconess when Miss Ruthven is gone. Your very presence has a subduing effect upon the little savages. I never knew them so quiet before so long a time," Arthur said to Lucy in a low tone, which, low as it was, reached

Anna's ear, but brought no pang of jealousy or sharp regret for what she felt was lost forever.

She was giving Lucy to Arthur Leighton, resolving that by every means in her power she would further her rival's cause, and the hot tears which dropped so fast upon Mrs. Hobbs's pillow while Arthur said the prayer were but the baptism of that vow, and not, as Lucy thought, because she felt so sorry for the suffering woman who had brought so much comfort to her.

"God bless you wherever you go," she said, "and if there is any great good which you desire, may He bring it to pass."

"He never will,—no, never," was the sad response in Anna's heart, as she joined the clergyman and Lucy, who were standing outside the door, the former pointing to the ruined slippers, and asking her how she ever expected to walk home in such dilapidated things.

"I shall certainly have to carry you," he said, "or your blistered feet will evermore be thrust forward as a reason why you cannot be my deaconess."

He seemed to be in unusual spirits that afternoon, and the party went gayly on, Anna keeping a watchful care over Lucy, picking out the smoothest places, and passing her arm round her waist as they were going up a hill.

"I think it would be better if you both leaned on me," the rector said, offering each an arm, and apologizing for not having thought to do so before.

"I do not need it, thank you, but Miss Harcourt does. I fear she is very tired," said Anna, pointing to Lucy's face, which was so white and ghastly and so like the face seen once before in Venice, that without another word, Arthur took the tired girl in his strong arms and carried her safely to the summit of the hill.

"Please put me down; I can walk now," Lucy pleaded; but Arthur felt the rapid beatings of her heart, and kept her in his arms until they reached Prospect Hill, were Mrs. Meredith was anxiously awaiting their return, her brow clouding with distrust when she saw Mr. Leighton, for she was constantly fearing lest her guilty secret should be exposed.

"I'll leave Hanover this very week, and remove her from danger," she thought, as she rose to say good-night.

"Just wait a minute, please. There's something I want to say to Miss Ruthven," Lucy cried, and leading Anna to her own room, she knelt down by her side, and looking up in her face, began:

"There's one question which I wish to ask, and you must answer me truly. It is rude and inquisitive, perhaps, but,—tell me,—has Arthur—ever—ever—"

Anna guessed what was coming, and with a sob, which Lucy thought was a long-drawn breath, she kissed the pretty, parted lips, and answered:

"No, darling, Arthur never did, and never will, but

some time he will ask you to be his wife. I can see it coming so plain."

Poor Anna! her heart gave one great throb as she said this, and then lay like a dead weight in her bosom, while with sparkling eyes and blushing cheeks, Lucy exclaimed:

"I am so glad,—so glad. I have only known you since Sunday, but you seem like an old friend, and you won't mind my telling you that ever since I first met Arthur among the Alps, I have lived in a kind of ideal world, of which he was the centre. I am an orphan, you know, and an heiress, too. There is half a million, they say; and Uncle Hetherton has charge of it. Now, will you believe me, when I say that I would give every dollar of this for Arthur's love if I could not have it without?"

"I do believe you," Anna replied, inexpressibly glad that the gathering darkness hid her white face from view as the childlike, unsuspecting girl went on: "The world, I know, would say that a poor clergyman was not a good match for me, but I do not care for that. Cousin Fanny favors it, I am sure, and Uncle Hetherton would not oppose me when he saw I was in earnest. Once the world, which is a very meddlesome thing, picked out Thornton Hastings, of New York, for me; but my! he was too proud and lofty even to talk to me much, and I would not speak to him after I heard of his saying that

'I was a pretty little plaything, but far too frivolous for a sensible man to make his wife.' Oh, wasn't I angry though, and don't I hope that when he gets a wife she will be exactly such a frivolous thing as I am."

Even through the darkness Anna could see the blue eyes flash, and the delicate nostrils dilate as Lucy gave vent to her wrath against the luckless Thornton Hastings.

"You will meet him at Saratoga. He is always there in the summer, but don't you speak to him, *the hateful*. He'll be calling you frivolous next."

An amused smile flitted across Anna's face as she asked, "But won't you too be at Saratoga? I supposed you were all going there."

"*Cela depend*," Lucy replied. "I would so much rather stay here, the dressing, and dancing, and flirting tire me so, and then you know what Arthur said about taking me for his deaconess in your place."

There was a call just then from the hall below. Mrs. Meredith was getting impatient of the delay, and with a good-by kiss, Anna went down the stairs, and stood out upon the piazza, where her aunt was waiting. Mr. Leighton had accepted Fanny's invitation to stay to tea, and he handed the ladies to their carriage, lingering a moment while he said his parting words, for he was going out of town to-morrow, and when he returned Anna would be gone.

"You will think of us sometimes," he said, still holding Anna's hand. "St. Mark's will be lonely without you. God bless you and bring you safely back."

There was a pressure of the hand, a lifting of Arthur's hat, and then the carriage moved away; but Anna, looking back, saw Arthur standing by Lucy's side, fastening a rose-bud in her hair, and at that sight the gleam of hope which for an instant had crept into her heart passed away with a sigh.

CHAPTER VII.

AT NEWPORT.

MOVED by a strange impulse, Thornton Hastings took himself and his fast bays to Newport instead of Saratoga, and thither, the first week in August, came Mrs. Meredith, with eight large trunks, her niece, and her niece's wardrobe, which had cost the pretty sum of eighteen hundred dollars.

Mrs. Meredith was not naturally lavish of her money, except where her own interests were concerned, as they were in Anna's case. Conscious of having come between her niece and the man she loved, she determined that in the procuring of a substitute for this man, no advantages which dress could afford should be lacking. Besides, Thornton Hastings was a perfect connoisseur in everything pertaining to a lady's toilet, and it was with him and his preference before her mind that Mrs. Meredith opened her purse so widely and bought so extensively. There were sun hats and round hats, and hats *à la cavalier*,—there were bonnets and veils, and dresses, and shawls of every color and kind, with the lesser matters of sashes, and gloves, and slippers, and fans, the whole making an array such as Anna had never seen before, and from which she had at first shrank back appalled and dismayed. But she was not now quite so much of a novice as when she first reached New York, the Saturday following the picnic at Prospect Hill. She had passed successfully and safely through the hands of mantua-makers, milliners, and hair-dressers since then. She had laid aside every article brought from home. She wore her hair in puffs and waterfalls, and her dresses in the latest mode. She had seen the fashionable world as represented at Saratoga, and sickening at the sight, had gladly acquiesced in her aunt's proposal to go on to Newport, where the air was purer, and the hotels not so densely packed. She had been called a beauty and a belle, but her heart was longing still for the leafy woods and fresh, green fields of Hanover; and Newport, she fancied, would be more like the country than sultry, crowded Saratoga, and never since leaving home had she looked so bright and pretty as the evening after her arrival at the Ocean House, when, invigorated by the bath she had taken in the morning, and gladdened by sight of the glorious sea and the soothing tones it murmured in her ear, she came down to the parlor, clad in simple white, with only a bunch of violets in her hair, and no other ornament than the handsome pearls her aunt had given to her. Standing at the open window, with the drapery of the lace curtain sweeping gracefully behind her, she did not look much like the Anna who led the choir in Hanover and visited the Widow Hobbs, nor yet much like the picture which Thornton Hastings had formed of the girl who he knew was there for his inspection. He had been absent the entire day, and had not seen Mrs. Meredith, when she arrived early in the morning, but he found her card in his room, and a smile curled his lip as he said:

" And so I have not escaped her."

Thornton Hastings had proved a most treacherous knight, and overthrown his general's plans entirely. Arthur's letter had affected him strangely, for he readily guessed how deeply wounded his sensitive friend had been by Anna Ruthven's refusal, while added to this was a fear lest Anna had been influenced by a thought of himself, and what might possibly result from an acquaintance. Thornton Hastings had been flattered and angled for until he had grown somewhat vain, and it did not strike him as at all improbable that the unsophisticated Anna should have designs upon him.

" But I won't give her a chance," he said, when he finished Arthur's letter. " I thought once I might like her, but I shan't, and I'll be revenged on her for refusing the best man that ever breathed. I'll go to Newport instead of Saratoga, and so be clear of the entire Meredith clique, the Hethertons, the little Harcourt, and all."

This, then, was the secret of his being at the Ocean House. He was keeping away from Anna Ruthven, who never had heard of him but once, and that from Lucy Harcourt. After that scene in the Glen, where Anna had exclaimed against intriguing mothers and their bold, shame-faced daughters, Mrs. Meredith had been too wise a manœuvrer to mention Thornton Hastings, so that Anna was wholly ignorant of his presence at Newport, and looked up in unfeigned surprise at the tall, elegant man whom her aunt presented as Mr. Hastings. With all Thornton's affected indifference, there was still a curiosity to see the girl who could say "no" to Arthur Leighton, and he did not wait long after receiving Mrs. Meredith's card before going down to find her.

"That's the girl, I'll lay a wager," he thought of a high-colored, showily dressed hoyden, who was whirling around the room with Ned Peters, from Boston, and whose corn-colored dress swept against his boots as he entered the parlor.

How, then, was he disappointed in the apparition Mrs. Meredith presented as "my niece," the modest, self-possessed young girl, whose cheeks grew not a whit the redder, and whose pulse did not quicken at the sight of him, though a gleam of something like curiosity shone in the brown eyes which scanned him so quietly. She was thinking of Lucy, and her injunction "not to speak to the *hateful* if she saw him;" but she did speak to him, and Mrs. Meredith fanned herself complacently as she saw how fast they became acquainted.

"You don't dance," Mr. Hastings said, as she declined an invitation from Ned Peters, whom she had met at Saratoga. "I am glad, for you will perhaps walk with me outside upon the piazza. You won't take cold, I think," and he glanced thoughtfully at the white neck and shoulders gleaming beneath the gauzy muslin.

Mrs. Meredith was in rhapsodies, and sat a full hour with the tiresome dowagers around her, while up and down the broad piazza Thornton Hastings walked with Anna, talking to her as he seldom talked to women, and feeling greatly surprised to find that what he said was fully appreciated and understood. That he was pleased with her he could not deny to himself, as he sat alone in his room that night, feeling more and more how keenly Arthur Leighton must have felt her refusal.

"But why did she refuse him?" he wished he knew, and ere he slept he resolved to study Anna Ruthven closely, and ascertain, if possible, the motive which prompted her to discard a man like Arthur Leighton.

The next day brought the Hetherton party, all but Lucy Harcourt, who, Fanny laughingly said, was just now suffering from clergyman on the brain, and, as a certain cure for the disease, had turned my Lady Bountiful, and was playing the pretty patroness to all Mr. Leighton's parishioners, especially a Widow Hobbs, whom she had actually taken to ride in the carriage, and to whose ragged children she had sent a bundle of cast-off party dresses; and the tears ran down Fanny's cheeks as she described the appearance of the elder Hobbs, who came to church with a soiled pink silk skirt, her black, tattered petticoat hanging down below, and one of Lucy's opera hoods upon her head.

"And the clergyman on her brain? Does he appreciate his situation? I have an interest there. He is an old friend of mine," Thornton Hastings asked.

He had been an amused listener to Fanny's gay badinage, laughing merrily at the idea of Lucy's taking an old woman out to air, and clothing her children in party dresses. His opinion of Lucy, as she had said, was that she was a pretty but frivolous plaything, and it showed upon his face as he asked the question he did, watching Anna furtively as Fanny replied:

"Oh yes, he is certainly smitten, and I must say I never saw Lucy so thoroughly in earnest. Why, she really seems to enjoy travelling all over Christendom to find the hovels and huts, though she is mortally afraid of the small-pox, and always carries with her a bit of chloride of lime as a disinfecting agent. I am sure she ought to win the parson. And so you know him, do you?"

"Yes; we were in college together, and I esteem him

so highly that, had I a sister, there is no man living to whom I would so readily give her as to him."

He was looking now at Anna, whose face was very pale, and who pressed a rose she held so tightly that the sharp thorns pierced her flesh, and a drop of blood stained the whiteness of her hand.

"See, you have hurt yourself," Mr. Hastings said. "Come to the water-pitcher and wash the stain away."

She went with him mechanically, and let him hold her hand in his while he wiped off the blood with his own handkerchief, treating her with a tenderness for which he could hardly account. He pitied her, and suspected she had repented of her rashness, and because he pitied her he asked her to ride with him that day after the fast bays, of which he had written to Arthur. Many admiring eyes were cast after them as they drove away, and Mrs. Hetherton whispered softly to Mrs. Meredith:

"A match in progress, I see. You have done well for your charming niece."

And yet matrimony, as concerned himself, was very far from Thornton Hastings' thoughts that afternoon, when, because he saw that it pleased Anna to have him do so, he talked to her of Arthur, hoping, in his unselfish heart, that what he said in his praise might influence her to reconsider her decision and give him a different answer. This was the second day of Thornton Hastings' acquaintance with Anna Ruthven, but as time went on, bringing the usual routine of life at Newport, the drives, the rides, the pleasant piazza talks, and the quiet moonlight rambles, when Anna was always his companion, Thornton Hastings came to feel an unwillingness to surrender even to Arthur Leighton the beautiful girl who pleased him better than any one he had known.

Mrs. Meredith's plans were working well, and so, though the autumn days had come, and one after another the devotees of fashion were dropping off, she lingered on, and Thornton Hastings still rode and walked with Anna Ruthven, until there came a night when they wandered farther than usual from the hotel, and sat down together on a height of land which overlooked the placid waters, where the moonlight lay softly sleeping. It was a most lovely night, and for awhile they listened in silence to the music of the sea, and then talked of the breaking-up which would come in a few days, when the hotel was to be closed, and wondered if next year they would come again to the old haunts and find them unchanged.

There was witchery in the hour, and Thornton felt its spell, speaking out at last, and asking Anna if she would be his wife. He would shield her so tenderly, he said, protecting her from every care, and making her as happy as love and money could make her. Then he told her of his home in the far-off city, which needed only her presence to make it a paradise, and then he waited for her answer, watching anxiously the limp, white hands, which, when he first began to talk, had fallen helplessly upon her lap, and then had crept up to her face, which was turned away from him, so that he could not see its expression, or guess at the struggle going on in Anna's mind. She was not wholly surprised, for she could not mistake the nature of the interest which, for the last two weeks, Thornton Hastings had manifested in her. But now that the moment had come, it seemed to her that she had never expected it, and she sat silent for a time, dreading so much to speak the words which she knew would inflict pain on one whom she respected so highly, but whom she could not marry.

"Don't you like me, Anna?" Thornton asked at last, his voice very low and tender, as he bent over her and tried to take her hand.

"Yes, very much," she answered; and emboldened by her reply, Thornton lifted up her head, and was about to kiss her forehead, when she started away from him, exclaiming:

"No, Mr. Hastings. You must not do that. I cannot be your wife. It hurts me to tell you so, for I believe you are sincere in your proposal; but it can never be. Forgive me, and let us both forget this wretched summer."

"It has not been wretched to me. It has been a very happy summer, since I knew you at least," Mr. Hastings said, and then he asked again that she should reconsider her decision. He could not take it as her final one. He had loved her too much, had thought too much of making her his own, to give her up so easily, he said, urging so many reasons why she should think again, that Anna said to him, at last:

".If you would rather have it so, I will wait a month, but you must not hope that my answer will be different then from what it is to-night. I want your friendship, though, the same as if this had never happened. I like you, because you have been kind to me, and made my stay in Newport so much pleasanter than I thought it could be. You have not talked to me like other men. You have treated me as if I at least had common-sense. I thank you for that; and I like you because—"

She did not finish the sentence, for she could not say " Because you are Arthur's friend." That would have betrayed the miserable secret tugging at her heart, and prompting her to refuse Thornton Hastings, who had also thought of Arthur Leighton, wondering if it were thus that she rejected him, and if in the background there was another love standing between her and the two men to win whom many a woman would almost have given her right hand. To say that Thornton was not piqued at her refusal would be false. He had not expected it, accustomed as he was to adulation; but he tried to put that feeling down, and his manner was even more kind and considerate than ever as he walked back to the hotel, where

Mrs. Meredith was waiting for them, her practised eye detecting at once that something was amiss. Thornton Hastings knew Mrs. Meredith thoroughly, and, wishing to shield Anna from her displeasure, he preferred stating the facts himself to having them wrung from the pale, agitated girl, who, bidding him good-night, went quickly to her room; so, when she was gone, and he stood for a moment alone with Mrs. Meredith, he said:

"I have proposed to your niece, but she cannot answer me now. She wishes for a month's probation, which I have granted, and I ask that she shall not be persecuted about the matter. I must have an unbiassed answer."

He bowed politely and walked away, while Mrs. Meredith almost trod on air as she climbed the stairs and sought her niece's chamber. Over the interview which ensued that night we pass silently, and come to the next morning, when Anna sat alone on the piazza at the rear of the hotel, watching the playful gambols of some children on the grass, and wondering if she ever could conscientiously say yes to Thornton Hastings' suit. He was coming towards her now, lifting his hat politely, and asking what she would give for news from home.

"I found this on my table," he said, holding up a dainty little missive, on the corner of which was written "In haste," as if its contents were of the utmost importance. "The boy must have made a mistake, or else he thought it well to begin at once bringing your letters to me," he continued with a smile, as he handed Anna the letter from Lucy Harcourt. "I have one, too, from Arthur, which I will read while you are devouring yours, and then, perhaps, you will take a little ride. The September air is very bracing this morning," he said, walking away to the far end of the piazza while Anna broke the seal of the envelope, hesitating a moment ere taking the letter from it, and trembling as if she guessed what it contained.

There was a quivering of the eyelids, a paling of the lips as she glanced at the first few lines, then with the low moaning cry, "No, no, oh no, not that," she fell upon her face.

To lift her in his arms and carry her to her room was the work of an instant, and then, leaving her to Mrs. Meredith's care, Thornton Hastings went back to finish Arthur's letter, which might or might not throw light upon the fainting-fit.

"Dear Thornton," Arthur wrote, "you will be surprised, no doubt, to hear that your old college chum is at last engaged; but not to one of the fifty lambs about whom you once jocosely wrote. The shepherd has wandered from his flock, and is about to take into his bosom a little stray ewe-lamb,—Lucy Harcourt by name—"

"The deuce he is," was Thornton's ejaculation, and then he read on:

"She is an acquaintance of yours, I believe, so I need

not describe her, except to say that she is somewhat changed from the gay butterfly of fashion she used to be, and in time will make as demure a little Quakeress as one could wish to see. She visits constantly among my poor, who love her almost as well as they once loved Anna Ruthven.

"Don't ask me, Thorne, in your blunt, straightforward manner if I have so soon forgotten Anna. That is a matter with which you've nothing to do. Let it suffice that I am engaged to another, and mean to make a kind and faithful husband to her. Lucy would have suited you better, perhaps, than she does me; that is, the world would think so, but the world does not always know, and if I am satisfied, surely it ought to be.

"Yours truly,

"A. LEIGHTON."

"Engaged to Lucy Harcourt! I never could have believed it. He's right in saying that she is far more suitable for me than him," Thornton exclaimed, dashing aside the letter and feeling conscious of a pang as he remembered the bright airy little beauty in whom he had once been strongly interested, even if he did call her frivolous and ridicule her childish ways.

She was frivolous, too much so by far to be a clergyman's wife, and for a full half-hour Thornton paced up and down the room, meditating on Arthur's choice and wondering how upon earth it ever happened.

CHAPTER VIII.

SHOWING HOW IT HAPPENED.

LUCY had insisted that she did not care to go to Saratoga. She preferred remaining in Hanover, where it was cool and quiet, and where she would not have to dress three times a day and dance every night until twelve. She was beginning to find that there was something to live for besides consulting one's own pleasure, and she meant to do good the rest of her life, she said; assuming such a sober, nun-like air, that no one who saw her could fail to laugh, it was so at variance with her entire nature. But Lucy was in earnest. Hanover had a greater attraction for her than all the watering-places in the world, and she was very grateful when Fanny threw her influence on her side and so turned the scale in her favor.

Fanny was glad to leave her dangerous cousin at home, especially after Mr. Bellamy decided to join their party at Saratoga; and as she carried great weight with both her parents it was finally decided to let Lucy remain at Prospect Hill in peace, and one morning in July she saw the family depart without a single feeling of regret that she was not of their number. She had far too much on her hands to spend her time in regretting anything: there was the parish school to visit, and a class of children to hear, children who were no longer ragged, for Lucy's money had been expended till even Arthur had remonstrated with her, and read her a long lecture on the subject of misapplied charity. Then there was Widow Hobbs waiting for the jelly which Lucy had promised, and for the chapter which Lucy now read to her, sitting where she could watch the road and see just who turned the corner, her voice always sounding a little more serious and good when the footsteps belonged to Arthur Leighton, and her eyes always glancing at the bit of a cracked mirror on the wall, to see that her dress and hair and ribbons were right before Arthur came in. It was a very pretty sight to see her thus and hear her as she read to the poor, whose surroundings she had so greatly improved; and Arthur always smiled gratefully upon her, and then walked back with her to Prospect Hill, where he lingered while she played or talked to him, or brought the luscious fruits with which the garden abounded.

This was Lucy's life, which she preferred to Saratoga, and they left her to enjoy it, somewhat to Arthur's discomfiture, for, much as he valued her society, he would rather she had gone where the Hethertons did, for he could not be insensible to the remarks which were being made by the curious villagers, who watched this new flirtation, as they called it, and wondered if their minister had forgotten Anna Ruthven. He had not forgotten her, and many a time was her loved name upon his lips and a thought of her in his heart, while he never returned from an interview with Lucy that he did not contrast the two, and sigh for the olden time when Anna was his coworker instead of pretty Lucy Harcourt. And yet there was about the latter a powerful fascination which he found it hard to resist. It rested him just to look at her, she was so fresh, so bright, and so beautiful; and then she flattered his self-love by the unbounded deference she paid to his opinions, studying all his tastes and bringing her will into perfect subjection to his, until she could scarcely be said to have a thought or feeling which was not a reflection of his own. And so the flirtation, which at first had been a one-sided affair, began to assume a more serious form, and the rector went oftener to Prospect Hill, while the Hetherton carriage stood daily at the gate of the parsonage, and people talked and gossiped, until Captain Humphreys, Anna's grandfather, concluded it was his duty as senior warden of St. Mark's, to talk with the young rector and know "what his intentions were."

"You have none?" he said, fixing his mild eyes reproachfully upon his clergyman, who recoiled a little beneath the gaze. "Then, if you have no intentions, my advice to you is that you quit it and let the gal alone, or you'll ruin her, if she ain't spoilt already, as some of the women folks say she is. It don't do no gal any good to have a chap, and 'specially a minister, gallivantin' after her, as I must say you've been after this one for the last few weeks. She's a pretty little creeter, and I don't blame you for liking her. It makes my old blood stir faster when she comes purring around me, with her soft ways and winsome face, and so I don't wonder at you, but when you say you've no intentions, I blame you greatly. You or'to have. Excuse my plainness; I'm an old man, and I like my minister, and don't want him to go wrong; and then I feel for her, left all alone by all her folks; more's the shame to them, and more's the harm to you, to tangle up her affections as you are doing if you are not in earnest; and so I speak for her just as I should want some one to speak for Anna!"

The old man's voice trembled a little here, for it had been a wish of his that Anna should occupy the parsonage, and he had at first felt a little resentment against the gay young creature who seemed to have supplanted her, but he was over that now, and in all honesty of heart he spoke both for Lucy's interest and that of his clergyman. And Arthur listened to him respectfully, feeling when he was gone that he merited the rebuke,—that he had not been guiltless in the matter,—that if he did not mean to marry Lucy Harcourt he should let her alone. And he would, he said,—he would not go to Prospect Hill again for two whole weeks, nor visit at the cottages where he was sure to find her; he would keep himself at home; and he did, and shut himself up among his books, not even going to make a pastoral call on Lucy when he heard that she was sick. And so Lucy came to him, looking dangerously charming in her blue riding-habit with the white feather streaming from her hat. Very prettily she pouted, too, as she chided him for his neglect, and asked why he had not been to see her nor anybody;—there was the Widow Hobbs, and Mrs. Briggs, and those miserable Donelsons, whom he had not been near for a fortnight.

"What is the reason?" she asked, beating her foot upon the carpet and tapping the end of her riding-whip upon the sermon he was writing. "Are you displeased with me, Arthur," she continued, her eyes filling with tears as she saw the expression of his face. "Have I done anything wrong; I am so sorry if I have."

Her voice had in it the grieved tones of a little child, and her eyes were very bright with the tears quivering on her long eyelashes. Leaning back in his chair, with his hands clasped behind his head, a position he usually assumed when puzzled and perplexed, the rector looked at her a moment before he spoke. He could not define to himself the nature of the interest he took in Lucy Harcourt. He admired her greatly, and the self-denials and generous exertions she had made to be of use to him since Anna went away, had touched a tender chord and made her seem very near to him. Habit with him was everything, and the past two weeks' isolation had shown him how necessary she had become to him. She did not satisfy his higher wants as Anna Ruthven had done. No one could ever do that, but she amused and soothed and rested him, and made his duties lighter by taking half of them upon herself. That she was more attached to him than he could wish he greatly feared, for since Captain Humphreys' visit he had seen matters differently from what he saw them before, and had unsparingly questioned himself as to how far he would be answerable for her future weal or woe.

"Guilty, verily I am guilty in leading her on if I meant nothing by it," he had written against himself, pausing in his sermon to write it just as Lucy came in, appealing to him to know why he had neglected her so long.

She was very beautiful this morning, and Arthur felt his heart beat rapidly as he looked at her, and thought any man who had not known Anna Ruthven would be glad to gather that bright creature in his arms and know she was his own. One long, long sigh to the memory of all he had hoped for once,—one bitter pang as he remembered Anna and that twilight hour in the church, and then he made a mad plunge in the dark and said :

"Lucy, do you know people are beginning to talk about my seeing you so much?"

"Well, let them talk; who cares?" Lucy replied, with a good deal of asperity of manner for her, for that very morning the house-keeper at Prospect Hill had ventured to remonstrate with her for "running after the parson." "Pray where is the wrong? What harm can come of it?"

"None, perhaps," Arthur replied, "if one could keep their affections under control. But if either of us should learn to love the other very much and the love was not reciprocated, harm would surely come of that. At least that was the view Captain Humphreys took of the matter when he was speaking to me about it."

There were red spots on Lucy's face, but her lips were very white and the buttons on her riding-dress rose and fell rapidly with the beating of her heart as she looked steadily at Arthur. Was he going to send her from him, —back to the insipid life she had lived before she knew him? It was too terrible to believe, and the great tears rolled slowly down her cheeks. Then as a flash of pride came to her aid, she dashed them away and said to him haughtily:

"And so for fear I shall fall in love with you, you are sacrificing both comfort and freedom, and shutting yourself up with your books and studies to the neglect of other duties. But it need be so no longer. The necessity for it, if it existed once, certainly does not now. I will not be in your way; forgive me that I ever have been."

Lucy's voice began to tremble as she gathered up her riding-habit and turned to find her gauntlets. One of them had dropped upon the floor between the table and the rector, and as she stooped to reach it her curls almost swept the young man's lap.

"Let me get it for you," he said, hastily pushing back his chair and awkwardly entangling his foot in her long sweeping dress, so that when she arose she stumbled backward and would have fallen, but for the arm he quickly passed around her.

Something in the touch of that quivering form completed the work of temptation, and he held it for an instant, when she said to him pettishly :

"Please let me go, sir."

"No, Lucy, I can't let you go. I want you to stay with me."

Instantly the drooping head was uplifted, and Lucy's eyes looked into his with such a wistful, pleading, wondering look that Arthur saw or thought he saw his duty plain, and gently touching his lips to the brow glistening so white within their reach, he continued:

"There is a way to stop the gossip and make it right for me to see you. Promise to be my wife, and not even Captain Humphreys can say aught against it."

Arthur's voice trembled now, for the mention of Captain Humphreys had brought a thought of Anna, whose eyes seemed for an instant to look reproachfully upon that wooing. But he had gone too far to retract; he had only to wait for Lucy's answer. There was no deception about her; hers was a nature as clear as crystal, and with a gush of glad tears she promised to be the rector's wife; and hiding her face on his bosom, told him, brokenly, how unworthy she was of him; how foolish, and how unsuited to the place, but promising to do the best she could not to bring him into disgrace on account of her shortcomings.

"With the knowledge that you love me I can do anything," she said, and her white hand crept slowly into the cold, clammy one which lay so listlessly on Arthur's lap.

He was already repenting, for he felt that it was sin to take that warm, trusting, loving heart in exchange for the cold, half lifeless one he should render in return, and in which scarcely a pulse of joy was beating, even though he held his promised wife; and she was fair and beautiful as ever promised wife could be.

"But I can make her happy, and I will," he thought, pressing the warm fingers which quivered to his touch.

But he did not kiss her again; he could not for the eyes, which still seemed looking at him and asking what he did. There was a strange spell about those phantom eyes, and they made him say to Lucy, who was now sitting demurely at his side :

"I could not clear my conscience if I did not confess that you are not the first woman whom I have asked to be my wife."

There was a start, and Lucy's face was pale as ashes, while her hand went quickly to her side, where the heart-beats were visible, warning Arthur to be careful how he startled one whose life hung on so slender a thread as Lucy's ; so, when she asked, " Who was it, and why did you not marry her ? Did you love her very much ? " he answered indifferently, " I would rather not tell you who it was, as that might be a breach of confidence. She did not care to be my wife, and so that dream was over and I was left for you."

He did not say how much he loved her who had discarded him, but Lucy forgot the omission, and asked, " Was she very young and pretty ? "

" Young and pretty both, but not as beautiful as you," Arthur replied, his fingers softly putting back the golden curls from the face looking so trustingly into his.

And in that he answered truly. He had seen no face as beautiful of its kind as Lucy's was, and he was glad that he could tell her so. He knew how that would please her and partly make amends for the tender words which he could not speak,—for the phantom eyes still haunting him so strangely.

And Lucy, who took all things for granted, was more than content, although she wondered that he did not kiss her again, and wished she knew the girl who had come so near being in her place. But she respected his wishes too much to ask after what he had said, and she tried to make herself glad that he had been so frank with her and not left his other love-affair to the chance of her discovering it afterwards, at a time when it might be painful to her.

"I wish I had something to confess," she thought; but from the score of her flirtations, and even offers, for she had not lacked for them, she could not find one where her own feelings had been enlisted in ever so slight a degree until she remembered Thornton Hastings, who for one whole week had paid her such attentions as had made her dream of him, and even drive round once on purpose to look at the house on Madison Square where the future Mrs. Hastings was to live.

But his coolness afterwards, and his comments on her frivolity had terribly angered her, making her think that she hated him, as she had said to Anna. Now, however, as she remembered the drive and the house, she nestled closer to Arthur and told him all about it, fingering the buttons on his dressing-gown as she told him it, and never dreaming of the pang she was inflicting as Arthur thought how mysterious were God's ways, and wondered that He had not reversed the matter and given Lucy to

Thornton Hastings, rather than to him, who did not half deserve her.

"I know now I never cared a bit for Thornton Hastings, though I might if he had not been so mean as to call me frivolous," Lucy said, as she arose to go; then suddenly turning to the rector, she added: "I shall never ask who your first love was, but would like to know if you have quite forgotten her?"

"Have you forgotten Thornton Hastings?" Arthur asked, laughingly; and Lucy replied, "Of course not; one never forgets, but I don't care a pin about him now, and did I tell you, Fanny writes that rumor says he will marry Anna Ruthven?"

"Yes,—no,—I did not know; I am not surprised;" and Arthur stooped to pick up a book lying on the floor, thus hiding his face from Lucy, who, woman-like, was glad to report a piece of gossip, and continued:

"She is a great belle, Fanny says; dresses beautifully and in perfect taste, besides talking as if she knew something, and this pleases Mr. Hastings, who takes her out to ride and drive, and all this after I warned her against him and told her just what he said of me. I am surprised at her!"

Lucy was drawing on her gauntlets, and Arthur was waiting to see her out, but she still lingered on the threshold, and at last said to him:

"I wonder you never fell in love with Anna yourself.

I am sure, if I were you I should prefer her to me. She knows something and I do not, but I am going to study; there are piles of books in the library at Prospect Hill, and you shall see what a famous student I will become. If I get puzzled will you help me?"

"Yes, willingly," Arthur replied, wishing that she would go, before she indulged in any more speculation as to why he did not love Anna Ruthven.

But Lucy was not done yet; the keenest pang was yet to come, and Arthur felt as if the earth was giving way beneath his feet, when, as he lifted her into the saddle and took her hand at parting, she said:

"You remember I am not going to be jealous of that other girl. There is only one person who could make me so, and that is Anna Ruthven; but I know it was not she, for that night we all came from Mrs. Hobbs's and she went with me up-stairs, I asked her honestly if you had ever offered yourself to her, and she told me you had not. I think you showed a lack of taste; but I am glad it was not Anna."

Lucy was far down the road ere Arthur recovered from the shock her last words had given him. What did it mean, and why had Anna said he never proposed? Was there some mistake, and he the victim of it? There was a blinding mist before the young man's eyes, and a gnawing pain at his heart as he returned to his study and went over again with all the incidents of Anna's refusal, even to the reading of the letter which he already knew by heart. Then, as the thought came over him that possibly Mrs. Meredith played him false in some way, he groaned aloud, and the great sweat-drops fell upon the table where he leaned his head. But this could not be, he reasoned. Lucy was mistaken. She had not heard aright. Somebody surely was mistaken, or he had committed a fatal error.

"But I must abide by it," he said, lifting up his pallid face. "God forgive the wrong I have done in asking Lucy to be my wife when my heart belonged to another. God help me to forget the one and love the other as I ought. She is a lovely little girl, trusting me so wholly that I can make her happy,—and I will!—but Anna,— O Anna!"

It was a despairing cry, such as a newly-engaged man should never have sent after another than his affianced bride; and Arthur thought so too, fighting back his first love with an iron will, and after that hour of anguish burying it so far from sight that he went that night to Captain Humphreys and told of his engagement; then called upon his bride-elect, and tried so hard to be satisfied, that, when at a late hour he returned to the parsonage, he was more than content; and by way of fortifying himself still more, wrote the letter which Thornton Hastings read at Newport.

And that was how it happened.

CHAPTER IX.

ANNA.

THROUGH the rich curtains which shaded the windows of a room looking out on Fifth Avenue the late October sun was shining; and as its red light played among the flowers on the carpet, a pale young girl sat watching it and thinking of the Hanover hills, now decked in their autumnal glory, and of the ivy on St. Mark's, growing so bright and beautiful beneath the autumnal frosts. Anna had been very sick since that morning in September when she sat on the piazza at the Ocean House and read Lucy Harcourt's letter. The faint was a precursor of fever, the physician said when summoned to her aid; and in a tremor of fear and distress Mrs. Meredith had had her removed at once to New York, and that was the last Anna remembered. From the moment her aching head had touched the soft pillows in Aunt Meredith's home, all consciousness had fled, and for weeks she had hovered so near to death that the telegraph-wires bore daily messages to Hanover, where the aged couple who had cared for her since her childhood wept, and prayed, and watched for tidings from their darling. They could not go to her, for Grandpa Humphreys had broken his leg, and his wife could not leave him; so they waited with what patience they could for the daily bulletins which Mrs. Meredith sent, appreciating their anxiety, and feeling glad withal of anything which kept them from New York.

"She had best be prayed for in church," the old man said; and so, Sunday after Sunday, Arthur read the prayer for the sick, his voice trembling as it had never trembled before, and a keener sorrow in his heart than he had ever known when saying the solemn words.

Heretofore the persons prayed for had been comparative strangers,—people in whom he felt only the interest a pastor feels in all his flock; but now it was *Anna*, whose case he took to God, and he always smothered a sob during the moment he waited for the fervent response the congregation made, the *Amen* which came from the pew where Lucy sat being louder and heartier than all the rest, and having in it a sound of the tears which dropped so fast on Lucy's book, as she asked that her dear friend might not die. Oh, how he longed to go to her! But this he could not do, and so he had sent Lucy, who bent so tenderly above the sick girl, whispering loving words in her ear, and dropping kisses upon the lips which uttered no response, save once, when Lucy said, "Do you remember Arthur?"

Then they murmured faintly: "Yes,—Arthur,—I remember him, and the Christmas song, and the gathering in the church. But that was long ago; there's much happened since then."

"And I am to marry Arthur," Lucy had said again; but this time there was no sign that she was understood, and that afternoon she went back to Hanover loaded with tickets for the children of St. Mark's and new books for the Sunday-school, and accompanied by Valencia, who, having had a serious difference with her mistress, Mrs. Meredith, had offered her services to Miss Harcourt, and been at once accepted.

That was near the middle of October; now it was the last, and Anna was so much better that she sat up for an hour or more and listened with some degree of interest to what Mrs. Meredith told her of the days when she lay so unconscious of all that was passing around her, never heeding the kindly voice of Thornton Hastings, who more than once had stood by her pillow with his hand on her feverish brow, and tokens of whose thoughtfulness were visible in the choice bouquets he sent each day, with notes of anxious inquiry when he did not come himself. Anna had not seen him yet since her convalescence. She would rather not see any one until strong enough to talk, she said. And so Thornton waited patiently for the interview she had promised him when she should be stronger, but every day he sent her fruit, and flowers, and books which he thought would interest her, and which always made her cheeks grow hot and her heart beat regretfully, for she knew of the answer she must give him when he came, and she shrank from wounding him.

"He is too good, too noble, to have an unwilling wife," she thought; but that did not make it the less hard to tell him so, and when at last she was well enough to see him, she waited his coming nervously, starting when she heard his step, and trembling like a leaf as he drew near her chair.

It was a very thin, wasted hand which he took in his, holding it for a moment between his own, and then laying it gently back upon her lap. He had come for the answer to a question put six weeks before, and Anna gave it to him,—kindly, considerately, but decidedly. She could not be his wife, she said, because she did not love him as he ought to be loved.

"It is nothing personal," she added, working nervously at the heavy fringe of her shawl. "I respect you more than any man I ever knew,—except one; and had I met you years ago,—before—before—"

"I understand you," Thornton said, coming to her aid. "You have tried to love me, but you cannot, because your affections are given to another."

Anna bowed her head in silence; then, after a moment, she continued:

"You must forgive me, Mr. Hastings, for not telling

you this at once. I did not know then but I could love you; at least, I meant to try, for you see this other one,"—the fingers got terribly tangled in the fringe as Anna gasped for breath and went on,—"he does not know, and never will,—that is,—he never cared for me, nor guessed how foolish I was to give him my love unsought."

"Then it is *not* Arthur Leighton, and that is why you refused him too," Mr. Hastings said involuntarily; and Anna looked quickly up, her cheeks growing paler than they were before, as she replied: "I don't know what you mean. I never refused Mr. Leighton,—never!"

"You never refused Mr. Leighton?" Thornton exclaimed, forgetting all discretion in his surprise at this flat contradiction. "I have Arthur's word for it, written to me last June, while Mrs. Meredith was there, I think."

"He surely could not have meant it, because it never occurred; there is some mistake," Anna found strength to say; and then she lay back in her easy-chair panting for breath, her brain all in a whirl as she thought of the possibility that she was once so near the greatest happiness she had ever desired, and which was lost to her now.

He brought her smelling-salts; he gave her ice-water to drink, and then, kneeling beside her, he fanned her gently, while he continued: "There surely *is* a mistake, and, I fear, a great wrong, too, somewhere. Were all your servants trusty? Was there no one who would withhold a letter if he had written? Were you always at home when he called?"

Thornton questioned her rapidly, for there was a suspicion in his mind as to the real culprit, but he would not hint it to Anna unless she suggested it herself. And this she was not likely to do. Mrs. Meredith had been too kind to her during the past summer, and especially during her recent illness, to allow of such a thought concerning her; and in a maze of perplexity she replied to his inquiries : " We keep but one servant,—Esther,—and she I know is trusty. Besides, who could have refused him for me? Grandfather would not, I know, because —because—" she hesitated a little, and her cheeks blushed scarlet as she added, " I sometimes thought he wanted it to be."

If Thornton had previously had a doubt as to the other man who stood between himself and Anna, that doubt was now removed, and laying aside all thoughts of self, he exclaimed:

" I tell you there is a great wrong somewhere. Arthur never told an untruth ; he thought that you refused him ; he thinks so still, and I shall never rest till I have solved the mystery. I will write to him to-day."

For an instant there swept over Anna a feeling of unutterable joy as she thought what the end might be; then, as she remembered Lucy, her heart seemed to stop its beating, and with a moan she stretched her hands towards Thornton, who had risen as if to leave her.

"No, no, you must not interfere," she said. "It is too late, too late. Don't you remember Lucy? don't you know she is to be his wife? Lucy must not be sacrificed for me. *I* can bear it the best."

She knew she had betrayed her secret, and she tried to take it back, but Thornton interrupted her with, "Never mind now, Anna. I guessed it all before, and it hurts my self-pride less to know that it is Arthur whom you prefer to me. I do not blame you for it."

He smoothed her hair pityingly, while he stood over her a moment, wondering what his duty was. Anna told him plainly what it was. He must leave Arthur and Lucy alone. She insisted upon having it so, and he promised her at last that he would not interfere. Then taking her hand, he pressed it a moment between his own and went out from her presence. In the hall below he met with Mrs. Meredith, who he knew was waiting anxiously to hear the result of that long interview.

"Your niece will never be my wife, and I am satisfied to have it so," he said; then, as he saw the lowering of her brow, he continued, "I have long suspected that she loved another, and my suspicions are confirmed, though there's something I cannot understand," and fixing his eyes searchingly upon Mrs. Meredith, he told what Arthur had written and of Anna's denial of the same. " Somebody played her false," he said, rather enjoying the look of terror and shame which crept into the haughty woman's eyes, as she tried to appear natural and express her own surprise at what she heard.

"I was right in my conjecture," Thornton thought as he took his leave of Mrs. Meredith, who could not face Anna then, but paced restlessly up and down her spacious rooms, wondering how much Thornton suspected, and what the end would be.

She had sinned for naught; Anna had upset all her cherished plans, and could she have gone back for a few months and done her work again, she would have left the letter lying where she found it. But that could not be now. She must reap as she had sown, and resolving finally to hope for the best and abide the result, she went up to Anna, who, having no suspicion of her, hurt her ten times more cruelly, by the perfect faith with which she confided the story to her, than bitter reproaches would have done.

"I know you wanted me to marry Mr. Hastings," Anna said, "and I would if I could have done so conscientiously, but I could not, for I may confess it now to you. I did love Arthur so much, and I hoped that he loved me."

The cold, hard woman, who had brought this grief upon her niece, could only answer that it did not matter. She was not very sorry, although she had wanted her to marry Mr. Hastings, but she must not fret about that now, or about anything. She would be better by and by, and forget that she ever cared for Arthur Leighton.

"At least," and she spoke entreatingly now, "you will not demean yourself to let him know of the mistake. It would scarcely be womanly, and he may have gotten over it. Present circumstances seem to prove as much."

Mrs. Meredith felt now that her secret was comparatively safe, and with her spirits lighter she kissed her niece lovingly and told her of a trip to Europe which she had in view, promising that Anna should go with her, and so not be at home when the marriage of Arthur and Lucy took place.

It was appointed for the 15th of January, that being the day when Lucy came of age, and the very afternoon succeeding Anna's interview with Mr. Hastings the little lady came down to New York to direct about her bridal trousseau making, in the city. She was brimming over with happiness and her face was a perfect gleam of sunshine, when she came next day to Anna's room, and throwing off her wrappings plunged at once into the subject uppermost in her thoughts, telling first how she and Arthur had quarrelled,—"not quarrelled as uncle and aunt Hetherton and lots of people do, but differed so seriously that I cried and had to give up, too," she said. "I wanted you for bridesmaid, and do you think, he objected;

not objected to you, but to bridesmaids generally, and he carried his point, so that we are just to stand up stiff and straight alone, except as you'll all be round me in the aisle. You'll be well by that time, and I want you very near to me," Lucy said, squeezing the icy hand, whose coldness made her start and exclaim, "Why, Anna, how cold you are, and how pale you are looking. You have been so sick, and I am so well; it don't seem quite right, does it? And Arthur, too, is so thin that I have coaxed him to raise whiskers to cover the hollows in his cheeks. He looks a heap better now, though he was always handsome. I do so wonder that you two never fell in love, and I tell him so most every time I see him, for I always think of you then."

It was terrible to Anna to sit and hear all this, and the room grew dark as she listened, but she forced back her pain, and stroking the curly head almost resting on her lap, and said kindly, " You love him very much, don't you, darling,—so much that it would be hard to give him up ? "

" Yes, oh yes, I could not give him up now, except to God. I trust I could do that, though once I could not, I am sure," and nestling closer to Anna, Lucy whispered to her of the hope that she was better than she used to be,—that daily intercourse with Arthur had not been without its effect, and now she believed she tried to do right from a higher motive than just to please him.

"God bless you, darling," was Anna's response, as she clasped the hand of the young girl, who was now far more worthy to be Arthur's wife than once she had been.

If Anna had ever had a thought of telling Arthur, it would have been put aside by that interview with Lucy. She could not harm that pure, loving, trusting girl, and she sent her from her with a kiss and a blessing, praying silently that she might never know a shadow of the pain which she was suffering.

CHAPTER X.

MRS. MEREDITH'S CONSCIENCE.

SHE had one years before, but since the summer day when she sent from her the white-faced man, whose heart she knew she had broken, it had been hardening,—searing over with a stiff crust which nothing, it seemed, could penetrate. And yet there were times when she was softened and wished that much which she had done might be blotted out from the great book in which even she believed. There was many a misdeed recorded there against her, she knew, and occasionally there stole over her a strange disquietude as to how she should confront them when they all came up before her. Usually she could cast such thoughts aside by a drive down gay Broadway, or at most by a call at Stewart's, but the sight of Anna's white face and the knowing what made it so white were a constant reproach, and conscience gradually wakened from its torpor, enough to whisper of the only restitution in her power, that of confession to Arthur. But from this she shrank nervously. She could not humble herself thus to any one, and she would not either, she said. Then came the fear lest by another than herself her guilt should come to light. What if Thornton Hastings should find her out? She was half afraid he suspected her now, and that gave her the heaviest pang of all, for she respected Thornton highly, and it would cost her much to lose his good opinion. She had lost him for her niece, but she could not spare him from herself, and so in sad perplexity, which wore upon her visibly, the autumn days went on until at last she sat one morning in her dressing-room and read in a foreign paper:

"Died at Strasburg, Aug. 31st, Edward Coleman, Esq. aged 46."

That was all, but the paper dropped from the trembling hands, and the proud woman of the world bowed her head upon the cold marble of the table and wept aloud. She was not Mrs. Meredith now, she was Julia Ruthven again, and she stood with Edward Coleman out in the grassy orchard where the apple-blossoms were dropping from the trees, and the air was full of the insects' hum and the song of mating birds. Many years had passed since then. She was the wealthy Mrs. Meredith now, and he was dead in Strasburg. He had been true to her to the last, for he had never married, and those who had met him abroad had brought back the same report of a "white-haired man, old before his time, and with a tired, sad look on his face." That look she had written there, and she wept on as she recalled the past and murmured softly: "Poor Edward, I loved you all the while, but I sold myself for gold, and it turned your brown locks snowy white,—poor darling,—" and her hands moved up and down the folds of her cashmere robe as if it were the brown locks they were smoothing just as they used to do. Then came a thought of Anna, whose face wore much the look which Edward's did when he went slowly from the orchard and left her there alone with the apple-blossoms dropping on her head, and the hum of the bees in her ear.

"I can at least do right in that respect," she said. "I can undo the past to some extent and lessen the load of sin upon my shoulders. I will write to Arthur Leighton; I surely need tell no one else,—not yet, at least, lest he has outlived his love for Anna. I can trust to his discretion and to his honor too; he will not betray me, unless it is necessary, and then only to Anna. Edward would bid me do it if he could speak; he was some like Arthur Leighton."

And so with the dead man in Strasburg before her eyes, Mrs. Meredith nerved herself to write to Arthur Leighton, confessing the fraud imposed upon him, imploring his forgiveness, and begging him to spare her as much as possible.

"I know from Anna's own lips how much she has always loved you," she wrote in conclusion, "but she does not know of the stolen letter, and I leave you to make such use of the knowledge as you shall think proper."

She did not put in a single plea for poor little Lucy dancing so gayly over the mine just ready to explode. She was purely selfish still with all her qualms of conscience, and only thought of Anna, whom she would make happy at another's sacrifice. So she never hinted that it was possible for Arthur to keep his word pledged to Lucy Harcourt, and as she finished her own letter and placed it in an envelope with the one which Arthur had sent to Anna, her thoughts leaped forward to the wedding she would give her niece,—a wedding not quite like that she had designed for Mrs. Thornton Hastings, but a quiet, elegant affair, just suited to a clergyman who was marrying a Ruthven.

CHAPTER XI.

THE LETTER RECEIVED.

ARTHUR had been spending the evening at Prospect hill. The Hethertons were there now, and would remain till after the 15th; and since they came the rector had found it even pleasanter calling there than it had been before with only his bride-elect to entertain him. Sure of Mr. Bellamy, Fanny had laid aside her sharpness and was exceedingly witty and brilliant, while, now that it was settled, the colonel was too thorough a gentleman to be otherwise than gracious to his future nephew, and Mrs. Hetherton was always polite and ladylike, so that the rector looked forward with a good deal of interest to the evenings he usually gave to Lucy, who, though satisfied to have him in her sight, still preferred the olden time when she had him all to herself, and was not disquieted with the fear that she was not learned enough for him, as she often was when she heard him talking with Fanny and her uncle of things she did not understand. This evening, however, the family were away and she received him alone, trying so hard to come up to his capacity, talking so intelligibly of the books she had been reading, and looking so lovely in her crimson winter dress, besides being so sweetly affectionate and confiding that for once since his engagement Arthur was more than content, and returned her modest caresses with a warmth he had not felt before. He was learning to love her very much, he thought, and when at last he took his leave and she went with him to the door there was an unwonted tenderness in his manner as he pushed her gently back, for the first snow of the season was falling and the large flakes dropped upon her hair, from which he brushed them carefully away.

"I cannot let my darling take cold," he said, and Lucy felt a strange thrill of joy, for never before had he called her his darling, and sometimes she had feared that the love she received was not as great as the love she gave.

But she did not think so now, and in an ecstasy of joy she stood in the deep recess of the bay-window watching him as he went away through the moonlight and the feathery cloud of snow, wondering why, when she was so happy, there should cling to her a haunting presentiment that she and Arthur would never meet again just as they had parted. Arthur, on the contrary, was troubled with no such presentiment. Of Anna he hardly thought, or, if he did, the vision was obscured by the fair picture he had seen standing in the door with the snow-flakes resting on its hair like pearls in a golden cabinet. And Arthur thanked his God that he was beginning at last to feel right, that the solemn vows he was so soon to utter would not be a mockery. It was Arthur's wish to teach to others how dark and mysterious are the ways of Providence, but he had not himself half learned that lesson in all its strange reality; but the lesson was coming on apace; each stride of his swift-footed beast brought him nearer and nearer to the great shock waiting for him upon his study-table, where his man had put it. He saw it the first thing on entering the room, but he did not take it up until the snow was brushed from his garments and he had seated himself by the cheerful fire blazing on the hearth. Then sitting in his easy-chair and moving the lamp nearer to him, he took Mrs. Meredith's letter and broke the seal, starting as if a serpent had stung him when in the note enclosed he recognized his own handwriting, the same he had sent to Anna when his heart was as full of hope as the brown stalks, now beating against his windows with a dismal sound, were full of fragrant blossoms. Both had died since then, the roses and his hopes, and Arthur almost wished that he, too, were dead when he read Mrs. Meredith's letter and saw the gulf he was treading. Like the waves of the sea his love for Anna came rolling back upon him, augmented and intensified by all that he had suffered, and by the terrible conviction that it could not be, although,

17

alas, "it might have been." He repeated these words over and over again, as, stupefied with pain, he sat gazing at vacancy, thinking how true was the couplet:

> "Of all sad words of tongue or pen,
> The saddest are these,—*it might* have been."

He could not pray at first, his brain was so confused; but when the white, quivering lips could move and the poor aching heart could pray, he only whispered: "God help me to do right," and by that prayer he knew that for a single instant there had crept across his mind the possibility of sacrificing Lucy, the girl who loved and trusted him so much; but only for an instant. He would not cast her from him, though to take her now, knowing what he did, was almost death itself. "But God can help me, and he will," he cried,—then falling upon his knees, with his face bowed to the floor, the rector of St. Mark's prayed as he had never prayed before, first for himself, whose need was greatest, then for Lucy, that she might never know what making her happy had cost him, and then for Anna, whose name he could not speak. "That other one," he called her, and his heart kept swelling in his throat and preventing his utterance so that the words he would say never reached his lips. But God heard them just the same, and knew his child was asking that Anna might forget him, if to remember him was pain,—that she might learn to love another far worthier than he had ever been. He did not think of Mrs. Meredith; he had no feeling of resentment then; he was too wholly crushed to care how his ruin had been brought about, and long after the woodfire on the hearth had turned to cold, gray ashes, he knelt upon the floor and battled with his grief; and when the morning broke it found him still in the cheerless room, where he had passed the entire night and from which he went forth strengthened as he hoped to do what he fully believed to be his duty.

This was on Saturday, and the Sunday following there was no service at St. Mark's. The rector was sick, the sexton said, hard sick, too, he had heard, and the Hetherton carriage with Lucy in it drove swiftly to the parsonage, where the quiet and solitude awed and frightened her as she entered the house and asked the housekeeper how Mr. Leighton was.

"It is very sudden," she said. "He was perfectly well when he left me on Friday night. Please tell him I am here."

The housekeeper shook her head. Her master's orders were that no one but the doctor should be admitted, she said, repeating what Arthur had told her in anticipation of just such an infliction as this. But Lucy was not to be denied; Arthur was hers; his sickness was hers; his suffering was hers, and see him she would.

"He surely did not mean me, when he asked that no

one should be admitted. Tell him it is I; it is Lucy," she said, with an air of authority, which in one so small, so pretty, and so childish only amused Mrs. Brown, who departed with the message, while Lucy sat down with her feet upon the stove and looked around the sitting-room, thinking that it was smaller and poorer than the one at Prospect Hill, and how she would remodel it when she was mistress there.

"He says you can come," was the word Mrs. Brown brought back, and with a gleam of triumph in her eye and a toss of the head which said, "I told you so," Lucy went softly into the darkened room and shut the door behind her.

Arthur had half expected this and had nerved himself to meet it, but the cold sweat stood on his face and his heart throbbed painfully as Lucy bent over him and said, " Poor, dear Arthur, I am so sorry for you, and if I could I'd bear the pain so willingly."

He knew she would; she was just as loving and unselfish as that, and he wound his arms around her and drew her closer to him, while he whispered, " My poor little Lucy, my poor little Lucy. I don't deserve this from you."

She did not know what he meant, and she only answered him with kisses, while her hands moved caressingly across his forehead, just as they had moved years ago in Rome when she soothed the pain away. There certainly was a mesmeric influence emanating from those hands, and Arthur felt its power, growing very quiet and at last falling away to sleep while the passes went on, and Lucy held her breath lest she should waken him. She was a famous nurse, the physician said, when he came, and he constituted her his coadjutor and gave his patient's medicine into her care.

It was hardly proper for her niece to stay at the rectory, Mrs. Hetherton thought, but Lucy was one who could trample down proprieties, and it was finally arranged that, in order to avoid all comment, Fanny should stay with her.

So, while Fanny went to bed and slept Lucy sat all night in the sick-room with Mrs. Brown, and when the next morning came she was looking very pale, and languid, but very beautiful withal. At least such was the mental compliment paid her by Thornton Hastings, who was passing through Hanover and stopped over a train to see his old college friend and perhaps tell him what he began to feel it was his duty to tell him in spite of his promise to Anna. She was nearly well now and had driven with him twice to the park, but he could not be insensible to what she suffered, or how she shrank from hearing the proposed wedding discussed, and in his intense pity for her he had half resolved to break his word and tell Arthur what he knew. But he changed his mind when he had been in Hanover a few hours and watched the little fairy, who, like some ministering angel, glided about the sick-room, showing herself every whit a woman, and making him repent that he had ever called her frivolous or silly. She was not either, he said, and with a magnanimity for which he thought himself entitled to a good deal of praise, he felt that it was very possible for Arthur to love the gentle little girl who smoothed his pillows so tenderly, and whose fingers threaded so lovingly the dark brown locks when she thought he—Thornton—was not looking on. She was very coy of *him*, and very distant towards him, for she had not forgotten his sin, and she treated him at first with a reserve for which he could not account. But as the days went on and Arthur grew so sick that his parishioners began to tremble for their young minister's life, and to think it perfectly right for Lucy to stay with him even if she was assisted in her labor of love by the stranger from New York, the reserve all disappeared, and on the most perfect terms of amity she and Thornton Hastings watched together by Arthur's side.

Thornton Hastings learned more lessons than one in that sick-room where Arthur's faith in God triumphed over the terrors of the grave which at one time seemed so near, while the timid Lucy, whom he had only known as a gay butterfly of fashion, dared before him to pray that God would spare her promised husband, or give her grace to say "Thy will be done." Thornton could hardly say that he was skeptical before, but any doubts he might have had touching the great fundamental truths on which a true religion rests were gone forever, and he left Hanover a changed man in more respects than one.

Arthur did not die, and on the Sunday preceding the week when the Christmas decorations were to commence he came again before his people, his face very pale and worn, and wearing upon it a look which told of a new baptism,—an added amount of faith which had helped to lift him above the fleeting cares of this present life. And yet there was much of earth clinging to him still, and it made itself felt in the rapid beatings of his heart when he glanced towards the pew where Lucy knelt and knew that she was giving thanks for him restored again.

Once in the earlier stages of his convalescence he had almost betrayed his secret by asking her which she would rather do, bury him from her sight, feeling that he loved her to the last, or give him to another now that she knew he would recover.

There was a frightened look in Lucy's eyes as she replied:

"I would ten thousand times rather see you dead, and know that even in death you were my own, than to lose you that other way. O Arthur, you have no thought of leaving me now?"

"No, darling, I have not. I am yours always," he said, feeling that the compact was sealed forever, and that God blessed the sealing.

He had written to Mrs. Meredith, granting her his forgiveness, and asking that if Anna did not already know of the deception she might never be enlightened. And Mrs. Meredith had answered that Anna had only heard a rumor that an offer had been made her, but that she regarded it as a mistake, and was fast recovering both her health and spirits. Mrs. Meredith did not add her surprise at Arthur's conscientiousness in adhering to his engagement, nor hint that her attack of conscience was so safely over; she was glad of it, for she still had hope of that house on Madison Square; but Arthur guessed at it and dismissed her from his mind, and waited with a trusting heart for whatever the future might bring.

CHAPTER XII.

VALENCIA.

VERY extensive preparations were making at Prospect Hill for the double wedding to occur on the 15th of January. After much debate and consultation, Fanny had decided to take Mr. Bellamy then, and thus she, too, shared largely in the general interest and excitement which pervaded everything. Both brides-elect were very happy, but in a widely different way, for while Fanny was quiet and undemonstrative Lucy seemed wild with joy and danced gayly about the house, now in the kitchen, where the cake was made, now in the chamber, where the plain sewing was done, and then flitting to her own room in quest of Valencia, who was sent on divers errands of mercy, the little lady thinking that as the time for her marriage was so near it would be proper for her to stop in-doors and not show herself in public quite so freely as she had been in the habit of doing. So she remained at home, and they missed her in the back streets and by-lanes, and the Widow Hobbs, who was still an invalid, pined for a sight of her bright face, and was only half consoled for its absence by the charities which

Valencia brought, the smart waiting-maid putting on a great many airs and making Mrs. Hobbs feel keenly how greatly she thought herself demeaned by coming to such a heathenish place. The Hanoverians, too, missed her in the streets, but for this they made ample amends by discussing the preparations at Prospect Hill and commenting upon the bridal trousseau, which was sent from New York the week before Christmas, thus affording a most fruitful theme of comment for the women and maids engaged in trimming the church. There were dresses of every conceivable fashion, it was said, but none were quite so grand as the wedding-dress itself,—a heavy white silk which " could stand alone," and trailed a full yard behind. It was also whispered that, not content with seeing the effect of her bridal robes as they lay upon the bed, Miss Lucy Harcourt had actually tried them on, wreath, veil, and all, and stood before the glass until Miss Fanny had laughed at her for being so vain and foolish, and said she was a pretty specimen for a sober clergyman's wife. For all this gossip the villagers were indebted mostly to Valencia Le Barre, who, ever since her arrival at Prospect Hill, had been growing somewhat dissatisfied with the young mistress she had expected to rule even more completely than she had ruled Mrs. Meredith. But in this she was mistaken, and it did not improve her never very amiable temper to find that she could not with safety appropriate more than half her mistress' handkerchiefs, collars, cuffs, and gloves, to say nothing of perfumery and pomades ; and as this was a new state of things with Valencia, she chafed at the administration under which she had so willingly put herself, and told things of her mistress which no sensible servant would ever have reported. And Lucy gave her plenty to tell. Frank and outspoken as a child, she acted as she felt and *did* try on the bridal dress, did scream with delight when Valencia fastened the veil and let its fleecy folds fall gracefully around her.

"I wonder what Arthur will think. I so wish he was here," she had said, ordering a glass brought, that she might see herself from behind, and know just how much her dress trailed, and how it looked beneath the costly veil.

She was very beautiful in her bridal robes, and she kept them on till Fanny began to chide her for her vanity, and even then she lingered before the mirror as if loth to take them off.

"I don't believe in presentiments," she said, "but do you know it seems to me just as if I should never wear this again," and she smoothed thoughtfully the folds of the heavy silk she had just laid upon the bed. "I don't know what can happen to prevent it, unless Arthur should die. He was so pale last Sunday, and seemed so weak that I shuddered every time I looked at him. I mean to drive round there this afternoon," she continued.

"I suppose it is too cold for him to venture out, and he has no carriage, either."

Accordingly she went to the rectory that afternoon, and the women in the church saw her as she drove by, the gorgeous colors of her carriage-blanket flashing in the wintry sunshine, and the long white feather in her hat waving up and down as she nodded to them. There was a little too much of the lady patroness about her to suit the plain Hanoverians, especially those who were neither high enough nor low enough to be honored with her notice; and as they returned to their wreath-making and gossip, they wondered under their breath if it would not on the whole have been better if their clergyman had married Anna Ruthven, instead of the fine city girl with her Parisian manners. As they said this, a gleam of intelligence shot from the gray eyes of Valencia Le Barre, who was there at work in a most unamiable mood.

"*She* did not like to stain her hands with the nasty hemlock, more than other folks," she had said, when, after the trying on of the bridal dress, Lucy had remonstrated with her for some duty neglected, and then bidden her go to the church and help if she was needed.

"I must certainly dismiss you unless you improve," Lucy had said to the insolent girl, who went unwillingly to the church, where she sat tying wreaths when the carriage went by.

She had thought many times of the letter she had read,

and more than once when particularly angry it had been upon her lips to tell her mistress that she was not Mr. Leighton's *first* choice, if indeed she was his choice at all; but there was something in Lucy's manner which held her back, besides which she was rather unwilling to confess to her own meanness in reading the stolen letter.

"I *could* tell them something if I would," she thought, as she bent over the hemlock boughs, and listened to the remarks; but for that time she kept her secret and worked on moodily, while the unsuspecting Lucy went her way, and was soon alighting at the parsonage-gate.

Arthur saw her as she came up the walk, and went out to meet her. He was looking very pale and miserable, and his clothes hung loosely upon him, but he welcomed her kindly, and lead her in to the fire, and tried to believe that he was glad to see her sitting there with her little high-heeled boots upon the fender, and the bright hues of her balmoral just showing beneath her dress of blue merino. She went all over the house as she usually did, suggesting alterations and improvements, and greatly confusing good Mrs. Brown, who trudged obediently after her, wondering what she and her master were ever to do with the gay-plumaged bird, whose ways were so unlike their own.

"You must drive with me to the church," she said at last to Arthur. "Fresh air will do you good, and you stay moped up too much. I wanted you to-day at Prospect Hill, for this morning the express from New York brought—" she stood up on tiptoe to whisper the great news to him, but his pulses did not quicken in the least, even when she told him how charming was the bridal-dress.

He was standing before the mirror, and glancing at himself, he said half laughingly, half sadly, " I am a pitiful-looking bridegroom to go with all that finery. I should not think you would want me, Lucy."

" But I do," she answered, holding his hand and leading him to the carriage, which took him swiftly to the church.

He had not intended going there as long as there was an excuse for staying away, and he felt himself grow sick and faint when he stood amid the Christmas decorations, and remembered the last year, when he and Anna had fastened the wreaths upon the wall. They were trimming the church very elaborately in honor of him and his bride-elect, and white artificial flowers, so natural that they could not be detected from the real, were mixed with scarlet leaves and placed among the mass of green. The effect was very fine, and Arthur tried to praise it, but his face belied his words, and after he was gone, the disappointed girls declared that he looked more like a man about to be hung, than one so soon to be married.

It was very late that night when Lucy summoned Valencia to comb out her long, thick curls, and Valencia was tired and cross and sleepy, and handled the brush so awkwardly, and snarled her mistress's hair so often, that Lucy expostulated with her sharply, and this awoke the slumbering demon, which, bursting into full life, could no longer be restrained, and in amazement which kept her silent, Lucy listened, while Valencia vulgarly taunted her with "standing in Anna Ruthven's shoes," and told all she knew of the letter stolen by Mrs. Meredith, and the one she carried to Arthur. But Valencia's anger quickly cooled, and she trembled with fear when she saw how deathly white her mistress grew, and even heard the loud beating of the heart which seemed trying to burst from its prison, and fall bleeding at the feet of the poor, wretched girl, around whose lips the white foam gathered as she motioned Valencia to stop, and whispered "I am dying."

She was *not* dying, but the fainting-fit which ensued was more like death than that which had come upon Anna when she heard that Arthur was lost. Once they really thought her dead, and in an agony of remorse Valencia hung over her, accusing herself as a murderess, but giving no other explanation to those around her than:

"I was combing her hair when the white froth spirted all over her wrapper, and she said that she was dying."

And that was all the family knew of the strange attack which lasted till the dawn of day, and left upon Lucy's face a look as if years and years of anguish had passed over her young head, and left its footprints behind. Early in the morning she asked to see Valencia alone, and the repentant girl went to her, prepared to take back all she had said, and declare the whole a lie. But something in Lucy's manner wrung the truth from her, and she repeated the story again so clearly, that Lucy had no longer a doubt that Anna was preferred to herself, and sending Valencia away, she moaned piteously :

"Oh, what shall I do ? What is my duty ?"

The part which hurt her most of all was the terrible certainty that Arthur did not love *her*, as he loved Anna Ruthven. She seemed intuitively to understand it all, and see how in an unguarded moment he had offered himself to save her good name from gossip, and how ever since his life had been a constant struggle to do his duty by her.

"Poor Arthur," she sobbed, "yours has been a hard lot, trying to act the love you did not feel; but it shall be so no longer, for I will set you free."

This was her final decision, but she did not reach it till a day and night had passed, during which she lay with her face turned to the wall, saying she wanted nothing except to be left alone.

"When I can, I'll tell you," she had said to Fanny and her aunt, who insisted upon knowing the cause of her distress. "When I can, I'll tell you all about it. Leave me alone till then."

So they ceased to worry her, but Fanny sat constantly in the room watching the motionless figure, which took whatever she offered, but otherwise gave no sign of life until the morning of the second day, when it turned slowly towards her, and the livid lips quivered piteously and made an attempt to smile as they said:

"I can tell you now. I have made up my mind."

Fanny's eyes were dim with the truest tears she had ever shed when Lucy's story was ended, and her voice was very low as she asked:

"And you mean to give him up at this late hour?"

"Yes, I mean to give him up. I have been over the entire ground many times, even to the deep humiliation of what people will say, and I have come each time to the same conclusion. It is right that Arthur should be released, and I shall release him."

"And what will *you* do?" Fanny asked, gazing in wonder and awe at the young girl, who answered: "I do not know; I have not thought. I guess God will take care of that."

And God *did* take care of *that*, and inclined the Hetherton family to be very kind and tender towards her, and kept Arthur from the house until the Christmas decorations were completed and the Christmas festival was held. Many were the inquiries made for Lucy on Christmas Eve, and many thanks and wishes for her speedy restoration were sent to her by those whom she had so bountifully remembered. Thornton Hastings, too, who had come to town and was present at the church on Christmas Eve, asked for her with almost as much interest as Arthur, who bade Fanny tell her that he should call on her on the morrow after the morning service.

"Oh, I cannot see him here! I must tell him at the rectory in the very room where he asked me to be his wife," Lucy said, when Fanny reported Arthur's message. "I am able to ride there, and it will be fine sleighing to-morrow. See, the snow is falling now," and pushing back the curtain Lucy looked drearily out upon the fast-whitening ground, sighing as she remembered the night when the first snow-flakes were falling, and she stood watching them with Arthur at her side.

Fanny did not oppose her cousin, and with a kiss upon the blue-veined forehead, she went to her own room and left her to think for the hundredth time *what* she should say to Arthur.

CHAPTER XIII.

CHRISTMAS DAY.

HE worshippers at St. Mark's on Christmas morning heard the music of the bells as the Hetherton sleigh dashed by, but none of them knew whither it was bound or dreamed of the scene which awaited the rector when after the services were over he started towards home. Lucy had kept to her resolution, and just as Mrs. Brown was looking at the clock to see if it was time to put her fowls to bake, she heard the hall door open softly, and almost dropped her dripping-pan in her surprise at the sight of Lucy Harcourt, who looked so mournfully at her as she said:

"I want to go to Arthur's room,—the library, I mean."

"Why, child, what is the matter? I heard you was sick, but did not s'spose 'twas anything very bad. You are paler than a ghost," Mrs. Brown exclaimed, as she tried to unfasten Lucy's hood and cloak and lead her to the fire.

But Lucy was not cold, and would rather go at once to Arthur's room. So Mrs. Brown made no objection, though she wondered if the girl was crazy as she went back to her fowls and Christmas pudding, and left Lucy to find her way alone to Arthur's study, which looked so like its owner, with his dressing-gown across the lounge just where he had thrown it, his slippers on the rug, and his arm-chair standing near the table, where he had sat when he asked Lucy to be his wife, and where she now sat down, panting heavily for breath and gazing drearily around with the look of a frightened bird when seeking for some avenue of escape from an appalling danger. There *was* no escape, and with a moan she laid her head upon the writing-table, and prayed that Arthur might come quickly while she had sense and strength to tell him. She heard his step at last, and rose up to meet him, smiling a little at his sudden start when he saw her there.

"It's only I," she said, shedding back the curls from her pallid face and grasping the chair to steady herself and keep from falling. "I am not here to frighten or worry you. I've come to do you good,—to set you free. O Arthur, you do not know how terribly you have been wronged, and I did not know it either till a few days ago! She never received your letter,—Anna never did. If she had she would have answered yes and been in my place now; but she is going to be there. I give you up to Anna. I'm here to tell you so. But O Arthur, it hurts,—it hurts—"

He knew it hurt by the agonized expression of her face, but he could not go near her for a moment, so great was his surprise at what he saw and heard. But when the first shock for them both was past, and he could listen to her more rational account of what she knew and what she was there to do, he refused to listen. He knew it all before, and he would not be free; he would keep his word, he said. Matters had gone too far to be so suddenly ended; he held her to her promise, and she must be his wife.

"Can you tell me truly that you love *me* more than Anna?" Lucy asked, a ray of hope dawning for an instant upon her heart, but fading into utter darkness as Arthur hesitated to answer her.

He *did* love Anna best, though never had Lucy been so near supplanting her as at that moment when she stood before him and told him he was free. There was something in the magnitude of her generosity which touched him closely, and made her dearer to him than she had ever been.

"I can make you very happy," he said at last, and Lucy replied, "Yes, but how with yourself? Would you be happy too? No, Arthur, you would not, and neither should I, knowing what I do. It is best that we should part, though it almost breaks my heart, for I have loved you so much."

She stopped for breath, and Arthur was wondering

what he should say next, when a cheery whistle sounded near, and Thornton Hastings appeared in the door. He had just returned from the post-office, whither he had gone after church, and not knowing any one but Arthur was in the library, had come there at once.

"I beg your pardon," he said, when he saw Lucy; and he was hurrying away, but Lucy called him back, feeling that in him she would find a powerful ally to aid her in her task.

Appealing to him as Arthur's friend, she repeated Valencia's story rapidly, and then went on: "Anna never knew of that letter,—or she would have answered yes. I know she loves him, for I can remember a thousand things which prove it, and I know he has loved her best all the time, even when trying so hard to love me. Oh, how it hurts me to think he had to *try* to love me who loved him so much. But that is all past now. I give him up to Anna, and you must help me as if I were your sister. Tell him it is best. He must not argue against me, for I feel myself giving way through my great love for him, and I know it is not right. Tell him, Mr. Hastings; plead my cause for me; say what a true woman ought to say, for, believe me, I am in earnest in giving him to Anna."

There was a ghastly hue upon her face, and her features looked pinched and rigid, but the terrible heartbeats were not there. God in His great mercy kept them back, else she had surely died under that strong excitement. Thornton thought she was fainting, and going hastily to her side, passed his arm around her and put her in the chair; then standing by her, he said just what first came into his mind to say. It was a delicate matter in which to interfere, but he handled it carefully, telling frankly what had passed between himself and Anna, and giving as his opinion, that she loved Arthur to-day just as well as before she left Hanover.

"Then it is surely right for Arthur to marry her, and he must!" Lucy exclaimed vehemently, while Thornton laid his hand pityingly upon her head, and said, "And only you be sacrificed."

There was something wonderfully tender in the tone of Thornton's voice, and Lucy glanced quickly at him while her eyes filled with the first tears she had shed since she came into the room.

"I am willing; I am ready; I have made up my mind, and I shall never unmake it," she answered, while Arthur put in a feeble remonstrance.

But Thornton was on Lucy's side, and did with his cooler judgment what she could not; and when at last the interview was ended, there was no ring on Lucy's forefinger, for Arthur held it in his hand, and their engagement was at an end. Stunned with what he had passed through, he stood motionless while Thornton drew Lucy's cloak about her shoulders, fastened her fur, tied on her satin hood, and took such care of her as a mother would take of a suffering child.

"It is hardly safe to send her home alone," he thought, as he looked into her face and saw how weak she was. "As a friend of both I ought to accompany her."

She was indeed so weak that she could scarcely stand, and Thornton took her in his arms and carried her to the sleigh; then springing in beside her, he made her lean her tired head upon his shoulder as they drove to Prospect Hill. She did not seem frivolous to him now, but rather the noblest type of womanhood he had ever met. Few could have done what she had, and there was much of warmth and fervor in the clasp of his hand as he bade her good-by, and went back to the rectory.

. . . . . .

Great was the consternation and surprise in Hanover when it was known that there was to be but one bride at Prospect Hill on the night of the 15th, and various were the surmises as to the cause of the sudden change; but strive as they might, the good people of the village could not get at the truth, for Valencia held her peace, while the Hethertons were far too proud to admit of their being questioned, and Thornton Hastings stood a bulwark of defence between the people and the clergyman, and managed to have the pulpit at St. Mark's supplied for a few weeks, while he took Arthur away, saying that his health required the change.

"You have done nobly, darling," Fanny Hetherton had said to Lucy when she received her from Thornton's hands and heard that all was over. Then, leading her half-fainting cousin to her own cheerful room, she made her lie down while she told her of the plan she had formed when first she heard what Lucy's intentions were. "I wrote to Mr. Bellamy asking if he would take a trip to Europe, so that you could go with us, for I knew you would not wish to stay here. To-day I have his answer saying he will go; and what is better yet, father and mother are going, too."

"Oh I am so glad! I could not stay here now," Lucy replied, sobbing herself to sleep, while Fanny sat by and watched, wondering at the strength which had upheld her weak little cousin in the struggle she had been through, and feeling, too, that it was just as well, for after all it was a mésalliance for an heiress like her cousin to marry a poor clergyman.

. . . . . .

There was a great wedding at Prospect Hill on the night of the 15th, but neither Lucy nor Arthur were there. He lay sick again at the St. Denis, in New York, and she was alone in her chamber fighting back her tears, and praying that now the worst was over she might be withheld from looking back and wishing the work undone. She went with the bridal party to New York, where she tarried for a few days, but saw no one but Anna, for whom she sent at once. The interview lasted more than an hour, and Anna's eyes were swollen with weeping when at last it ended; but Lucy's face, though white as snow, was very calm and quiet, and wore a peaceful, placid look which made it like the face of an angel. Two weeks later, and the steamer Java bore her away across the water, where she hoped to outlive the storm which had beaten so piteously upon her. Thornton Hastings and Anna went with her on board the ship, and for their sakes she tried to appear natural, succeeding so well that it was a very pleasant picture, which Thornton kept in his mind, of a frail little figure standing upon the deck, holding its water-proof together with one hand, and with the other waving a smiling adieu to Anna and himself.

More than a year later Thornton Hastings followed that figure across the sea, and found it in beautiful Venice, sailing again through the moonlit streets, and listening to the music which came so oft from the passing gondolas. It had recovered its former roundness, and the face was even more beautiful than it had been before, for the light frivolity was gone, and there was in its stead a peaceful, subdued expression which made Lucy Harcourt more attractive than she had ever been. At least so Thornton Hastings thought, and he lingered at her side, and felt glad that she gave no outward token of agitation when he said to her:

"There was a wedding at St. Mark's in Hanover just

before I left. Can you guess who the happy couple were?"

"Yes, Arthur and Anna. She wrote me they were to be married on Christmas eve. I am so glad it has come around at last."

Then she questioned him of the bridal,—of Arthur,—and even of Anna's dress, her manner evincing that the old wound had healed, or was healing very fast, and that soon only a scar would remain to tell where it had been.

And so the days went on beneath the sunny Italian skies, until one glorious night in Rome, when they sat together amid the ruins of the Colosseum, and Thornton spoke his mind, alluding to the time when each had loved another, expressing himself as glad that in his case the matter had ended as it did, and then asking Lucy if she could conscientiously be his wife.

"What! You marry a frivolous plaything like me?" Lucy asked, her woman's pride flashing up once more, but this time playfully, as Thornton knew by the joyous light in her eye.

She told him what she meant, and how she had hated him for it, and then they laughed together, but Thornton's kiss smothered the laugh on Lucy's lips, for he guessed what her answer was, and that this, his second wooing, was more successful than his first had been.

• • • • • •

"MARRIED, in Rome, on Thursday, April 10th, THORNTON HASTINGS, ESQ., of New York City, to MISS LUCY HARCOURT, also of New York, and niece of Colonel James Hetherton."

Anna was out in the rectory garden bending over a bed of hyacinths when Arthur brought her the paper and pointed to the notice.

"Oh, I am so glad, so *glad*, so GLAD!" she exclaimed, emphasizing each successive glad a little more, and setting down her foot as if to give it force. "I have never dared be quite as happy with you as I might," she continued, leaning lovingly against her husband, "for there was always a thought of Lucy, and what a fearful price she paid for our happiness. But now it is all as it should be, and, Arthur, am I very vain in thinking that she is better suited to Thornton Hastings than I ever was, and that I do better as your wife than Lucy would have done?"

A kiss was Arthur's only answer, but Anna was satisfied, and there rested upon her face a look of perfect content as all that warm spring afternoon she walked in her pleasant garden, thinking of the newly married pair in Rome, and glancing occasionally at the open window of the library where Arthur was, busy with his sermon, his pen moving all the faster for the knowing that Anna was just within his call,—that by turning his head he could see her dear face, and that by and by, when his work was done, she would come in to him, and with her loving words and winsome ways make him forget how tired he was, and thank Heaven again for the great gift bestowed when it gave him Anna Ruthven.

THE END.

NEW BOOKS
AND NEW EDITIONS,
RECENTLY ISSUED BY

G. W. CARLETON & Co., Publishers,
Madison Square, New York.

The Publishers, upon receipt of the price in advance, will send any book on this Catalogue by mail, *postage free*, to any part of the United States.

All books in this list [unless otherwise specified] are handsomely bound in cloth board binding, with gilt backs, suitable for libraries.

Mary J. Holmes' Works.

TEMPEST AND SUNSHINE	$1 50	DARKNESS AND DAYLIGHT	$1 50
ENGLISH ORPHANS	1 50	HUGH WORTHINGTON	1 50
HOMESTEAD ON THE HILLSIDE	1 50	CAMERON PRIDE	1 50
'LENA RIVERS	1 50	ROSE MATHER	1 50
MEADOW BROOK	1 50	ETHELYN'S MISTAKE	1 50
DORA DEANE	1 50	MILLBANK	1 50
COUSIN MAUDE	1 50	EDNA BROWNING	1 50
MARIAN GRAY	1 50	WEST LAWN......(new)	1 50

Marion Harland's Works.

ALONE	$1 50	SUNNYBANK	$1 50
HIDDEN PATH	1 50	HUSBANDS AND HOMES	1 50
MOSS SIDE	1 50	RUBY'S HUSBAND	1 50
NEMESIS	1 50	PHEMIE'S TEMPTATION	1 50
MIRIAM	1 50	THE EMPTY HEART	1 50
AT LAST	1 50	TRUE AS STEEL......(new)	1 50
HELEN GARDNER	1 50	JESSAMAINE....(just published)	1 50

Charles Dickens' Works.
"Carleton's New Illustrated Edition."

THE PICKWICK PAPERS	$1 50	MARTIN CHUZZLEWIT	$1 50
OLIVER TWIST	1 50	OUR MUTUAL FRIEND	1 50
DAVID COPPERFIELD	1 50	TALE OF TWO CITIES	1 50
GREAT EXPECTATIONS	1 50	CHRISTMAS BOOKS	1 50
DOMBEY AND SON	1 50	SKETCHES BY "BOZ"	1 50
BARNABY RUDGE	1 50	HARD TIMES, etc.	1 50
NICHOLAS NICKLEBY	1 50	PICTURES OF ITALY, etc.	1 50
OLD CURIOSITY SHOP	1 50	UNCOMMERCIAL TRAVELLER	1 50
BLEAK HOUSE	1 50	EDWIN DROOD, etc.	1 50
LITTLE DORRIT	1 50	CHILD'S ENGLAND, and CATALOGUE	1 50

Augusta J. Evans' Novels.

BEULAH	$1 75	ST. ELMO	$2 00
MACARIA	1 75	VASHTI......(new)	2 00
INEZ	1 75		

G. W. CARLETON & CO.'S PUBLICATIONS.

Captain Mayne Reid—Illustrated.
SCALP HUNTERS .... $1 50 | WHITE CHIEF................. $1 50
WAR TRAIL..................... 1 50 | HEADLESS HORSEMAN........... 1 50
HUNTER'S FEAST................ 1 50 | LOST LENORE................. 1 50
TIGER HUNTER.................. 1 50 | WOOD RANGERS................ 1 50
OSCEOLA, THE SEMINOLE......... 1 50 | WILD HUNTRESS............... 1 50
THE QUADROON.................. 1 50 | THE MAROON.................. 1 50
RANGERS AND REGULATORS........ 1 50 | RIFLE RANGERS............... 1 50
WHITE GAUNTLET................ 1 50 | WILD LIFE................... 1 50

A. S. Roe's Works.
A LONG LOOK AHEAD............. $1 50 | TRUE TO THE LAST............ $1 50
TO LOVE AND TO BE LOVED....... 1 50 | LIKE AND UNLIKE............. 1 50
TIME AND TIDE................. 1 50 | LOOKING AROUND.............. 1 50
I'VE BEEN THINKING............ 1 50 | WOMAN OUR ANGEL............. 1 50
THE STAR AND THE CLOUD........ 1 50 | THE CLOUD ON THE HEART...... 1 50
HOW COULD HE HELP IT.......... 1 50 | RESOLUTION...... (new)...... 1 50

Hand-Books of Society.
THE HABITS OF GOOD SOCIETY. The nice points of taste and good manners,
and the art of making oneself agreeable....................................$1 75
THE ART OF CONVERSATION.—A sensible work, for every one who wishes to be
either an agreeable talker or listener..................................... 1 50
THE ARTS OF WRITING, READING, AND SPEAKING.—An excellent book for self-
instruction and improvement.. 1 50
A NEW DIAMOND EDITION of the above three popular books.—Small size,
elegantly bound, and put in a box.. 3 00

Mrs. Hill's Cook Book.
MRS. A. P. HILL'S NEW COOKERY BOOK, and family domestic receipts..........$2 00

Charlotte Bronte and Miss Muloch.
SHIRLEY.—Author of Jane Eyre....$1 75 | JOHN HALIFAX, GENTLEMAN......$1 75

Mrs. N. S. Emerson.
BETSEY AND I ARE OUT—And other Poems. A Thanksgiving Story.........$1 50

Louisa M. Alcott.
MORNING GLORIES—A beautiful juvenile, by the author of "Little Women"..... 1 50

The Crusoe Books—Famous "Star Edition."
ROBINSON CRUSOE.—New illustrated edition..................................$1 50
SWISS FAMILY ROBINSON.   Do.   Do 1 50
THE ARABIAN NIGHTS.   Do.   Do 1 50

Julie P. Smith's Novels.
WIDOW GOLDSMITH'S DAUGHTER....$1 75 | THE WIDOWER.................$1 75
CHRIS AND OTHO................ 1 75 | THE MARRIED BELLE........... 1 75
TEN OLD MAIDS......[in press].. 1 75 |

Artemus Ward's Comic Works.
ARTEMUS WARD—HIS BOOK........$1 50 | ARTEMUS WARD—IN LONDON.....$1 50
ARTEMUS WARD—HIS TRAVELS..... 1 50 | ARTEMUS WARD—HIS PANORAMA.. 1 50

Fanny Fern's Works.
FOLLY AS IT FLIES.............$1 50 | CAPER-SAUCE......(new).......$1 50
GINGERSNAPS................... 1 50 | A MEMORIAL—By JAMES Parton.. 2 00

Josh Billings' Comic Works.
JOSH BILLINGS' PROVERBS.......$1 50 | JOSH BILLINGS FARMER'S ALMINAX, 25 cts.
JOSH BILLINGS ON ICE.......... 1 50 | (In paper covers.)

Verdant Green.
A racy English college story—with numerous comic illustrations............$1 50

Popular Italian Novels.
DOCTOR ANTONIO.—A love story of Italy. By Ruffini........................$1 75
BEATRICE CENCI.—By Guerrazzi. With a steel Portrait...................... 1 75

M. Michelet's Remarkable Works.
LOVE (L'AMOUR).—English translation from the original French.............$1 50
WOMAN (LA FEMME).   Do.   Do.   Do. 1 50

G. W. CARLETON & CO.'S PUBLICATIONS.

May Agnes Fleming's Novels.
GUY EARLSCOURT'S WIFE.........$1 75 | A WONDERFUL WOMAN.......... $1 75
A TERRIBLE SECRET............. 1 75 |

Ernest Renan's French Works.
THE LIFE OF JESUS..............$1 75 | LIFE OF SAINT PAUL............$1 75
LIVES OF THE APOSTLES......... 1 75 | BIBLE IN INDIA. By Jacolliot.... 2 00

Geo. W. Carleton.
OUR ARTIST IN CUBA............$1 50 | OUR ARTIST IN AFRICA. (In press.) $1 50
OUR ARTIST IN PERU............ 1 50 | OUR ARTIST IN MEXICO. Do. 1 50

Popular Novels, from the French.
SHE LOVED HIM MADLY. Borys...$1 75 | SO FAIR YET FALSE. By Chavette.$1 75
A FATAL PASSION. By Bernard.. 1 75 |

Maria J. Westmoreland's Novels.
HEART HUNGRY..................$1 75 | CLIFFORD TROUPE. (New).......$1 75

Sallie A. Brock's Novels.
KENNETH, MY KING.............$1 75 | A NEW BOOK. (In press.)........

Don Quixote.
A BEAUTIFUL NEW 12MO EDITION. With illustrations by Gustave Dore.....$1 50

Victor Hugo.
LES MISERABLES.—English translation from the French. Octavo..........$2 50
LES MISERABLES.—In the Spanish language............................... 5 00

Algernon Charles Swinburne.
LAUS VENERIS, AND OTHER POEMS.—An elegant new edition.............$1 50
FRENCH LOVE-SONGS.—Selected from the best French authors................ 1 50

Robert Dale Owen.
THE DEBATEABLE LAND BETWEEN THIS WORLD AND THE NEXT............$2 00
THREADING MY WAY.—Twenty-five years of Autobiography................... 1 50

The Game of Whist.
POLE ON WHIST.—The late English standard work......................$1 00

Mansfield T. Walworth's Novels.
WARWICK......................$1 75 | STORMCLIFF.....................$1 75
LULU.......................... 1 75 | DELAPLAINE.................... 1 75
HOTSPUR....................... 1 75 | BEVERLY. (New.).............. 1 75

Mother Goose Set to Music.
MOTHER GOOSE MELODIES.—With music for singing, and illustrations........$1 50

M. M. Pomeroy "Brick."
SENSE—(a serious book).........$1 50 | NONSENSE—(a comic book).......$1 50
GOLD-DUST do. .... 1 50 | BRICK-DUST do. 1 50
OUR SATURDAY NIGHTS.......... 1 50 | LIFE OF M. M. POMEROY......... 1 50

John Esten Cooke.
FAIRFAX.......................$1 50 | HAMMER AND RAPIER............$1 50
HILT TO HILT.................. 1 50 | OUT OF THE FOAM............... 1 50

Feydeau and Cazenave.
FEMALE BEAUTY AND THE ARTS OF PLEASING.—From the French.............$1 50

Joseph Rodman Drake.
THE CULPRIT FAY.—The well-known fairy poem, with 100 illustrations......$2 00
THE CULPRIT FAY. Do. superbly bound in turkey morocco.. 5 00

Richard B. Kimball.
WAS HE SUCCESSFUL?............$1 75 | LIFE IN SAN DOMINGO...........$1 50
UNDERCURRENTS OF WALL STREET. 1 75 | HENRY POWERS, BANKER.......... 1 75
SAINT LEGER................... 1 75 | TO-DAY........................ 1 75
ROMANCE OF STUDENT LIFE...... 1 75 | EMILIE. (In press.)...........

Author "New Gospel of Peace."
CHRONICLES OF GOTHAM.—A rich modern satire. (Paper covers)...........25 cts.
THE FALL OF MAN.—A satire on the Darwin theory. Do. ....50 cts.

Celia E. Gardner's Novels.
STOLEN WATERS (in verse).......$1 50 | TESTED......(in prose)..........$1 75
BROKEN DREAMS do. .... 1 50 | RICH MEDWAY....do............. 1 75

4   G. W. CARLETON & CO.'S PUBLICATIONS.

Ann S. Stephens.
PHEMIE FROST'S EXPERIENCES.—Author of "Fashion and Famine" $1 75

Anna Cora Mowatt.
ITALIAN LIFE AND LEGENDS......$1 50 | THE CLERGYMAN'S WIFE.—A novel.$1 75

Mrs. C. L. McIlvain.
EBON AND GOLD.—A new American novel................. ....$1 50

Dr. Cummings's Works.
THE GREAT TRIBULATION........$2 00 | THE GREAT CONSUMMATION......$2 00
THE GREAT PREPARATION........ 2 00 | THE SEVENTH VIAL............... 2 00

Cecelia Cleveland.
THE STORY OF A SUMMER; OR, JOURNAL LEAVES FROM CHAPPAQUA.........$1 50

Olive Logan.
WOMEN AND THEATRES.—And other miscellaneous sketches and topics.......$1 50

Miscellaneous Works.
TALES FROM THE OPERAS........$1 50	NORTHERN BALLADS.—Anderson...$1 00
BELDAZZLE'S BACHELOR STUDIES.. 1 00	PLYMOUTH CHURCH.—1847 to 1873. 2 00
LITTLE WANDERERS.—Illustrated.. 1 50	O. C. KERR PAPERS.—4 vols. in 1... 2 00
GENESIS DISCLOSED.—T. A. Davies 1 50	CHRISTMAS HOLLY-Marion Harland 1 50
COMMODORE ROLLINGPIN'S LOG.... 1 50	DREAM MUSIC.—F. R. Marvin.... 1 50
BRAZEN GATES.—A juvenile 1 50	POEMS.—By L. G. Thomas....... 1 50
ANTIDOTE TO GATES AJAR........25 cts	VICTOR HUGO.—His life.......... 2 00
THE RUSSIAN BALL (paper).......25 cts	BEAUTY IS POWER............... 1 50
THE SNOBLACE BALL do ....25 cts	WOMAN, LOVE, AND MARRIAGE.... 1 50
DEAFNESS.—Dr. E. B. Lighthill.. 1 00	WICKEDEST WOMAN in New York..25 cts
A BOOK ABOUT LAWYERS.......... 2 00	SANDWICHES.—By Artemus Ward.25 cts
A BOOK ABOUT DOCTORS......... 2 00	REGINA.—Poems by Eliza Cruger.. 1 50
SQUIBOB PAPERS.—John Phœnix.. 1 50	WIDOW SPRIGGINS.—Widow Bedott 1 75

Miscellaneous Novels.
A CHARMING WIDOW.—Macquoid..$1 75	ROBERT GREATHOUSE.—J. F. Swift $2 00
TRUE TO HIM EVER.—By F. W. R. 1 50	FAUSTINA.—From the German..... 1 50
THE FORGIVING KISS.—By M. Loth. 1 75	MAURICE.—From the French..... 1 50
LOYAL UNTO DEATH.............. 1 75	GUSTAV ADOLF.—From the Swedish 1 50
BESSIE WILMERTON.—Westcott.... 1 75	ADRIFT WITH A VENGEANCE....... 1 50
PURPLE AND FINE LINEN.—Fawcett. 1 75	UP BROADWAY.—By Eleanor Kirk. 1 50
EDMUND DAWN.—By Ravenswood, 1 50	MONTALBAN...................... 1 75
CACHET.—Mrs. M. J. R. Hamilton, 1 75	LIFE AND DEATH................ 1 50
MARK GILDERSLEEVE.—J.S.Sauzade 1 75	CLAUDE GUEUX.—By Victor Hugo. 1 50
FERNANDO DE LEMOS.—C. Gayaree 2 00	FOUR OAKS.—By Kamba Thorpe.. 1 75
CROWN JEWELS.—Mrs. Moffat..... 1 75	ADRIFT IN DIXIE.—Edmund Kirke. 1 50
A LOST LIFE.—By Emily Moore... 1 50	AMONG THE GUERILLAS. Do. . 1 50
AVERY GLIBUN.—Orpheus C. Kerr. 2 00	AMONG THE PINES Do. . 1 50
THE CLOVEN FOOT.— Do. . 1 50	MY SOUTHERN FRIENDS. Do. . 1 50
ROMANCE OF RAILROAD.—Smith... 1 50	DOWN IN TENNESSEE. Do. . 1 50

Miscellaneous Works.
WOOD'S GUIDE TO THE CITY OF NEW YORK.—Beautifully and fully illustrated..$1 00
BILL ARP'S PEACE PAPERS.—Full of comic illustrations...................... 1 50
A BOOK OF EPITAPHS.—Amusing, quaint, and curious. (New).............. 1 50
SOUVENIRS OF TRAVEL.—By Madame Octavia Walton LeVert............... 2 00
THE ART OF AMUSING.—A book of home amusements, with illustrations...... 1 50
HOW TO MAKE MONEY; and how to keep it.—By Thomas A. Davies......... 1 50
BALLAD OF LORD BATEMAN.—With illustrations by Cruikshank (paper).......25 cts
BEHIND THE SCENES; at the "White House."—By Elizabeth Keckley........ 2 00
THE YACHTSMAN'S PRIMER.—For amateur sailors. T. R. Warren (paper)....50 cts
RURAL ARCHITECTURE.—By M. Field. With plans and illustrations......... 2 00
LIFE OF HORACE GREELEY.—By L. U. Reavis. With a new steel Portrait.... 2 00
WHAT I KNOW OF FARMING.—By Horace Greeley............................ 1 50
PRACTICAL TREATISE ON LABOR.—By Hendrick B. Wright................... 2 00
TWELVE VIEWS OF HEAVEN.—By Twelve Distinguished English Divines...... 1 50
HOUSES NOT MADE WITH HANDS.—An illustrated juvenile, illust'd by Hoppin. 1 00
CRUISE OF THE SHENANDOAH—The Last Confederate Steamer................ 1 50
MILITARY RECORD OF CIVILIAN APPOINTMENTS in the U. S. Army 5 00
IMPENDING CRISIS OF THE SOUTH.—By Hinton Rowan Helper................ 2 00
NEGROES IN NEGROLAND   Do.   Do.   Do. (paper covers).. 1 00

CHARLES DICKENS' WORKS.

A New Edition.

Among the numerous editions of the works of this greatest of English Novelists, there has not been until now *one* that entirely satisfies the public demand. .... Without exception, they each have some strong distinctive objection, ... either the shape and dimensions of the volumes are unhandy—or, the type is small and indistinct—or, the paper is thin and poor—or, the illustrations [if they have any] are unsatisfactory—or, the binding is bad—or, the price is too high.

A new edition is *now*, however, published by G. W. Carleton & Co. of New York, which, it is believed, will, in every respect, completely satisfy the popular demand. ... It is known as

"Carleton's New Illustrated Edition."

The size and form is most convenient for holding, .. the type is entirely new, and of a clear and open character that has received the approval of the reading community in other popular works.

The illustrations are by the original artists chosen by Charles Dickens himself ... and the paper, printing, and binding are of the most attractive and substantial character.

The publication of this beautiful new edition was commenced in April, 1873, and will be completed in 20 volumes—one novel each month—at the extremely reasonable price of $1.50 per volume, as follows:—

1—THE PICKWICK PAPERS.	11—MARTIN CHUZZLEWIT.
2—OLIVER TWIST.	12—OUR MUTUAL FRIEND.
3—DAVID COPPERFIELD.	13—TALE OF TWO CITIES.
4—GREAT EXPECTATIONS.	14—CHRISTMAS BOOKS.
5—DOMBEY AND SON.	15—SKETCHES BY "BOZ."
6—BARNABY RUDGE.	16—HARD TIMES, ETC.
7—NICHOLAS NICKLEBY.	17—PICTURES OF ITALY, ETC.
8—OLD CURIOSITY SHOP.	18—UNCOMMERCIAL TRAVELLER.
9—BLEAK HOUSE.	19—EDWIN DROOD, ETC.
10—LITTLE DORRIT.	20—ENGLAND and CATALOGUE.

Being issued, month by month, at so reasonable a price, those who *begin* by subscribing for this work, will imperceptibly soon find themselves fortunate owners of an entire set of this *best edition of Dickens' Works*, almost without having paid for it.

A Prospectus furnishing specimen of type, sized-page, and illustrations, will be sent to any one *free* on application—and specimen copies of the bound books will be forwarded by mail, *postage free*, on receipt of price, $1.50, by

G. W. CARLETON & Co., Publishers,
Madison Square, New York.

THREE VALUABLE BOOKS,
All Beautifully Printed and Elegantly Bound.

I.—The Art of Conversation,

With Directions for Self-Culture. An admirably conceived and entertaining work—sensible, instructive, and full of suggestions valuable to every one who desires to be either a good talker or listener, or who wishes to appear to advantage in good society. Every young and even old person should read it, study it over and over again, and follow those hints in it which lead them to break up bad habits and cultivate good ones. *** Price $1.50. Among the contents will be found chapters upon—

ATTENTION IN CONVERSATION.—SATIRE.—PUNS.—SARCASM.—TEASING.—CENSURE.—FAULT-FINDING.—EGOTISM.—POLITENESS.—COMPLIMENTS.—STORIES.—ANECDOTES.—QUESTIONING.—LIBERTIES.—IMPUDENCE.—STARING.—DISAGREEABLE SUBJECTS.—SEL-

FISHNESS.—ARGUMENT.—SACRIFICES.—SILENT PEOPLE.—DINNER CONVERSATION.—TIMIDITY.—ITS CURE.—MODESTY.—CORRECT LANGUAGE.—SELF-INSTRUCTION.—MISCELLANEOUS KNOWLEDGE.—LANGUAGES.

II.—The Habits of Good Society.

A Handbook for Ladies and Gentlemen. With thoughts, hints, and anecdotes concerning social observances, nice points of taste and good manners, and the art of making oneself agreeable. The whole interspersed with humorous illustrations of social predicaments, remarks on fashion, etc. *** Price $1.75. Among the contents will be found chapters upon—

GENTLEMEN'S PREFACE.
LADIES' PREFACE.—FASHIONS.
THOUGHTS ON SOCIETY.
GOOD SOCIETY.—BAD SOCIETY.
THE DRESSING-ROOM.
THE LADIES' TOILET.—DRESS.
FEMININE ACCOMPLISHMENTS.
MANNERS AND HABITS.
PUBLIC AND PRIVATE ETIQUETTE.
MARRIED AND UNMARRIED LADIES.
DO   DO GENTLEMEN.
CALLING ETIQUETTE.—CARDS.
VISITING ETIQUETTE.—DINNERS.
DINNER PARTIES.

LADIES AT DINNER.
DINNER HABITS.—CARVING.
MANNERS AT SUPPER.—BALLS.
MORNING PARTIES.—PICNICS.
EVENING PARTIES.—DANCES.
PRIVATE THEATRICALS.
RECEPTIONS.—ENGAGEMENTS.
MARRIAGE CEREMONIES.
INVITATIONS.—DRESSES.
BRIDESMAIDS.—PRESENTS.
TRAVELLING ETIQUETTE.
PUBLIC PROMENADE.
COUNTRY VISITS.—CITY VISITS.

III.—Arts of Writing, Reading, and Speaking.

An exceedingly fascinating work for teaching not only the beginner, but for perfecting every one in these three most desirable accomplishments. For youth this book is both interesting and valuable; and for adults, whether professionally or socially it is a book that they cannot dispense with. *** Price $1.50. Among the contents will be found chapters upon—

READING & THINKING.—LANGUAGE.—WORDS, SENTENCES, & CONSTRUCTION.
WHAT TO AVOID.—LETTER WRITING.
PRONUNCIATION.—EXPRESSION.—TONE
RELIGIOUS READINGS.—THE BIBLE.—
PRAYERS.—DRAMATIC READINGS.—THE
ACTOR & READER.—FOUNDATIONS FOR
ORATORY AND SPEAKING.—WHAT TO

SAY.—WHAT NOT TO SAY.—HOW TO BEGIN.—CAUTIONS.-DELIVERY.—WRITING A SPEECH.—FIRST LESSONS.—PUBLIC SPEAKING.—DELIVERY.—ACTION.
ORATORY OF THE PULPIT.—COMPOSITION.—THE BAR.—READING OF WIT & HUMOR.—THE PLATFORM.—CONSTRUCTION OF A SPEECH.

These works are the most perfect of their kind ever published; fresh, sensible, good-humored, entertaining, and readable. Every person of taste should possess them, and cannot be otherwise than delighted with them.

☞ A beautiful new miniature edition of these very popular books has just been published, entitled "THE DIAMOND EDITION," three little volumes, elegantly printed on tinted paper, and handsomely bound in a box. Price $3.00.
*** These books are all sent by mail, *postage free*, on receipt of price, by

G. W. CARLETON & CO., Publishers, Madison Square, New York.

www.ingramcontent.com/pod-product-compliance
Lightning Source LLC
Chambersburg PA
CBHW022110290426

44112CB00008B/616